THE HUMAN DIMENSION IN PSYCHOANALYTIC PRACTICE

THE HUMAN DIMENSION IN PSYCHOANALYTIC PRACTICE

Edited by

KENNETH A. FRANK, PH.D.

Assistant Professor of Clinical Psychology
Department of Psychiatry
College of Physicians and Surgeons
of Columbia University
and
Co-Director of Training
National Institute for the Psychotherapies
New York, N.Y.

GRUNE & STRATTON
A Subsidiary of Harcourt Brace Jovanovich, Publishers
New York   San Francisco   London

Library of Congress Cataloging in Publication Data

Main entry under title:

The Human dimension in psychoanalytic practice.

    Includes bibliographical references and index.
    1. Psychoanalysis—Addresses, essays, lectures.
2. Psychotherapist and patient—Addresses, essays,
lectures.   I. Frank, Kenneth A.
RC509.H86   616.8'914   77-10165
ISBN 0–8089–1039–6

Grune & Stratton, Inc.
111 Fifth Avenue
New York, New York 10003

Distributed in the United Kingdom by
Academic Press, Inc. (London) Ltd.
24/28 Oval Road, London NW 1

Library of Congress Catalog Number 77–10165
International Standard Book Number 0–8089–1039–6
Printed in the United States of America

to Linda and Sara

CONTENTS

ACKNOWLEDGEMENTS

So many people have played an important role in the genesis of this book that I am able to mention relatively few by name. Initially, of course, I must thank the patients with whom I have worked. Not one has ever failed to help me to grow, personally as well as professionally. In a similar vein, the students whose work I have supervised in a variety of settings, have helped me to formulate the idea for this book. I am indebted to them.

The National Institute for the Psychotherapies has offered a particularly stimulating atmosphere for the development of this book. Conflict between my relatively traditional position and other more unconventional points of view at the Institute has caused me to deepen and explore my personal interests, but never to inhibit them. It is an unusual setting, indeed, which can, in the context of close collaboration, produce relatively traditional volumes such as this, as well as others dealing with highly esoteric aspects of psychotherapy. I am especially grateful to Drs. James Fosshage, Henry Grayson, Clemens A. Loew, Henry Lowenheim and Paul Olsen for helping to create this rich atmosphere.

I would also like to extend my appreciation to Drs. Stanley S. Heller and Donald S. Kornfeld, my closest associates within the Department of Psychiatry at the Columbia University College of Physicians & Surgeons, whose support has increased as my professional interests have expanded.

My personal psychoanalyst, Dr. Saul D. Miller, helped me to grapple with a number of crucial personal and professional issues such as those addressed in this book. It may have been my attempt to separate personal from professional attributes of his, so profoundly helpful to me, which provided the initial incentive to undertake this volume.

More formally, I would like to thank Mrs. Bertha Guntrip, widow of the late Harry Guntrip, for permitting me to re-publish the highly relevant article he wrote shortly before his death. As a great admirer of Dr. Guntrip, I would have felt this volume to be incomplete, especially given its specific theme, without a contribution from him. The article reproduced here first appeared in the International Review of Psycho-Analysis, volume 2, pages 145–156 in 1975. I also wish to thank Dr. Joseph Sandler, Editor of the International Review, for his cooperation.

Dr. Greenson's article appeared previously in the Journal of the American Psychoanalytic Association, volume XIV, No. 1, pages 9–27 in January, 1966. I would like to thank the author, the Journal, and the publisher, International Universities Press, for their permission to re-publish it. I am very pleased to include Dr. Greenson's paper in the book for he, perhaps more than any other prominent orthodox American analyst, has addressed the issues of the psychoanalyst as a person and the real, human relationship between patient and analyst.

Mr. Khan's article appeared in French in the Nouvelle Revue de Psychanalyse, No. 14, November, 1976. I would like to thank the author and the publisher for permitting me to include the author's English translation in the volume, published here for the first time.

Dr. Searles' paper was presented as the author's contribution to the Ninth Annual Symposium on Psychotherapy of the Department of Psychiatry of Tufts University School of Medicine in Boston on April 26, 1974. The title of the Symposium was "The Role of Hope in Psychotherapy." Given the relevance of this paper to the theme of the book, and Dr. Searles' outstanding contribution to this specific area, I am extremely pleased to publish the paper, for the first time, in this book.

Passages from Truax and Mitchell in the Introduction are reprinted by permission of John Wiley & Sons, Inc.

Finally, I would like to thank my wife, Linda Reckler Frank, for her editorial assistance, as well as her patience and understanding in supporting my work on this volume. That assistance is symbolic of the enduring source of inspiration and support she has become for me.

PREFACE

I have had a growing conviction that most traditional theoretical and technical papers about psychoanalysis and psychoanalytic psychotherapy, while perhaps contributing significantly to therapeutic understanding and efficacy, have failed to address a highly significant area: the personal experience, attitudes and involvement of the analyst, which contribute importantly to the interpersonal subtleties and uncharted techniques which may, in fact, constitute the effective core of psychotherapy.

Currently, there is a saturation of objective writing in the field concentrating on theoretical and technical aspects of the diadic interaction, psychopathological manifestations of the patient, and to a lesser degree, conceptualizations about the analyst's internal processes. But there is a dearth of responsible, highly personal articles by technically competent psychoanalysts, emphasizing self-disclosure and addressing the informative issues of the analyst's personal involvement in his work and his real, human relationship with his patients. I have attempted here to compile such a volume of papers, written by a diverse sampling of highly competent practitioners. It is my belief that this investigation will offer much to students and practitioners in the field about the true foundations of psychotherapy. I must stress that while this volume is subjective in emphasis, it is in no way intended in an anti-scientific spirit, but rather to enrich a literature which has given insufficient attention to an important investigative area.

CONTRIBUTOR LIST

Basescu, Sabert, Ph.D.
Adjunct Professor of Psychology, Graduate School of Arts and Sciences and Postdoctoral Program in Psychotherapy and Psychoanalysis, New York University; Director of Training, Westchester Center for the Study of Psychoanalysis and Psychotherapy; Private Practice, Larchmont, N.Y.

Ben-Avi, Avrum, Ph.D.
Adjunct Professor of Psychology and Training Analyst, Graduate School of Arts and Sciences, New York University; Faculty, Westchester Center for the Study of Psychoanalysis and Psychotherapy; Private Practice, New York City and White Plains, N.Y.

Bruch, Hilde, M.D.
Professor of Psychiatry, Department of Psychiatry, Baylor College of Medicine, Texas Medical Center, Houston, Texas.

Frank, Kenneth A., Ph.D.
Assistant Professor and Coordinator of Internship Training in Clinical Psychology, College of Physicians & Surgeons of Columbia University; Co-Director of Training, National Institute for the Psychotherapies, New York City; Private Practice, New York City and Tenafly, New Jersey.

Greenson, Ralph R., M.D.
Training/Supervising Analyst, Los Angeles Psychoanalytic Society and Institute.

Guntrip, Harry, Ph.D.
Former Psychotherapist and Lecturer, Leeds University Department of Psychiatry, England; Former Member, British Psychoanalytical Society; Deceased.

Kelman, Harold, M.D., Med. Sc.D.
Dean Emeritus, Specialty Program in Psychoanalytic Medicine, Postgraduate Center for Mental Health, New York City; Past President, The American Academy of Psychoanalysis; Former Dean, The American Institute for Psychoanalysis; Deceased.

Khan, M. Masud R., B. A. (Hons.), M.A.
Member, British Psychoanalytical Society, London, England.

Olsen, Paul, Ph.D.
Director of Intern Training and Publications, National Institute for the Psychotherapies, New York City; Director of Clinical Psychology Training, The

Roosevelt Hospital, New York City; Clinical Associate, Department of Psychiatry, College of Physicians & Surgeons of Columbia University.

Rosenfeld, Herbert A., M.D.

L.R.C.P., L.R.C.S. (Edinburgh), L.R.F.P.S. (Glascow), F.R.C.Psych.; Member, British Psychoanalytical Society, London, England

Searles, Harold F., M.D.

Supervising and Training Analyst, The Washington Psychoanalytic Institute; Clinical Professor of Psychiatry, Georgetown University School of Medicine, Washington, D.C.; Consultant in Psychiatry, National Institute of Mental Health, Bethesda, Maryland

Shainberg, David, M.D.

Dean, Specialty Program in Psychoanalytic Medicine, Post-graduate Center for Mental Health, New York City.

Singer, Erwin, Ph.D.

Fellow, Faculty, Training and Supervising Analyst, William Allanson White Institute of Psychiatry, Psychoanalysis and Psychology; Visiting Professor, New York University; Professor Emeritus, City College of New York.

THE HUMAN DIMENSION
IN PSYCHOANALYTIC PRACTICE

Kenneth A. Frank, Ph.D.

Introduction

There is a compelling point of rapprochment developing between the psychoanalytic literature and academic psychotherapy research. Among psychoanalysts, Guntrip has said that, "In the last resort good therapists are born not trained, and they make the best use of training."[1] * From a research position, Truax has stated emphatically that, "Basically, the personality of the therapist is more important than his techniques. Conversely, however, techniques . . . can be quite potent in the hands of a therapist who is inherently helpful. . . ."[2]

Summarizing the psychotherapy research, Truax has said further, "These studies taken together suggest that therapists or counselors who are accurately empathic, nonpossessively warm in attitude, and genuine, are indeed effective."[3] Again reflecting a convergence of the two literatures, Greenson has emphasized that, "As for the analyst, it is his consistent and unwavering pursuit of insight *plus* his concern, respect, and care for the totality of the patient's personality, sick and healthy, that contributes to the working alliance."[4] "The *reliable* core of the working alliance is the real object relationship between the patient and his psychoanalyst . . . It is only when . . . the analyst has perceived the patient as a whole human being *and* has permitted himself to be perceived as a human being . . . only then do we have a living, ongoing analysis."[5]

This evidence suggests clearly that the techniques of the analyst are

---

* The article in which this quote originally appeared is reproduced in this volume, pp. 49–68 (cf. p. 491).

optimally effective only when implemented within the context of a real, caring, human relationship between patient and analyst. Yet most published material about psychoanalysis and psychoanalytic psychotherapy,* while perhaps contributing significantly to psychotherapeutic understanding and efficacy, fails to recognize the positive role of the analyst's personal involvement and thus can be misleading about the true nature of psychoanalysis. The personal, subjective experience and attitudes of the analyst, especially while conducting treatment, contribute importantly to those interpersonal subtleties and uncharted techniques which may, in fact, comprise the effective core of all psychotherapy. The paucity of such material in the psychoanalytic literature is, I believe, the result of a phobic attitude toward the inner life of the analyst as he functions professionally, resulting in a failure to address the "human dimension in psychoanalytic practice."

Currently, there is a saturation of traditional scientific and technical writing in the field of psychoanalysis, but a dearth of highly personal articles, written by highly competent psychoanalysts, stressing self-disclosure. Although there has been an encouraging increase in the number of more personal articles, clinical examples still tend to reflect the guarded manner of the past, when the therapist was portrayed as an omniscient analyst-technician rather than a caring analyst-person. While few experienced psychoanalysts would deny the value of their subjective responses to their patients as crucial data in conducting psychotherapy, nevertheless such responses have received relatively little attention in the literature. Further, the way in which we use secondary process to draw upon our personal reactions for the benefit of our patients is not integrated into the literature either, although recent attempts to clarify this complex subject matter have been rewarding.[6,7,8,9] A highly personal volume, consisting of self-revelatory statements by accomplished psychoanalysts about their personal involvement in their work is timely and, by shedding light on the human dimension in psychoanalytic practice, may offer much to students of the field about the true foundations of psychotherapy.

Ideally, personal material such as that included in these pages ought to be discussed routinely in the context of case seminars, supervision and courses on technique. Yet, this kind of biographical material is rarely emphasized formally and often is not even shared informally among col-

---

* Throughout the paper I shall refer to psychoanalysis and psychoanalytic psychotherapy, the analyst and the therapist, interchangeably. Clearly, there are theoretical and technical distinctions between the two processes. However, I believe this approach is reasonable within the present context. It enables me to avoid awkward and redundant clarifications and, more importantly, I believe that the real relational core is essential to both processes and that the subjective emotional responses of the psychoanalyst and psychoanalytic psychotherapist have essentially similar origins, manifestations and treatment implications.

leagues. Writing two decades ago, Searles[10] observed that the psychoanalytic community and literature reflected normative attitudes which were apt to cause the analyst to feel troubled at finding himself to be experiencing strong but natural feelings toward a patient. Twenty years later this criticism is still relevant. Why, for so long, has psychoanalysis placed such heavy stress on theory and technique, minimizing the analyst's personal experience as a legitimate subject for study?

Let us look to the origins of psychoanalysis to more fully understand the problem. Freud was a brilliant man whose creative genius and contribution to modern knowledge rank with those of Copernicus, Darwin, and others who have substantially changed man's view of himself and of his world. Above all Freud was a scientist, trained in the natural scientific framework and grounded in the scientific tradition of medicine. Indeed, Freud was a humanist also, but to a lesser degree. The scientific origins of Freud's psychoanalysis have been a mixed blessing. On the one hand, Freud's attempt to integrate depth psychological insights with the natural scientific framework of his time initiated a scientific psychoanalysis which provided a respectable and perhaps otherwise unattainable foundation for subsequent developments in the field. It has also afforded objective study of its concepts and rendered them teachable. The psychoanalytic viewpoint, permitting the derivation of psychodynamic formulations, probably goes further than any other known system toward an understanding of personality. On the other hand, a major drawback of Freud's psychoanalysis is that it was limited by the natural scientific tradition as to which aspects of man constitute proper subject for study. It has been criticized by humanistic, existential and object-relations spokesmen for its failure to provide a model from which to appreciate fully the wholeness and uniqueness of the individual person.[11,12,13]

An exclusive emphasis on the scientific aspects of psychoanalysis, and on formal technique, is terribly misleading to students as it deprives psychoanalysis, and the analyst alike, of essential qualities of humanness. In its best sense, psychoanalysis is a profoundly human encounter and not merely the analysis of resistances, of imagos projected onto the analyst, the neutralization of preconscious derivatives of the id, and the like—all of which smack of sterile intellectual reductionism and dilution of the living experience. At least equally as important, psychoanalysis is, I believe, a uniquely caring, extraordinarily personal (vs. technical) collaboration. While this conviction must be universally implemented by *effective* practitioners of all orientations, nevertheless the literature continues to promote a largely unrealistic image of the aloof analyst-technician, rather than that of the caring analyst-person.

Returning to Freud, it is useful to draw a distinction between Freud as theorist and as practitioner. Freud's disciplined, objective orientation to theory-building, and even his papers on technique, are at variance with his actual reported work as an analyst. Racker[14] has pointed out that Freud's technical concepts such as "evenly-suspended attention," the "surgeon's attitude" and "the mirror," lend themselves to misunderstanding. Freud's actual work with patient "Dora"[15] and with "The Rat Man,"[16] cases about which Freud left the most extensive notes, reveals his freedom, activity and expressiveness in session, characteristics which Racker draws upon in asserting the *need* for a "positive countertransference" in successful psychoanalytic work. According to Racker, Freud could hardly be identified as a "classical" analyst.

These considerations notwithstanding, the fiction of the anonymous technician-analyst has prevailed in the literature for all too long, with disclosures of the analyst's personal responses to his patients limited primarily to "countertransference" manifestations and viewed in a generally pejorative way. It is my impression that at this time in its development, psychoanalysis is experiencing a period of "humanization," with psychoanalyst generally moving toward a position of fuller appreciation of the "real" relationship in psychoanalytic work.[17] The recent influence of object-relations theory[18,19,20] on American psychoanalytic thought has been strong in this regard.* This humanization brings with it a revitalization such that psychoanalysis may better respond to the challenge of modern times, including that of more efficient psychotherapeutic modalities which may act more swiftly, but only in relation to a fragmented man. A more truly humanistic psychoanalysis is emerging—one which reiterates its uniquely human and transcendant capabilities on the spectrum of conventional Western psychotherapeutic modalities. This humanization is also responsive to the changing needs of people living in modern times as compared with those of the Victorian era which provided the social context for the original psychoanalysis. Currently, problems of alienation, rather than of incest predominate, rendering the analyst-technician even more obsolete as a model.

Reflecting this shift, a trend can be readily noted in the literature on countertransference, the development of which has been chronologically documented by Hunt.[21] For purposes of discussion I shall draw upon the distinctions made by Kernberg[9] and by Sandler, Holder and Dare[22] who, in their reviews of the literature, identify two groups of authors on countertransference: the *classicists,* including Glover,[23] Reich[24] and Fliess,[25] and the *totalists,* or *modernists* according to Hunt, who include

---

* Dr. Guntrip's article published herein exemplifies this thinking about the therapeutic relationship.

Fromm-Reichman,[26] Racker[27] and Winnicott.[28] In general, the classicists view countertransference as a problem in the analysis and seek its origins in the unconscious response of the analyst to the patient's transference. The totalists' broader view of countertransference includes, but is not limited to, the classicist interpretation. The totalists see countertransference as the analysts's total emotional response to the patient in the psychoanalytic situation, including conscious as well as unconscious reactions. The totalistic definition also provides for responses to the reality of the patient, as well as to his transference, and includes responses originating from the analyst's realistic, as well as neurotic, needs. Although the two views of countertransference overlap, they reflect different emphases. Like the classicists, the totalists believe that countertransference is definitely to be resolved, but that it is nevertheless very useful to an understanding of the patient. The classicists, on the other hand, emphasize the need for resolution of the countertransference and minimize its usefulness.

This discussion of countertransference is quite revealing; for one sees that it is almost entirely under the rubric of countertransference that psychoanalysis has, in the past, considered the person of the psychoanalyst—that is, as one's personal responses have become problematic in, and detrimental to, treatment. Thus it becomes clear why more personal disclosure in the literature, and even experiencing, has been suppressed. The modernist view gives the analyst permission to experience fully, and to use constructively, his subjective reactions to his patient. They are, in effect, legitimized, thus releasing a fuller psychotherapeutic potentiality. One can see why Racker[14] has termed countertransference the "Cinderella" of psychoanalysis.

With the humanistic influence to augment, but surely not to replace the scientific study of theoretical and technical psychoanalysis, the highest goals of applied psychoanalysis can be truly served. However, the liberation of the feeling person-analyst must go hand in hand with cautions against technical abuses resulting from undisciplined and irresponsible emotional expressions by the analyst within the therapy. But this is a minor point relative to the general significance of the emergence of the modernist position. Far more importantly, it marks the movement within psychoanalysis toward a fuller recognition of the psychoanalyst as an involved person, rather than as a detached technician or an omniscient being, and of the essential human core of the psychoanalytic endeavor. This trend is responsive to the remarks of Anna Freud, made some 20 years ago:

But—and this seems important to me—to the extent to which the patient has a healthy part of his personality, his real relationship to the analyst is never wholly submerged. With due respect for the necessary strictest handling and interpretation of transference, I still feel that somewhere we should leave room for the realization that analyst and patient are also two real people, of equal adult status, in a real personal relationship to each other.[29]

The viability of psychoanalytic psychotherapy depends upon the recognition, minimized in the past, that even the most perceptive possible grasp of the patient's psychodynamics, combined with optimally timed and focused interpretation, is of limited value unless implemented within a relationship characterized by an affectional bond of mutual trust and respect, and where the analyst is willing to fully experience and to be experienced, on an authentically human level. Consequently, the ultimate developmental task of the psychoanalyst is the integration of theory and technique with his unique person. This is necessarily a challenging and lifelong task. But it need not be a secret struggle.

REFERENCES

1. Guntrip H: My experience of analysis with Fairbairn and Winnicott (How complete a result does psychoanalytic therapy achieve?). Int Rev Psychoanal 2:145–156, 1975, p. 145.
2. Truax CB, Mitchell KM: Research on certain therapist interpersonal skills in relation to process and outcome. In Bergin AE, Garfield SL (eds): Handbook of Psychotherapy and Behavior Change: An Empirical Analysis. New York, John Wiley, 1971, pp. 299–344, p. 341.
3. ———— ibid., p. 310.
4. Greenson RR, Wexler MW: The non-transference relationship in the psychoanalytic situation. Int J Psychoanal 50:27–39, 1969, p. 29.
5. Gumbel E (Chairman): Discussion of the non-transference relationship in the psychoanalytic situation. Int J Psychoanal 51:143–150, 1970, p. 144.
6. Aaron R: The analyst's emotional life during work (panel report). J Am Psychoanal Assoc 22:160–169, 1974.
7. Beres D, Arlow J: Fantasy and identification in empathy. Psychoanal Q 43:26–50, 1974.
8. Greenson RR: The psychoanalytic situation. In: The Technique and Practice of Psychoanalysis, vol 1. New York, International Universities Press, 1967, pp. 358–411.
9. Kernberg O: Countertransference. In: Borderline Conditions and Pathological Narcissism. New York, Jason Aronson, 1975, pp. 49–67.
10. Searles H: Oedipal love in the countertransference. Int J Psychoanal 40:180–190, 1959.
11. Maslow A: The Farther Reaches of Human Nature. New York, Viking Press, 1971.
12. May R, Angel E, Ellenberger HF (eds): Existence: A New Dimension in Psychiatry and Psychology. New York, Basic Books, 1958.

13. Guntrip H: Psychoanalytic Theory, Therapy and the Self. New York, Basic Books, 1971.
14. Racker H: Transference and Countertransference. New York, International Universities Press, 1968.
15. Freud S: Fragment of an analysis of a case of hysteria (1905). *In* Strachey J (ed): The Standard Edition of the Complete Psychological Works of Sigmund Freud, vol 7. London, Hogarth Press, 1961.
16. Freud S: Notes upon a case of obsessional neurosis (1909). *In* Strachey J (ed): The Standard Edition of the Complete Psychological Works of Sigmund Freud, vol. 10. London, Hogarth Press, 1961.
17. Greenson RR: Beyond transference and interpretation. Int J Psychoanal 53:213–217, 1972.
18. Fairbairn WRD: On the nature and aims of psychoanalytic treatment. Int J Psychoanal 39:374–385, 1958.
19. Guntrip H: Schizoid Phenomena, Object-Relations and the Self. New York, International Universities Press, 1968.
20. Winnicott DW: The Maturational Processes and the Facilitating Environment. London, Hogarth Press, 1965.
21. Hunt W: The transference-countertransference system. Unpublished manuscript.
22. Sandler J, Holder A, Dare C: Basic psychoanalytic concepts: IV. Countertransference. Br J Psychiatry 117:83–88, 1970.
23. Glover E: The Technique of Psychoanalysis. New York, International Universities Press, Inc., 1955.
24. Reich A: Further remarks on countertransference. Int J Psychoanal 41:389–395, 1960.
25. Fliess R: The metapsychology of the analyst. Psychoanal Q 11:211–227, 1942.
26. Fromm-Reichman F: Principles of Intensive Psychotherapy. Chicago, University of Chicago Press, 1950.
27. Racker H: The meaning and uses of countertransference. Psychoanal Q 2:303–357, 1957.
28. Winnicott DW: Hate in the countertransference. Int J Psychoanal 30:69–75, 1949.
29. Freud A: Widening scope of indications for analysis (1954). *In* Freud A: The Writings of Anna Freud, vol 4. New York, International Universities Press, 1968, p. 373.

Harold F. Searles, M.D.

The Development of Mature Hope
in the Patient-Therapist Relationship

Hope is generally assumed to be a "good" emotion, just as hate is assumed to be a "bad" one. We as adults cling to our cherished illusion that our hope is innately as good, as pure and virtuous as is that of the infant or little child who, at least so our concept would have it, is hoping that his momentarily absent good mother will imminently return. The realm of hope seems to us a last repository of such innate goodness as human beings possess. One of the harshest maturational tasks the individual must accomplish to become truly adult is to realize and accept that his hope is "impure" in two vast ways: first, it is not unitary in nature but multifarious and permeated with ambivalence, with conflict (such that no one hope or set of hopes is completely fulfillable, for it is opposed by powerfully contrasting hopes); and, secondly, many of these hopes are devoted not to living, but rather to destructive, ends.

Thus, since hope tends to be a realm into which we are most reluctant to allow, so to speak, our conscious ambivalence to enter, it is one of our most tenaciously clung-to refuges for our repressed fantasies of omnipotence. One of the major dimensions of genuine adulthood is living in the full knowledge that many of one's private hopes are mutually irreconcilable and are far less loving in nature than one's ideal self would have them be.

Realistic hope can come into existence, be maintained, and grow only insofar as one has become able to integrate one's multifarious, and at many areas conflictual, hopes into a more coherent and predominant hope-nucleus. This aspect of ego-integration involves our working through of our disappointments, and above all of our infantile-omnipotence-based frustration-rage and grief, as regards those of our hopes which we have had to relinquish. Put somewhat differently, this hope aspect of ego-integration requires our working through of our rage, grief, disappointment, and so on, at having to recognize, and accept, that human relatedness inescapably involves ambivalence. This is a never-finally-completed maturational process but, rather, a route which every therapist, for example, traverses in terms of the evolution of his own personal feelings in relation to each of the patients with whom he becomes deeply and sustainedly involved.

If the therapist's and patient's mutual therapeutic endeavor is to prove successful, the patient must come to discover in himself heretofore unconscious hopes which do violence to his long-conscious hope for relief from his symptoms, or for personal fulfillment in life; and the therapist himself, must discover, over and over again, repressed hopes within himself which are violently at odds with his conscious hope of becoming a successfully and lastingly helpful therapist for the patient.

I have a vivid memory of an experience of mine as a patient in analysis, more than twenty years ago, when I became conscious of a previously repressed hope entirely at odds with what I had felt to be my singlemindedly hoped for goal—namely, my parting from the analyst. From very early on in the analysis, my feelings about being there had oscillated between a conviction that I was on the verge of such overwhelming insanity that, as I frequently admonished the analyst, "You'd better get a bed ready for me at Chestnut Lodge" (one measure of my true nuttiness being that I assumed that, for anyone so special as an analytic candidate, the Institute would arrange free treatment at that expensive place, where I had not yet gone to work), and a conviction, on the other hand, that I was so manifestly and totally well that the analysis had now become absurdly superfluous.

At the time the incident in question occurred, my self-evaluations had pretty much stopped oscillating and I had long since settled into a consistent, unremittent bellyaching that the analyst was refusing to let me have done with this idiotically unnecessary analysis. He indicated the end of the session during which, for the nth time, I had been carping thus. I got up from the couch, as usual.

The next thing I knew, I was walking toward him; he was standing by his chair, no doubt preparatory to my walking out the door as usual. As I walked the couple of steps to him, I did so suffused with romantic love of which I had been entirely unaware, but which had a quality of having been there all along. I embraced him and said, fondly, pleadingly, companionably, and above all romantically, "Ernest, *when* are we going to get this analysis over with?" I referred to the analysis, here, clearly as being in the nature of some inherently meaningless courtship-ritual which was being imposed from without upon both of us, and which we had to get behind us in order, at long last, to consumate our fully-mutual love for one another. For all my gripingly impatient hope of getting the analysis over with, it was now immediately clear to me that I unconsciously had not had the slightest intention of leaving him; my unconscious hope had been, on the contrary, for us fully to possess one another.

Incidentally, I give him high marks, indeed, for his reaction to all this. His neither returning my embrace nor saying a word, left me free to make this discovery without his being, on any mature and realistic level, rejecting or scornful of me, or threatened by what I was doing. I assume that he had long been aware of my unconscious romantic attachment to him, for he showed not the slightest trace of surprise.

Before going on to the next aspect of this paper, I shall present a second bit of relevant patient-data from my own analysis. When I went to Dr. Ernest Hadley for my initial interview, I went with the conscious hope of finding relief from a great deal of severe anxiety and despair and, far less importantly to me, of discharging successfully the training-analysis requirement for graduation from the analytic institute. He was standing outside the door of his office when I walked toward it from the waiting room. I had the distinct sense—not a delusion, but a nonetheless vivid fantasy—that he, standing there, was Cerberus, the three-headed dog which guards the entrance to Hades.

I have remembered this impression many times during the more than quarter century since, and have never thought much about it, beyond preening myself a bit at this evidence of some familiarity with mythology. Only during the last few years have I found it significant that I was not so afraid, after all, that Dr. Hadley would not let me *escape from* his office (Hell), but rather that he would not *let me into* it. You see, early in our third session, my first training analyst had suddenly stood up and permanently dismissed me. The despair which I brought into the first session with Dr. Hadley was despair lest I would prove hopelessly unable to communicate my innermost feelings to any human being. At the end of that first session, during which I had sat, following his direction, in a chair opposite him, I asked, "Do you see any reason why we can't work together?" He assured me, briefly but emphatically, "Hell, no!"

The point I am trying to make here is that it was only a few years ago that I realized that the Cerberus-Hell imagery indicated that, at the time, I unconsciously *hoped* the analysis would prove to be hell, a sought-for hell which I feared that its guardian, Cerberus, would prevent me from entering. It would take me too far afield, here, to pursue in detail the determinants of my hope that the analysis would be hell. My often terrifyingly enraged mother made life hell for me much of the time in her kitchen and environs, where I cowered like a frightened animal in a corner at the end of an alley under her cook-stove, a refuge where I could be near her but where she could not readily get at me. Although much of the time she was loving indeed, she was often, particularly when I was a very small child, hell to live with. Thus any longing to recapture my early-mothering experience was impossible to differentiate from a hope to be living again in hell. Further, during much of the time in the subsequent years of my upbringing, when I was more in the orbit of my father, I found him to be living largely in his private hell—a hell comprised of an endless succession of excruciatingly painful psychosomatic symptoms, depression, fear of insanity, and other torments. As regards my analysis, I do not doubt, in retrospect, that I hoped fully to join my father in hell, not only because I hated him and had much unconscious guilt to atone for, in relation to his suffering, but also because I loved him and wanted to rescue him from his hell.

The next general point I want to make is that a healthy hopefulness needs to be distinguished clearly from an essentially manic repression of feelings of loss and despair. The mother in one of the most tragic families I have ever encountered, in which one after another of the children grew up to meet suicidal, chronically psychotic, and similarly tragic ends, had written a book entitled, *Joy is the Banner;* it seemed clear that she unconsciously had instilled her despair into her children, who came in course of time to provide her with the ground of tragedy above which her joyful banner could continue, by way of contrast, to fly undyingly high. The determinedly optimistic therapist coerces, similarly, his patients into experiencing the depression which he is too threatened to feel within himself.

A healthy capacity for hope is founded, quite in contrast to a manic denial of depression, in past experiences of the successful integrating of disappointments—that is, past experiences of successful grieving. Hope emerges through the facing of feelings of disappointment, discouragement, and despair. This is analogous to the kind of archaeological uncovering of successive layers of affects which I described in my paper entitled, "Scorn, Disillusionment, and Adoration in the Psychotherapy of Schizophrenia,"[1] in which I reported that one helps the schizophrenic patient to achieve a derepression of his feelings of adoration only by traversing first, in succession, the strata of his scorn and his feelings of disillusionment.

In other words, any realistic hope—as contrasted to unconscious-denial-based, unrealistic hopefulness—must be grounded in the ability to experience loss. One who has survived the griefs over losses, over disappointments, in the past has known what it is for hope to triumph over—

to survive—despair. He also knows that hoped-for changes which the future may bring, no matter how "favorable" or "healthy" (in psychotherapeutic terms) these changes may prove to be will inevitably bring a concomitant sense of loss in various regards—since, as he knows from his past experiences, the fulfillment of one hope is accompanied by loss-feelings stemming from the necessary discarding of the hopes which have been opposing it. In this same regard, hope comes into being when one discovers that such feelings as disappointment and despair can be shared with a fellow human being—when one discovers, that is, that the sharing of such feelings can foster one's feeling of relatedness with one's fellow human beings, rather than stigmatizing one as something less than human, something alien and unqualified to be included among human beings.

At Chestnut Lodge, many of the schizophrenic patients with whom my colleagues and I worked would have been considered to be, by reason of the severity and chronicity of their illnesses, hopeless. One of the lessons which my experience with these patients taught me is that *any* gratifications which the therapist can come to experience (referring here primarily to the realm of feeling, rather than that of observable behavior) in his work with the patient—no matter how lustful or sadistic or murderously rageful or what-not these gratifications may be in nature, nor how largely springing from countertransference sources in the therapist (so long as the therapist proves capable of gaining access to the relevant areas of his own repressed memories)—engender hope in both participants that the therapy will prove meaningful and will eventuate well and relatively successfully. It is essential, therefore, that the therapist become as open as possible, within himself, to the experiencing of whatever gratifications this work, which innately tends to be so deprivational, so engendering of feelings of futility and discouragement, can come to afford him, no matter how tabooed such gratifications are in relation to our time-honored concept of the analyst who experiences in response to the patient naught but affective neutrality and evenly hovering attentiveness.

Two of the ways in which hope (or hopefulness) and sadism are related deserve to be detailed here. First, one of the more formidable ways of being sadistic toward the other person is to engender hope, followed by disappointment, in him over and over. Secondly, the presenting of a hopeful demeanor under some circumstances can comprise, in itself, a form of sadism toward the other person, for it can be expressing, implicitly and subtly, cruel demands upon him to fulfill the hopes which are written upon one's face. One finds both these forms of sadism at work in many patients, whether schizophrenic or neurotic, and in many therapists also.

For many years now I have stressed, in my writings, that the chronically schizophrenic patient derives enormous gratification, sadistic in na-

ture, from watching the recurrently-hopeful therapist make eager and vigorous, but increasingly anguished, attempts to rescue the seemingly
so-tormented patient from the latter's schizophrenia. By now I have learned
that, whenever I am finding the course of work with any patient (whether
psychotic or non-psychotic) to prove recurrently and painfully disappointing to me, I am alerted to the presence of more sadism in the treatment
relationship than I had suspected previously.

I have come also, with some regret, to be conscious of the likelihood
that if a person walks into the interview-room with a too-naively-hopeful
look on his or her face, and particularly if I know the person to be a
borderline schizophrenic patient who is a veteran of a number of treatment
efforts, I am perceiving not merely a youthfully and healthily-hopeful
person, but an accomplished and formidable sadist. I came to this rueful
conclusion in the course of several hundred demonstration interviews at
a number of hospitals, particularly at Sheppard Pratt. These interviews
were held in a one-way mirror viewing room and observed by the residents
and other staff-members. Stressful as many of the interviews have been
with, for example, dilapidated, manifestly psychotic, hopeless-appearing
patients, even more stressful in some regards have been those interviews
with relatively youthful, healthy-appearing patients who have been diagnosed accurately as schizophrenic but who come into the room appearing
filled with hope that I shall somehow put, in that single interview, the
specter of mental illness out of their lives. I know, when I see one of
them walking into the room with such a demeanor, that by the end of
the interview I shall have been given to feel that I am an inhuman monster
for having so cruelly disappointed him or her.

Only about six months ago did I realize that I had been doing this
oftentimes, unconsciously, to a chronically schizophrenic patient who has
been in intensive psychotherapy with me, four hours per week, for more
than 21 years now. I had noticed that frequently, when she looked at
my face upon my showing her into my office from the waiting room,
she would give a helpless shrug. It finally occurred to me that this was
her reaction to the radiantly hopeful expression she saw on my face.

In the instance of another, much less ill but highly sadistic woman
with whom I have worked for several years, it recently occurred to me
that the vigorously hopeful manner I presented on inviting her into my
office from the waiting room on one occasion, a manner so inappropriate
to the glacial slowness with which the analysis advances, was in essence
a hopefulness that I would succeed, this time, in giving her the sort of
anguishedly difficult time—particularly as regards a torture of disappointment—which she had given me, innumerable times, over the past years
of our work together.

A thirty-seven-year-old divorced woman, upon her transfer to Chestnut Lodge after a year in another hospital, although clearly suffering from paranoid schizophrenia seemed, nonetheless, far less ill than most of the patients with whom I worked there. Only gradually did the true depth of her illness become evident and likewise the integral role, in her psychodynamics, of tantilization and disappointment.

Her verbally expressed emotions were largely limited, for at least two years, to expressions of her feeling threatened in a paranoid fashion and, in particular, to her intense, bitter and oftentimes acid disapproval and condemnation, always self-righteous, of practically everyone and everything about her. Only after some two years did I begin to see, during our sessions, that the paranoid hate and fear she typically expressed was subtly becoming differentiated into a wider gamut of underlying feelings, feelings against which her paranoid ways of relating could be seen to comprise an unconscious defense system. In particular, such emotions as *disappointment,* hurt, and grief began to be discernible in her. That is, I found I was no longer met by a demeanor of unbroken, threatened (and at times threatening) paranoid hate but could detect that she tended to feel disappointed or hurt by something I had just said or failed to say. But rather than her experiencing, as yet, the fullness of these human emotions, she evidently experienced instead, on such occasions, a heightened perception of me as being hateful and threatening.

Incidentally, I have found reliably in a number of much less ill patients—patients with, variously, borderline ego-functioning or a schizoid or narcissistic ego-structure—that only after several years of analysis, during which an essentially paranoid blamingness, reproachfulness, and hostile passive-competitiveness holds sway in their relationship to the analyst, do they finally start experiencing the fullness of their long-repressed disappointment—disappointment with the analyst, with the significant persons in their childhood, and with themselves.

In the early stages, then, of the derepression of the feelings of disappointment, one can at times clearly see these feelings to be in conflict with the more usual paranoid way of responding. For example, one woman whose expressions of emotions had been largely limited, for years of analytic work, to a monochromatic, paranoid-tinged ragefulness, resentment, and dissatisfaction, came to say of her young son, ". . . Billy—God damn dirty trick that he was born a boy . . ." There was *some* note of disappointment in her tone as she said this, but there was, still, a much more predominantly paranoid note in it—implying that Billy had played, omnipotently, a viciously dirty trick on his mother by causing himself to be born a boy rather than a girl.

A man whose ego-functioning was essentially similar in this regard had recounted many things in a session when, characteristically for him, he suddenly became intensely exasperated and said, "Oh, I'm all mixed up!" On some such occasions in the past, his exasperation would be so overwhelming that he would beat his head with his fists; but his self-destructiveness had decreased somewhat by now. I suggested, ironically, "I've spoiled everything by not responding at the right times?" He replied, "No. . . . You spoil everything by *being* here! . . . People ruin *everything;* they really *do!* They have *nothing* to recommend them . . ." When he said, "*People* ruin *everything;* they really *do!*" his tone was one of intense disappointment—a significant sign of analytic progress—but there was discernible, simultaneously, a paranoid element, expressive of his semiconviction that all the rest of humanity was in a plot against him, a plot to ruin everything he cared about.

The previously mentioned divorcée became relatively soon—for Chestnut Lodge patients—sufficiently well to seem tantalizingly on the verge of being able to move to out-patient living, and I was highly aware of needing, for statistical as well as for many more personal reasons, for one of my bevy of Chestnut Lodge veterans to become an out-patient. Finally after three years, she was moved out into a long-ready apartment in nearby Rockville, but almost immediately became frankly psychotic again, and was back in the sanitarium within less than twenty-four hours. She quickly regained her previously achieved level of ego-functioning, and resumed her snail-like progress. For example, in one building at Chestnut Lodge where relatively well patients were housed, she refused for three full years ever to set foot in the living room of the building, sure (for reasons well-founded, indeed, in her childhood-family life) that, were she to do so, she would instantly be held responsible for all that was transpiring and would transpire thereafter in that room.

Not until more than twelve years after her initial Chestnut Lodge admission did she again move out, and this time successfully. Those twelve-plus years had involved a succession of some eight or ten administrative psychiatrists, each of whom found reason to hope, as I did, that the carefully made plans for her moving out would imminently be crowned with successful fulfillment. Each administrator in turn was disappointed. For most of those years I, slowly becoming acquainted with the existence and subtle workings of her sadism, subsisted on the aphorism, which occurred to me in many of our sessions, that "Most men live lives of quiet desperation." I looked up this quotation in preparing these comments, and found that it was Thoreau who, in *Walden,* first opined this, and that I unknowingly had been misremembering, for twelve-plus years, his precise statement, that "The mass of men lead lives of quiet desperation." But then, although I really still can't accept it, nothing is perfect.

I regard it as significant that, some time prior to her becoming established in out-patient living, I had become sufficiently able to integrate my essentially infantile-omnipotence-based disappointment, as regards the lack of fulfillment of my multifarious goals in my efforts with her, so that I was no longer threatened by the possibility that she might never be able to live outside the Lodge. By now I have experienced analogous turning points (or, better, phases) in my work with one patient after another. It seems, in each instance, that the patient's successful individuation cannot occur until it has become clear that the patient's life is, in a sense, in his own hands: the contemplated next major move (whatever it is in any particular case, whether graduation from the analytic institute, or marriage, or termination of the analysis, or whatever) is experienced by the patient not primarily as some feather in the cap of the analyst's narcissism, coerced out of the patient in conformity to some omnipotence-based ego-ideal on the analyst's part, but primarily, rather, as a step in fulfillment of the patient's individual self.

A forty-year-old man whom I shall call Bill had been hospitalized constantly for eleven years, including five years at Chestnut Lodge, when I became his individual therapist. He had long since established a durable social role there as a chronically hebephrenic patient who seemed to remember nothing of his prepsychotic past, a past which I knew from other sources to have been marked by promiscuous homosexuality, transvestitism, physical violence, alcoholism, and reckless driving. Over the years at the Lodge he had lived a highly stereotyped life largely as an apathetic vegetable, lying on a couch at the end of the ward-corridor and leaving it only briefly to walk rapidly, with an effeminate gait, to the nurse's station, swearing explosively on the way at apparently random hallucinatory figures, and then getting a cigarette and returning to his couch. He was generally looked upon as being one of the least promising among the Lodge's nucleus of severely and chronically schizophrenic patients.

During approximately the first two years of our work, while he spent the sessions lying or sitting on his bed, silent except for his frequent loud farting and occasional launches into frighteningly unexpected, brief but vitriolically furious tirades at me, neither of us seemed to find any great reason for hope. But over the total of nine and a half years of our individual psychotherapy together, prior to my leaving the Chestnut Lodge staff, he manifested really memorable progress. This progress occurred in proportion to my becoming able to recognize, within myself, a succession of intense feelings regarding him, feelings each of which was at first formidably opposed to my superego standards and my sense of personal identity. These feelings included intense envy of his inherited millions of dollars and of the various forms of contentment which his hebephrenic mode of living afforded him, as I perceived that mode of life; murderous rage toward him, rage born of his behaving in a psychotically violent way toward me on innumerable occasions (an atmosphere of intense murderousness permeated the room for a number of years); unmistakable indications (from my dreams and various daily life data) of feelings of violent sexual lust in myself toward him; and, in the later years of the work, increasingly freely conscious romantic feelings toward him, as well as dependent feelings toward him as a good mother, and friendly, brotherly feelings.

Early in our work, his vitriolic tirades at me had typically been of this order: "Shut up, you black bastard!" or "Shut up, you slimy son of a bitch, or I'll knock your teeth out!" His contempt as well as his fury was barely controllable. After some years, during which I had become relatively well aware of my contempt as well as my rage toward him, I took to resorting, with excellent therapeutic results, to goading him, contemptuously, about his defiant pseudo-stupidity. When he would utter some verbal stereotype in a spirit of being defiantly idiotic—when, in short, he would play dumb—I would inquire with ironic politeness, "Do you find that it [i.e., your head] echoes when you talk?" On other such occasions, I would remind him, ironically, that "the trouble with *acting like* an imbecile so much is that you're apt to really *become* an imbecile." On one occasion, when his long silence was broken by a loud fart I said to him in furious contempt, "Why don't you just *shit* here on the floor? Why don't you just make yourself comfortable? I don't understand why you go to the toilet if you're trying to be an animal." After years of his threatening furiously to knock my teeth out, I replied with equivalent rage, "You'd better *not* hit me, or I'll knock you right through that wall there!"

As Bill's psychotic ragefulness found thus an interpersonal context for its expression, so over the same years did his hebephrenic manifestations of homosexual lust evolve into something finer. Early in our work he asked invitingly, while lying in his bed, "Do ya wanta see my banana?" which I politely declined in my most conventionally obsessive-compulsive manner. A bit later in the work, he sat on his bed open-mouthed, leering at me, with a wad of sputum on his tongue. On another early occasion, he sat on his bed looking like a fat, veteran prostitute, and I heard him murmur voluptuously to himself, "Mm—it's a beauty; shove it up." He frequently appeared close to panic, on the other hand, lest I had come there to homosexually assault and/or kill him. He misidentified me more than once as being "Pretty Boy" Floyd, a notorious gangland killer of the 1930's, and on one occasion he said to himself in quick reassurance as I walked into his room, "That's all right, Dearie; that ain't one of the Fuller Brush ones."

It required some years before I realized, during one of the silences which still predominated during our sessions, that it had now become conceivable for me to be tangibly related to him without my having to either fuck him or kill him. It was some time thereafter that we went through a phase of predominantly romantic feelings toward one another and mutually experienced fantasies of becoming happily married to one another. I believe that he was fairly consistently the bride in these hopeful fantasies. In my actual marriage during that era, I most uncharacteristically forgot, until the following day, my wife's and my fourteenth wedding anniversary. My first thought as to why I had forgotten it was a feeling that my wife stood between me and Bill. It was a feeling of such power that, although I had been aware for some time of romantic feelings about Bill, the realization hit me very forcibly.

In a staff conference which occurred five years after my having become Bill's individual therapist, his then-current administrative psychiatrist reported,

I do feel he's changing . . . Certainly his relationship to me is quite different. In the first year I was administrator [of his ward] he never spoke to me, and regarded me as more not there than anything else. He was the only patient who never attended the group meetings. Now he's one of the most faithful patients; he never misses a group meeting. He enjoys it a great deal, and participates, verbally, as well as listens. A lot of humor comes out, which is quite new. . . ."

Two years later still, Bill's younger sister and her husband came to visit him for the first time in several years; he had received no visits from relatives in that interim. His sister and brother-in-law were nothing less than astonished at how much healthier they found him to be this time, and they began to give serious consideration to the possibility of his coming to visit them at their distant home. Meanwhile, during these later years, Bill, who used to be unable to endure any sustained physical proximity to me, had come to spend at least 80 percent of the time during the psychotherapy sessions sitting in his room with me, within arm's length, and with the door to the corridor closed. His demeanor clearly was one of attaching great importance to our sessions, and of being very attentive to what was occurring between us. He was able to provide enough meaningful data to enable me to make transference interpretations.

During the early years of our work I, as well as various members of the ward-staff, heard him say, many times, "I came here to die," and this hopeless statement seemed then all too well-founded. But after a few years, during one of our sessions, he said, "I came here to reminisce"; and in the latter years of our work his hopefulness had grown still further, such that he now said, "I came to join," which clearly had a connotation of joining in mature human interrelatedness.

Miss Susan Johnson was only twenty-one years old—relatively young, that is, among the Chestnut Lodge patient population at that time—upon her transfer to the Lodge from a hospital in her home city to which she had been admitted six months previously. But her illness, which had developed insidiously prior to its first manifestations about two years before, proved to be more severe than that of any other Chestnut Lodge patient with whom I worked. She had, upon admission, the appearance of a hopelessly chronic, back-ward hebephrenic patient. Her Lodge administrative psychiatrist, a man with decades of mental hospital experience, considered her to be the sickest patient he had ever seen, the nurse or attendant assigned initially to "special" her said she looked "at times like a demon." I found her appearance and behavior initially to be grotesque, indeed, and only after a number of years did her sense of identity as a human being come to prevail at all durably over a galaxy of "nonhuman" identity components—whether as some kind of demon, or a circus freak, or a horse, or a dog, or whatever. When, after eleven years of my working with her, I left Chestnut Lodge, she was still, despite a number of dramatic but transitory periods of improvement, deeply schizophrenic.

At the time of her admission to the Lodge, it was learned that each of her parents had confided to her, during the previous few years, the hope that she would never marry, for the expressed reason that the three of them—the girl and her parents—had such good times together. She had been in many ways socially popular but each of her parents had disapproved of all of her boyfriends. I found it shockingly incongruous when the father of this grievously ill young woman, housed in a seclusion room some floors above my office, told me thoughtfully, "My daughter has had two love affairs that didn't materialize, I think fortunately for her," and went on to speak critically of the two young men in question.

There was abundant case history data to indicate that she and her parents were involved in a deeply pathological, symbiotic relatedness. But I, and the other personnel-members who worked with her, had little reason to feel superior to her mother and father in this regard, for she was to become involved, over the years of her hospital stay, in equally formidable, pathologically symbiotic modes of relatedness with us as well. Of specific relevance for this paper, I learned over and over, in my work with her, that at the heart of my own recurrent feelings of hopelessness about her was a symbiotic infantile-dependency on my part, toward her, which I found appalling in its depth and power.

It was relatively easy, of course, for me to see the other personnel-members' symbiotic dependency upon her—to see, that is, their unconscious stake in her remaining ill. For example, one of the veteran female aides who worked much with her during the early years said to me with enthusiastic warmth and fondness, one day when I came upon the locked

ward for my session with Susan, "All of us up here love Susan so much
. . . ," detailing something about the endearing things she did there with
them, and then added, with an intonation of intended sadness about the
tragedy of Susan's long illness, "You don't think she'll ever get well, do
you?" But the way this question was actually asked was in the form of
a request for reassurance from me—reassurance that Susan would never
become well and reassurance, therefore, that this aide (and the others
among the ward-personnel) need not fear ever losing her.

I well remember one session which occurred after several years of
my work with her, at a time when the ward administrator was planning
to move the majority, and hopefully all, of the patients to a nearby small
building which had been readied for them and where, it was hoped, they
would come to live in a generally less regressed, more autonomous, fashion.
It had not been decided whether Susan was sufficiently well to make this
move. I realized, sitting there in her room, that I was *unable to want*
her to be able to make this move. This realization was accompanied by
intense feelings of personal humiliation and helplessness, for it ran entirely
counter to my better judgment—namely, that the move would be conducive
to her recovery. I still believe, in retrospect, that this reaction of mine
was less a function of my hatred toward her—I was quite accustomed
to hating her with at times shocking intensity—than of the enormous
loss-feelings, at a repressed level, which the prospect of the move aroused
in me. Incidentally, she did make the move, along with all her fellow
patients.

There emerged much evidence that Susan had functioned as a kind
of unofficial and unacknowledged family therapist in her family, just as
she did on the ward. I remember my amazement at the demeanor of
her mother upon the latter's return from a visit which she and Susan's
brother had just had with her grotesquely and tragically ill daughter.
The mother was laughing gaily and exclaimed delightedly, "She just kept
us in stitches!" Nearly three years later, at a time when Susan was very
markedly improved, her mother was looking, in my office, very like a
little girl who has lost her mother. This was at a time when another
therapist on the staff conveyed to me his astonishment upon noting, during
his own visits to the locked ward for interviews with a patient of his
there, that Susan appeared no longer grotesquely ill but, instead, "like a
girl from a fine Eastern school," as she indeed was.

The father's symbiotic stake in her illness became revealed in the
evolution of the transference, as well as elsewhere. In one of our sessions,
for example, Susan clearly perceived me as being dead and said of her
father later in the session, "He's alive when he gives to me." I had become,
indeed, deeply dependent upon her allowing me to give something to her—

if not an interpretation, then at least some orange juice; it is hardly an overstatement to say that it felt to me that my life depended upon her being willing to accept *something* from me.

It was commonplace at the Lodge to find that marked improvement in this or that patient, was greeted with manifestations of repressed loss-reactions on the parts of those most concerned with the patient; but this was true with extraordinary intensity in Susan's instance. For example, at the end of the fifth year of Susan's stay at the Lodge, both the head nurse of the ward and a nighttime attendant, expressed to me, on the same day, their feelings of being *stunned* by her improvement.

In sessions when she was appearing markedly more healthy, I myself reacted, more often than not, with feelings of overwhelming awe and envy of her healthy, young giantess quality, her Junoesque quality, her quality of radiating an innate social superiority over me. On such occasions I would feel personally, in contrast to her, overwhelmingly puny and socially inferior, and would have no sense whatever that I had made any contribution, however small, to the improvement in her.

On one occasion in the middle of the fifth year, I realized that my then-prevailing feelings of hopelessness about her prognosis were springing, at least in part, from previously repressed feelings of hopelessness about my ever being able to satisfy my sexual desires toward her, she being in this regard, I realized at the same time, the personification of my early mother. Presumably until then I had been hopeless about ever becoming able to *acknowledge* to myself such a desire.

Sometimes Susan clearly manifested all the loss feelings herself, in our symbiotic relationship, in reaction to clinical improvement in her which I consciously welcomed. For example, early in the fifth year, when she was sufficiently improved to be able, for the first time in all our work, to spend the entire session in my office, I felt jubilant about this development, while she clearly was bereft. On another occasion she gave me to know that the loss of her accustomed room, when she came over to my office for the session, was equivalent to the loss of her *self*. I strongly surmise that it was this very kind of primitive loss reaction on my own part which rendered me unable to want her to be able to make the above-mentioned move to the other building: her accustomed room on the locked ward, where our sessions had long been held, presumably had become, at an unconscious level in me, equivalent to my self.

I am implying with these clinical vignettes the principle that the better aware the therapist can become of his heretofore repressed emotional investment in the perpetuation of the patient's illness, the more will there grow a realistic hope for the patient's recovery. I am trying to show that this unconscious investment can exist in many forms, whether in the form of symbiotic dependency, sexual lust, vindictiveness and envy, or whatever. It is obviously important for the other staff-members to become as aware as possible, likewise, of their respective, heretofore unconscious investments in the perpetuation of the patient's illness. The patient's own most crucial unconscious stake in his remaining ill cannot become conscious and eventually resolved if the therapist, at least, cannot face his own hopes for the illness to continue.

My infantile-omnipotence-based feelings of personal guilt concerning Susan's illness impelled me unwittingly to make enormously heavy, coercive demands upon her toward improved functioning and to remain largely oblivious of the progress which, in her individual way, she was actually making. I expressed the latter aspect of this realization in a staff conference near the end of the third year. As I told my colleagues, I had realized recently that I had been

underestimating how much she has put into her therapy—how much progress, relatively, she has gained. I have been so awed by the depth of this illness. For instance, two or three months ago, coming up to see her at five o'clock and she was lying on the floor [in one of the ward's few seclusion rooms] in her slip and menstrual blood was all over her—she was reeking with menstrual blood—and things like this are such that I haven't realized how badly she needs acknowledgment for what [i.e., what forward moves] she *has* been doing.

The above realization had come only a week before when, in a session which involved little meaningful verbal contact, she had asked me laconically, in a shy, eagerly hopeful way, "Strides?", which I heard as her first clear request for recognition, from me, that she was making strides in overcoming her illness. I could see, upon hearing this, that she was indeed making strides in various subtle and seemingly small ways but I had been feeling too burdened, in an agonizedly guilt-ridden way, at the immensity of the task yet before us to have paid any heed to these "little" steps of hers.

During one of the infrequent walks we took together—not really much together, actually—on the hospital grounds during the early years of her treatment (and these ventures had been quite beyond her during the first several months at least), she suddenly dragged me by the hand while she went racing through a kind of dense thicket of low overhanging tree branches which whipped against me. It was a frightening and confusing experience for me but she managed, thus, to communicate to me the idea that this was characteristically the way I made her feel in our sessions, when I tried—without realizing it—to drag her pell-mell and headlong toward health.

On one occasion in those early years, she was able to make a verbal communication of the same order; I was shocked at hearing her say, "Bob [her father's nickname], he dragged me behind a car." This statement, like so many of her cryptic comments, seemed to have a myriad of meanings, many of them unfathomable; but the one shockingly clear meaning it conveyed was that he had (figuratively speaking) dragged her, on a rope, from a car which he was driving. I had long known that all her many accomplishments—athletic, social, and so on—prior to her psychosis had fallen far short of his perfectionistic goals for her. What shocked me in her statement was, more precisely, the realization that my own demands upon her, in her psychotherapy, felt to her to be fully as callous, impossible, and dangerously uncontrollable.

In this era, my enormous, superego-based demands upon her interfered with, if not precluded, the development of realistic hopefulness in her. But, to say a word here on my own behalf, I could not realistically hope to satisfy the extremely ambivalent demands which she was making upon me, for whereas on the one hand she was giving me to feel that I was placing cruelly impossible demands upon her, on the other hand, in ways too numerous and varied to elaborate here, she was conveying to me urgently anguished pleas *for* me to intervene actively in her tragic plight.

I must have become appreciably less superego-tormented for the following development to have taken place in her during the seventh year of our work. She had moved to the previously mentioned small building something like a year before, and the session was being held, as usual, in her room there. She was lying on her bed, as was often the case. The notes I dictated (as was customary) immediately after the session reported that,

In this hour occurred a beautiful example of the development of autonomy [partly through, I would now add, the formation of a healthy identification].

"We were on relatively close and friendly terms in this hour, as has been the case now for some weeks. . . .

In the course of this hour she got to talking about Emily, the [black] maid, and mentioned Emily's last name, which I had not known—"Miller." She said, "Her job is not hard," indicating that she, Susan, has lain there watching Emily do her job. There was no criticism implied in Susan's remarks. She feels fond of Emily, as I have known for several weeks or months, and I, also, admire Emily. Emily, it has seemed to me, has stood in refreshing contrast to my conceited self, from Susan's point of view. Emily is a mature, unassuming, friendly person whom it is easy to respect as a human being.

A bit later on in the hour (there being verbalizations from both of us pretty much throughout the hour), she said something about "dust on the table," indicating the table in her room—or dresser, or something like that—to which I replied, "Yes, that's Emily's job: dusting," again without any criticism of Emily in my tone, simply an acknowledgment that that is Emily's province.

A few minutes later, after other verbalizations about apparently other subjects from both of us, she said, "It's *my* job, *my* place, to grow up, as the years go on," in a tone of quiet, prideful assertion of autonomy, a tone of pleasureful self-possession. There was no defiance implied in this, nor any kind of stiff-arming me away as though to say in any defiant tone, "You stay out of my business." One of the components of this remark was a realization that this is not going to be accomplished in a day or a month, but that it is within her capacity and that it will happen. This struck me as a beautiful example of her identifying usefully with the maid, who has a job which is within the latter's own capacity.

Needless to say, I was tremendously pleased to hear this, and felt at the end of the hour, not many minutes later, like giving her a very warm hug and kiss on the cheek.

This represented a tremendous advance beyond a session in which, while lying hopelessly on the same bed in the same room, she asked me in despair as I walked in and sat down in my usual chair, "Did you come to look at your hole?" This remark had much less of any adult sexual meaning than a meaning referable to the pathologically symbiotic components of our relationship, in terms of which one of her meanings to me was as the personification of my own hopelessness about myself, my feelings of being empty of any personal worth. It seems to me that I must have become, at the time of the above quoted session, at least to some limited degree assured that the function of being psychotherapist to her was within my capacity or she could scarcely have felt, and said, what she did.

Speaking more generally for a moment, it seems to me that the realm of realistic hope, in the doing of psychoanalysis and intensive psychother- apy, becomes more tangible insofar as the therapist can discover meanings, or previously undiscerned meanings, in what is transpiring during the session. In the instance of so tragically ill a patient as Susan, the therapist tends to feel too guiltily and anguishedly enmeshed in the patient's illness to be able to achieve enough of separateness—of objectivity, of distance— to be able to see the meanings in the processes which have both the patient and himself in their grip. In another session in the same room of Susan's to which I just referred, she was standing near her bed, by which I was sitting as usual. She reached down and touched her patterned bedspread and said to me quietly, "Patterns?" Ostensibly she was asking whether I saw the patterns in her bedspread; but I realized that she was asking also whether I was aware of the patterns in our ways of relating to one another which were evident to her. She was not yet well enough to verbalize in more detail about this; but the fact that she had become able to communi- cate on such a level of differentiation surprised and impressed me.

This young woman's illness proved tenacious and severe despite brief improvements which enabled her, for example, successfully to visit her parental home and function capably as hostess at a large cocktail party attended by some fifty of her former friends and acquaintances—a visit from which she had returned to the locked ward looking like the sole survivor of a mining disaster.

Several years later I finally sought weekly supervision—something I had not done at the Lodge, or elsewhere, in several years. I began meeting with one of the few persons higher in the sanitarium staff hierarchy. One of Susan's more troublesome symptoms at the time was her pulling out her scalp hair, one by one, in patches, and eating them. This had gone on for years and contributed greatly to her circus-freak appearance, as well as to my own feelings of helplessness, embarrassment, guilt, and hatred of her.

The supervision had been going on for a few months when I reported a new development in my work with Susan. While sitting on her bed, she had quietly leaned forward so that I could readily look directly at her present bald spot; I had no doubt that she was carefully showing it to me. I noticed that it was an amazingly perfect square. Parenthetically, at this writing, I have little doubt that she was nonverbally conveying to me—among whatever other meanings—her conviction that I am a square; another chronically schizophrenic woman, this one from New York City, used to speak in passing of Herald Square with, I thought, more than merely passing significance.

At any rate, what was new in my work with Susan was that I had become sufficiently free from being enmeshed in guilt so that I could view this symptom from a vantage point, now, of a kind of esthetic interest, although I did not spell all this out to the supervisor. When I reported to him my amazement at seeing how perfect a square she had created on her scalp, his response was to push himself back from his large desk where he sat across from me, look at me condemningly, and ask, heavily, "Just what do you regard as your responsibility to this woman?" With that, I stopped getting supervision from him for, having suffered for years from a kind of malignant overconscientiousness in the work, this response was precisely what I did *not* need. To his credit, he did not take steps to discharge me from the case; but I have never found reason to seek any formal supervision, from anyone, since then.

SUMMARY

Maturation involves one's coming to realize and accept that one's hopes are multifarious, devoted variously to destructive as well as constructive ends, permeated with ambivalence and in many regards mutually irreconcilable, and inherently, therefore, far from wholly fulfillable at best.

Thus the accomplishment of this maturational task requires the recognition and large-scale relinquishment of one's erstwhile unconscious fantasies of omnipotence.

The integration in awareness of previously unintegrated and largely unconscious feelings of hopefulness proceeds in pace with the working through of progressively intense feelings of disappointment, discouragement, despair, grief, and infantile-omnipotence-based frustration-rage. This is a maturational process which is never finally completed but which comprises, rather, the route traversed by every therapist, for example, in terms of the evolution of his own personal feelings in relation to each of the patients with whom he becomes deeply and sustainedly involved. These and additional related psychodynamic principles have been illustrated by two of the author's personal experiences as an analysand and, mainly, by material from his work with borderline and chronically schizophrenic patients. Also discussed was the role of unconscious sadism, on the part of either patient or therapist, in evoking feelings of recurrent and intense disappointment in both participants.

In the therapist's work with those patients who initially feel largely hopeless and who give him much reason, indeed, to write them off as "hopeless cases," it is essential that he become as open as possible, within himself, to experiencing whatever gratifications this work, which innately tends to be so deprivational, so engendering of feelings of futility and discouragement, can afford him, no matter how tabooed these gratifications may be in relation to our time-honored concept of the analyst who experiences in response to the patient naught but affective neutrality and evenly hovering attentiveness. The therapist's becoming aware of these gratifications comes to engender hope in both participants that the therapy will prove meaningful and will eventuate well and relatively successfully.

REFERENCES

1. Searles, H. F. Scorn, disillusionment and adoration in the psychotherapy of schizophrenia. Psychoanal and the Psychoanal Rev, 49:39–60, 1962. Reprinted in Collected Papers on Schizophrenia and Related Subjects. London, Hogarth Press and The Institute of Psycho-Analysis, 1965; and New York International Universities Press, 1965, pp. 605–625.

Herbert A. Rosenfeld, M.D., F.R.C.Psych.

Personal Experiences in Treating Psychotic Patients

At a time when the psychotherapeutic and analytic treatment of psychoses, particularly schizophrenia, has begun to become more firmly established in many countries, particularly in the United States, it may be of interest to hear about the difficulties and struggles that accompanied those first attempts to oppose orthodox or established concepts of treatment in psychiatry. Relevant to this are some of my own personal experiences which helped me to contribute in a decisive way to the fundamental change in the understanding and treatment of psychotic illness. I also want to draw attention to the factors that I regard as essential in the interrelationship between patient and therapist, on which the success or failure of psychoanalytic treatment in general, but particularly the treatment of psychosis, may depend.

From the age of fifteen I began to take a great interest in medicine and read about medical problems in any books that I managed to obtain. My interest in psychology was stimulated by the work of Klages who wrote books on characterology and graphology. My father was a businessman and was hoping that I would follow in his footsteps, but he was also a very open-minded man who supported my intense curiosity to find out everything I could about medicine and psychology. But I soon found that studying both psychology and medicine was practically impossible, and so I started to concentrate first on my medical studies, trying whenever possible to hear lectures on psychological subjects. However, the lectures on psychology at Munich University were usually mostly related to experimental psychology rather than to the development of character or personal-

ity or to the understanding of the mind that I was searching for. There
were occasionally a few lectures on Freud which were not very satisfactory,
so I concentrated mainly on reading Freud, in addition to Jung and Adler
and some of their followers. At that time I felt that there was probably
some truth in most of the books I was studying, and I attempted to keep
an open mind. The professor of psychiatry at Munich University was
Oswald Bumke, who had written an important textbook on psychiatry.[1]
His course of lectures was quite detailed, as he taught two 2-hour classes
a week for a whole term of three to four months. He largely followed
Kraepelin[2] and completely ignored Freud or any dynamic psychology in
his lectures. I found out afterwards that he had written some very critical
articles on Freud in the early part of his career.

After Hitler came to power in the spring of 1933, it was impossible
for me, as a Jew, to work on a psychiatric ward or on any medical ward
in order to acquire more personal contact with patients, because under
the Nazi racial laws, Jewish students were forbidden any work in hospitals.
I was, however, allowed to continue my theoretical studies and to finish
my final medical examinations in Germany. I was also allowed to submit
my M.D. thesis on a psychological subject, "Multiple Absences in Childhood." I was assisted in this work by a Professor Benjamin, a Jew who,
until the end of 1934, had still been able to keep open his small private
hospital (Kinderheim) near Munich for the treatment of psychologically
disturbed children. Then I had to leave Germany, as qualification in medicine was being withheld and, of course, any practical work was impossible.
I was accepted at Guy's Hospital in London for one year's clinical work,
which was the minimum time necessary to take the English qualifying
examination at Edinburgh University. At Guy's Hospital, I made some
contact with Dr. R. D. Gillespie, whose teaching was psychodynamically
oriented, as he had been influenced by Adolf Meyer. I also found that
the Henderson Gillespie textbook on psychiatry,[3] which introduced a dynamic orientation into psychiatric teaching, was a welcome change from
Oswald Bumke.

In January and June 1936, I took the preliminary examinations in
pharmacology, pathological anatomy, bacteriology, public health, and so
forth and in the autumn of that year, I took the qualifying examinations
in Edinburgh in midwifery, surgery, and medicine. I then hoped to do
some practical medicine and afterwards to specialize in psychiatry as I
had always intended. However, immediately after qualification my permit
to stay in England was cancelled. I was offered work in Australia or
India, since only medical specialists of reputation or specialists in disciplines
where there was still some shortage were permitted to stay in England.

I decided to become a psychotherapist, which I had always wanted to be, and was accepted for a two-year training course in psychotherapy at the Tavistock Clinic in the autumn of 1937. During the remaining nine months, I worked first at the Royal Infirmary, Edinburgh, in the medical wards and afterwards for several months at the Postgraduate Hospital at Hammersmith, the Littlemore Mental Hospital near Oxford, and the Maudsley Hospital in London. Treatment of mental patients in England in 1936 was almost nonexistent and was primarily related to taking physical care of the patients and keeping them locked up. For example, at the Littlemore Mental Hospital near Oxford, where I was engaged as a locum, I had to look after 350 patients, which was half the patient population of the hospital. There were only three doctors—the superintendent, who was in charge of the hospital and administration, a senior colleague, and myself—to look after about 700 patients. A senior doctor who had been working in the psychiatric hospital service for many years and who introduced me to my job explained to me that there was very little work to do. After occasionally seeing a new admission, I would have to do rounds of the wards which would take not more than one and a half hours in the morning and then I would generally be free for the rest of the day, except for inquiring in the afternoon or evening whether there was any problem that I had to attend to. He explained to me that the art of being a doctor in a mental hospital was to do as little work as possible and then one would be free to relax. He also told me that the present superintendent's predecessor at Littlemore had spent a great deal of his time talking to the patients in the hospital, obviously attempting some psychotherapy, which my colleague thought was rather cranky. This man had attempted to keep the wards of the hospital unlocked to make the patients feel as free as possible.

I could not trace any of the patients whom the retired superintendent had treated at Littlemore, but I looked around among the new admissions for any of the less chronic cases or any whom I felt to be suitable for psychotherapy. I selected a catatonic patient who had severe attacks every four weeks which lasted only one week. He had been in the hospital for over a year, and the staff complained that he was uncooperative, would not do any work in the wards, and was at times violent. However, he seemed to be quite friendly to me. I asked the superintendent if I could do some simple psychotherapy with this patient. I also asked him whether he would agree to connect any improvement in the patient's condition with the treatment I gave him. Since nobody at this time believed that psychotherapy could have any appreciable effect, any improvement was always called a "remission." I did not doubt that remissions were common, but there was obviously a difference between a spontaneous remission and one that resulted from some external positive influence such as a psychotherapeutic approach. But such a hypothesis would imply that schizophrenia might have a psychogenic basis, which at this time was not acceptable to psychiatrists in England, apart perhaps from R. D. Gillespie and one or two others, such as Clifford Scott whom I had not met at that time.

In talking to this patient, he explained to me that he had to endure electric shocks every night when he was going to bed. This occurred every few weeks and made him feel very disturbed. In other words, he suffered from a delusion of being influenced by a machine, a condition that Tausk described in 1919 in his paper on the "Origins of the Influencing Machine in Schizophrenia."[4] The patient asked me many questions, was friendly, and readily listened to my explanations about his physical sensations, which I thought were mainly sexual feelings that were troubling him. He seemed to be completely ignorant about sex and being informed about it seemed to enable him to become less frightened and more accepting of his sexual feelings. He was very appreciative and asked me what he could do for me. I told him that it would be useful if he could show his appreciation by cooperating in the ward, which would make it much easier for everybody, and he proceeded to do so. From this time onward, his periodic excitement ceased. When I left Littlemore Hospital a month or two after this, the patient had not been discharged, but when I returned six months later, I asked the superintendent whether he had found this patient improved and whether he felt more convinced about the possibility of any psychological approach. The superintendent was surprised by my question. He said the patient had been discharged. It had been an unexpected remission.

I gradually became used to this response, which I met in almost everybody. Working afterwards at the Maudsley Hospital for a few months, I had the opportunity to talk with Dr. Eliot Slater and Dr. Gutman, a well-known German psychiatrist. I explained to Dr. Gutman that I was interested not only in taking detailed case histories, which he was quite willing to allow me to do, but that I also wanted to follow up the patients for a while and to talk to them regularly. He did not object to this but felt that it was a complete waste of my time, because I surely had to realize that schizophrenia was an organic disease. Any apparent conflicts or traumatas were simply aspects created by the patient's organic illness and had no causal effect on the appearance of the illness.

While I was working at the Maudsley, I kept an open mind and I observed a young schizophrenic girl of age sixteen who was severely withdrawn and refused to talk to anybody or take part in any occupation. She explained to me that it was impossible for her to be part of a world where horrible things were going on, such as the fact that she had been born through a hole in her mother's body which disgusted her and made her feel that life was impossible for her to accept. She had discovered this fact just a short time before her illness developed, and she had turned violently against her mother. Unfortunately, I was not allowed to treat this girl, whose case seemed similar to the young catatonic whom I had treated for a short period in the Littlemore Hospital and who had responded to a very simple psychological approach.

I only saw a few of the Maudsley patients regularly. For example, one highly intelligent patient suffered from paranoid delusions and was very withdrawn. He apparently took very little notice of me. He had had two or three schizophrenic attacks that lasted a few months, followed by a spontaneous remission. When I left the Maudsley, he did not seem to have improved, but two years later, when I was working privately, I was contacted by the patient's father. The patient had apparently been talking to his father about my visits to him in the hospital, and during the intervening two years, he had asked his father again and again to try to find out whether he could come to see me. Since my leaving the Maudsley the patient had had two further, quite severe schizophrenic paranoid attacks. I saw the patient for a consultation, and he was very pleased to see me and asked to come and see me regularly. I arranged to see him twice a week. He was generally very carelessly dressed and unshaven, but he always came on time and reported some problems relating to himself. I do not remember the details of my talks with him, but I recognized that many of the stories he told me had some symbolic meaning which I explained to him. At that time, I did not know anything about transference analysis, and very little of that would have entered into this treatment.

After about six months the patient started to dress very much better and appeared in the consulting room cleanly shaven. He was very eager to do some work that he had not been able to do for many years, and a boarding school that he had left about seven years before was eager to have him as a teacher. He felt eager to accept. This seemed rather risky, but in fact he decided without any hesitation to do so, and the job was a great success. But from this time onward he was reluctant to see me because he was afraid that returning to me would remind him again of his previous illness. His father reported to me from time to time that he was getting on well, but I had to accept the patient's need to keep his split-off schizophrenic state in control by avoiding seeing me. This is perhaps a typical response of patients who achieve an improvement by psychotherapy but do not sufficiently work through the process in a transference analysis. It is only when the psychotic process, particularly the splitting mechanisms, is thoroughly worked through in psychoanalytic treatment that the patient feels that returning to visit the therapist not only reminds him of the previous illness but also of the help that he had been able to get.

It seems necessary here to make an attempt to clarify how I was treating schizophrenic patients at the beginning of my career and how it was possible to achieve the few successes that sound almost like a kind of miracle cure. My approach was very simple, as I had no knowledge of psychotherapy or analysis and analyzing the transference. I always felt quite at ease and adopted a very open attitude with the hope that the patient would communicate with me. In this I was almost always successful, and even persistently mute patients often talked to me. I also adopted an empathic attitude and tried to put myself as much as possible into the patient's state of mind. The few patients who responded well to this simple treatment probably felt helped by my closeness and capacity to hold them together. As far as the patient was concerned, these occasional striking improvements were, of course, very superficial, and the "mechanics" of this "cure" were probably based on the idealization of the therapist and the idealization of the patient-therapist relationship. In addition, there was most certainly a deepening of the split between the saner and the more psychotic part of the patient's self, leading to an isolation of the psychotic process. This means that there was a great danger that the split-off psychosis might suddenly reemerge, which would no doubt have overwhelmed the nonpsychotic part of the patient. At this early time, I was unaware of the dangers of an unskilled therapeutic approach to the psychosis, as the importance of analyzing the transference and the psychotic mechanisms was still a closed book to me. It is also important to realize that unskilled psychotherapy of the psychosis is a danger to the therapist's personality, as it inevitably stimulates his feelings of omnipotence. Fortunately, it was quite obvious to me that there were only very few schizophrenic patients who were able to respond to this simple empathic understanding with temporary or even long lasting improvement. At the time, it confirmed to me the importance of psychological factors in schizophrenia. Since many may doubt the diagnosis of schizophrenia in the cases that I treated at that time, I want to stress that all the cases I reported here were typical schizophrenias regarded from the psychiatric point of view. The patients suffered from delusions and hallucinations and had typical schizophrenic thought disorders.

After two months at the Maudsley Hospital, I returned to Littlemore Hospital for a few months, and then I began my psychotherapeutic course at the Tavistock Clinic. Training at the Tavistock Clinic in psychotherapy consisted of some form of personal analysis by somebody on the staff or outside the clinic and treatment of several patients who were seen three times a week and were supervised once a week by a member of the staff. One could not choose one's supervisor. One of the German colleagues I had worked with for the examination in Edinburgh had recommended to me an analyst from Berlin who had recently come to England. He was a pleasant man, and I started analysis with him. However, I would regard his technique and understanding of psychoanalysis by present standards and even by the standards of that period (1937) as rather primitive. He did not follow the transference very clearly and altogether interpreted very little, apart from indicating that the problems related to castration anxieties or oedipal questions, and so forth. Analysis gave me very little understanding and was rather frustrating, but nevertheless I conscientiously went to him for some time.

One of my first patients at the Tavistock Clinic had been diagnosed as suffering from obsessions. Most patients were treated on the couch, but this patient refused to lie down. He formed a strong positive transference and had very little resistance in talking to me. He was fascinated by cancer and cancer research, and he was also very interested in experimenting with death. For example, he turned on the gas at his home and was measuring the time that it would take until he might be overcome by the fumes and lose consciousness. He tried to turn off the gas just before this event occurred. This was obviously a very dangerous way of behaving, and it also became apparent that he was not suffering simply from obsessional thoughts and behavior, but that behind this were real psychotic thought disorders. My senior colleagues at the Tavistock Clinic were convinced that he was schizophrenic, and they were probably right. They asked me to discontinue the treatment, but this was rather painful for both the patient and myself. At that time, I was not sufficiently clear whether I could help the patient and if I would prevent him from possibly killing himself in one of these experiments, so I reluctantly persuaded him to go to a mental hospital for treatment. The patient eventually agreed and wrote me pathetic letters from the hospital, telling me that he was not better and that he felt deserted by me. He did not return to me for treatment after leaving the hospital, and I do not blame him for this. I clearly had a very meager knowledge of psychopathology and offered a rather primitive form of treatment. Yet despite this, I gradually became more and more convinced that the psychological factors in the schizophrenias I had come across played an important, indeed, probably a predominant part in this disease. I was also impressed by the fact that the psychotic patient, particularly the schizophrenic one, was quite capable of forming a relationship with the therapist when he felt understood.

I also decided that whenever possible I would try again to treat any schizophrenic patient who was offered to me for treatment and would continue with them whenever possible. When I was allowed private work with patients in the autumn of 1938, a senior colleague of the Tavistock Clinic, Dr Bevan-Brown, sent me a schizophrenic patient whom he had treated for many years. The patient had had an acute breakdown and had been hospitalized more than ten years ago. Ever since, he had been treated by Dr. Bevan-Brown, whose psychotherapeutic technique was rather unorthodox. At this time, my colleague felt rather stuck with the patient. The patient came from a Quaker family and as a young man was very ignorant and frightened about sex. When he was about twenty-five years old, he developed a delusion that his mother wanted him to have sexual intercourse with her to teach him about sex. When the patient proceeded to creep into bed with her one night, she abruptly rejected him, and soon afterward he attempted suicide. The patient was sent to Bowden House, a private hospital near London, where Dr. Bevan-Brown had worked as an assistant to Dr. Crighton-Miller.

The patient had paranoid delusions of reference for many years after the acute schizophrenic episode had passed, and Dr. Bevan-Brown attempted to treat the patient mainly by reeducation, encouragement, and friendly social relations. Over a period of more than ten years, there had been some improvement, but fundamentally the patient felt misunderstood and rejected by the too-active treatment, which he experienced as intrusion and seduction. Dr. Bevan-Brown had obviously recognized that the schizophrenic breakdown by the patient had a psychogenic origin, and his own approach was, of course, purely intuitive.

I treated this patient from 1937 onward. He discussed in great detail the ambivalent relationship that existed with the previous therapist, which had become his main obsession, and it was obvious that he idealized my own nonintrusive approach with which he felt more comfortable. During the first years of the war the patient attended only occasionally, but then he came regularly for at least another ten years and afterward only from time to time. He gradually became more able to work as a caretaker in a psychiatric nursing home, and his relationship with other people improved. He had a woman friend for many years, but he never achieved a really close relationship with her. He remained in touch with me all his life and wrote to me after he had retired from his job at the age of 70. He had never felt at ease with his family or his sister, probably because of his sexual preoccupations, but now he told me that he was happy to be with his sister as part of his family and felt contented to spend his remaining years living with her in the country.

For a short period in 1930, I treated a young girl who had sexual delusions of somebody wanting to marry her. The delusions during the treatment showed very clearly an oedipal coloring. I interpreted her incestuous sexual phantasies, which were only too obvious, and occasionally I made a transference interpretation. For example, after she told me that a voice had just told her that she was going to get married in a month's time, I pointed out to her that she had begun to care for me and hoped that I would marry her. Unfortunately, these transference interpretations made her very much worse. Her delusions increased, and she had to go into a mental hospital for a long time. I felt very bad about this result, but it enabled me to realize that interpretations of openly oedipal material were very dangerous in schizophrenia. I only found out later that this was mainly due to the concreteness of the schizophrenic's way of thinking and feeling, which distorted interpretations so that they were misheard as actual suggestions. For this reason, interpretations of sexual material in the transference were experienced by the patient as seduction. However disturbing this worsening of the patient's condition had been, it also convinced me that the psychological approach was very powerful: if psychotherapy was able to make a patient so much worse, it should also be able to make him or her better. This was probably the first time that I attempted to analyze sexual delusions in a woman patient by interpreting those delusions both in relation to her father and to the transference. In other words, I treated her as if she were one of the neurotic patients whom I had treated at the Tavistock Clinic. The earlier treatments with the Littlemore Hospital patient and the Maudsley patient had been much simpler, and this had obviously been an advantage, because I did not stir up problems which I could not deal with at the time.

During the war, I first worked full time for the Tavistock Clinic in their wartime home at Westfield College with other members on the staff who had not been called up. I had several borderline patients in treatment, and I occasionally saw schizophrenic and manic-depressive patients for consultation. But I had become increasingly dissatisfied with the kind of therapy I was doing and was reluctant at that time to accept psychotic patients for treatment. I realized that my training had been very imperfect, and I had become quite certain that psychoanalysis was the treatment I wanted to follow. However, the relationship between the Tavistock Clinic staff and the members of the Institute of Psychoanalysis was a mutually critical one, and most psychoanalysts were regarded by my colleagues at Tavistock as being rigid and rejecting to the patient. One of my colleagues at the Tavistock Clinic impressed me as being both human and perceptive in his analytic approach, and he was willing to take me into analysis until he was called up. This short experience, lasting only a few months, was valuable to me because it combined some transference analysis with analysis of projective mechanisms, which was quite new to me.

In my discussions with colleagues at the Tavistock Clinic, Melanie

Klein and her way of thinking and interpreting were frequently discussed. It seemed generally accepted that she had made very important contributions to psychoanalysis and psychotherapy, but in spite of using her terminology, none of the therapists at the Tavistock Clinic at the time had had an analysis from her or from her closest colleagues. My wife needed treatment at this time, and a colleague of the Tavistock Clinic sent her to a close co-worker of Melanie Klein. My wife frequently discussed her treatment with me, and I was astonished by the understanding and insight that she rapidly gained. I also found that I could apply quite a lot of what she was telling me to my difficult patients, and I realized even more forcefully how limited my own knowledge was. I heard at this time that Melanie Klein was returning to London from Pitlochry, Scotland, and as it was not likely that I would be called up to the Forces since I was considered an enemy alien, albeit a friendly one, I decided to apply for training at the Institute of Psychoanalysis. I saw Melanie Klein, who accepted me for analysis, and members of the Training Committee of the British Psycho-Analytic Society accepted me for training. My analysis with Melanie Klein was a revelation to me from the beginning, since at that time I felt particularly receptive to analysis. Melanie Klein had the capacity to understand immediately the anxieties and problems that were preoccupying me and to interpret them in a very direct way. I not only experienced the benefits of the analysis in myself but many of my patients also improved with the widening of my personal psychoanalytic experience.

My second training case at the Institute turned out to be a schizophrenic state with depersonalization. I have published my experiences with this patient in the first chapter of my book on psychotic states.[5] The patient, Mildred, had been suffering from what she called influenza for four to five months when I first saw her. She said she felt tired and ill and could not get up in the morning. She also had difficulty in feeling and thinking because her head felt so heavy. During the early stages of the analysis, she described her sensations and feelings in great detail. She said she felt dim and sleepy, half unconscious, and could hardly keep awake. At times, there was something like a blanket separating her from the world, and she felt dead, "not here," and cut off from herself. She also indicated her awareness of the danger of insanity, because she frequently said that if she tried to join up with this self, it might force her mind completely out of joint. My supervisor for this patient was Dr. Sylvia Payne, who was very experienced diagnostically and psychoanalytically. She warned me that the patient was suffering from a latent psychosis and thought the analysis would mobilize a schizophrenic state, so that I would very likely find myself with an acute schizophrenic patient who would need hospitalization. For this reason, she tried to persuade me to stop the analysis. I fully agreed with Dr. Payne about the danger of mobilizing the schizophrenic state and the responsibility I had toward the patient. But I also remembered vividly my first patient at the Tavistock Clinic whom I had been forced to terminate. I felt very strongly that I could not repeat the experience of terminating a treatment which might have even more severe consequences of driving the patient deeper into her illness than would be likely if I were to continue seeing her. She presented me frequently with the sort of barrier or stonewall that Freud described as characteristic of the treatment of psychotic and narcissistic patients. I now had more hope that with better understanding and with the help of my own analysis I would find a way to make contact with this patient's psychotic state. So I decided to continue my treatment of Mildred, and Dr. Payne agreed that this patient could remain my training case for the time being, and I continued to report to her.

In order to be able to treat a patient, it is first necessary to make enough contact with the patient's feelings and thoughts so that one can feel and experience, oneself, what is going on in the patient. These processes have been examined very sensitively in Money-Kyrle's paper, "Normal Counter Transference and Some of its Deviations."[6] He stressed there that the analyst's empathy and insight, as distinct from his theoretical knowledge, depend on his capacity to identify himself with aspects of the patient's self, for example, his infantile self. He also described the unconscious interplay between the patient's and the analyst's mental processes and the need of the analyst to be conscious of what is going on in the patient and in himself in order to disentangle and interpret to the patient the aspects belonging to the patient. My success in treating psychotic patients so far had probably been due to my capacity to make sufficient contact with my psychotic patients and so make some interaction between them and me possible. However, this was extremely difficult in a patient such as Mildred who was emotionally blocked and negativistic. In the first year of Mildred's analysis, I found it very difficult to understand Mildred's relationship to me. In other words, I could not recognize her transference reactions because they were so peculiar. As I realized that my own mind and my own responses to the patient were the only guide to getting a better understanding, I examined my own "countertransference" to the patient much more fully, and my analysis not only helped me to understand my own reactions to the patient but it also mobilized those areas in me that corresponded to the infantile levels at which the patient was functioning. This could then be worked through in my own analysis. I gradually began to experience in myself a number of the defense mechanisms that were particularly prominent in Mildred, namely the schizoid mechanisms of splitting the self and projecting both the good and bad aspects of the self onto other people, particularly onto the analyst, a process that Melanie Klein[7] described in 1946 as "projective identification." I realized that a great deal of my difficulty with Mildred was related to her intense projection of parts of her self onto me and her persecutory fears of retaliation. When I myself felt less blocked and defensive, not only was I able to understand Mildred better but she seemed to be able to show her own feelings more openly because she probably noticed that I was more receptive to what was going on in her.

In 1946, Melanie Klein elaborated on her earlier work in a paper on "Schizoid Mechanisms"[7] which she read to the British Society. Previously, in 1935, Mrs. Klein[8] had described in some detail early infantile object-relations, experiences, and ego-mechanisms and defenses characteristic for certain phases of infantile development. The earliest phase, lasting approximately four to six months, she called "the paranoid position," because of the quality of the anxieties predominating at that early time. A later phase, which she thought started somewhere between the fourth or sixth month, she called "the depressive position," since during this time infantile anxieties and object-relations assumed a depressive quality. She felt that the early anxieties of the infant had similarities to the psychotic illnesses developing later in life. She actually referred to the early infantile anxieties as "psychotic anxieties," which she believed were regressively revived in the later psychotic illnesses. Now, in her 1946 paper, Melanie Klein described in much greater detail the anxieties and particularly the mechanisms, such as splitting of the ego and projective identification, denial and omnipotence, that were characteristic of the earliest infantile phase which she now renamed "paranoid schizoid position," emphasizing the importance of the schizoid mechanisms that she had discovered. She stressed that if the early paranoid anxieties and schizoid mechanisms continued and were not sufficiently modified during the later depressive position, there was a danger that schizoid or schizophrenic illnesses would develop in later life.

In my paper[5] on "The Schizophrenic State with Depersonalization," written in 1947, I fully applied Mrs. Klein's findings to my own experiences and understanding of Mildred's psychotic illness. This paper came to be regarded as a fundamental paper in the history of the treatment of schizophrenia, as it describes the importance of analyzing the infantile object-relations and mechanisms in the *transference psychosis* which Mildred developed during her analysis. The importance of recognizing and analyzing the psychotic transference phenomena during the analysis of psychotic patients is a crucial aspect of my work with psychotic patients. Through helping students and analysts to recognize these phenomena during the analysis of psychotic patients, some of the mystery of treating psychotic patients by psychotherapy and psychoanalysis has disappeared, and there is now a sounder basis for teaching analysts how to treat psychotic patients psychoanalytically.

From 1947, I always had a few psychotic patients in analysis. In 1949[9] and 1950,[10] I reported on the treatment of a paranoid schizophrenic patient who was a manifest homosexual. In 1952,[11] I described the observation of a superego conflict of a severe catatonic, hallucinating patient whom I was treating in a private mental hospital. The treatment of this patient presented a number of difficulties because he was violent and had difficulty in speaking. Unfortunately, his violence was generally acted out with female and male nurses in the hospital. The patient never referred to this himself, and I could only assume that it had something to do with the patient's difficulties in making himself understood and also with his feelings of humiliation at being so disturbed, which would come out into the open with the nursing staff more than with myself. In spite of his delusions and hallucinations, he always cooperated in the analysis, but when the patient's mother insisted on second opinions about the patient's state, the psychoanalytic treatment became completely disorganized. The patient became aggressive and violent toward me, and he would no longer talk to me.

During the very early period of my attempts to treat psychotic patients, I naturally felt very isolated and alone, as there was nobody who could give me advice on how to proceed, and I was left almost entirely to my own resources. From 1950 onward, Dr. Hanna Segal and Dr. W. Bion started treatment with psychotic patients, but at first we did not share our experiences because we all wanted to pursue and establish our own findings until they became sufficiently clarified to become a conviction we could use for publication. After that the sharing of our experiences was most useful, and I began to conduct seminars and supervisions to help all those interested in the treatment of psychotic patients. It seemed to me essential to give support and advice to all the analysts who attempted to treat psychotic patients, and there was now that possibility, so that we could gradually create a more established form of psychoanalytic treatment of the psychoses, one that would be recognized by the English school of psychiatry.

The resistance of English psychiatrists to psychoanalytic treatment of psychosis has lessened a little over the years, but even today it is far from being accepted by English psychiatrists as a whole. Psychiatric cooperation in establishing more fully the psychotherapeutic and psychoanalytic treatment of psychosis in the hospital is still very limited. So far, only in the Maudsley Hospital in London have in-patient and out-patient units been established where patients can be treated with analytic psychotherapy by the staff. However, there has been an increase in the number of well-trained psychiatrists who apply for psychoanalytic training. There is hope that some change will occur over the years. My own appeal in papers and elsewhere for research funds to enable further work on schizophrenia has not been successful, so I have persisted in continuing with my own research in those cases that were sent to me privately. The supervisory work of the psychotic patients of colleagues has also been of considerable help.

After my paper on analysis of the superego conflict,[11] written in 1952, American psychiatrists and analysts became increasingly interested in my work. In 1953, at the London Congress of Psychoanalysis, I had the opportunity to discuss the treatment of psychosis with a number of American analysts, including for example, Bychowski. Bychowski and I agreed that psychotics could be analyzed, and he also agreed with many of my findings. He was, however, surprised that some of the problems that were encountered in our psychotic patients could also be found in our ordinary psychoanalytic patients who were, at times, merely neurotic or borderline psychotic. He did not agree that it was necessary to analyze psychoanalytic candidates more deeply. More recently, some of the American analysts have changed their opinion; for example, when I was working for a few days in Topeka, some training analysts confided to me that many of the candidates in training had severe narcissistic disturbances, and they were worried as to whether this could be altered by analysis. So there was at least a recognition that narcissistic problems are as common in psychiatrists as in other people—and that they need analysis. There is evidence that some candidates in psychoanalytic training turn out to have borderline problems, and occasionally psychotic illnesses have been discovered. However, what I want to stress here is that at the time of talking with Bychowski in 1953, I was convinced, not only from my own experience in analysis but also from my analytic experience with patients, that there were psychotic anxieties in everyone, though, of course, the degree and intensity of the problems varied from case to case.

From 1962 onward the American Psychiatric Association became interested in my work with psychotic patients. In 1962, they invited me to discuss the treatment of depressive patients at a meeting of American psychiatrists at Montreal.[12,13] They repeated this invitation in 1964 when they asked me to talk in Boston about recent research into psychoanalytic treatment of schizophrenic patients.[14] In the Boston meeting, I was stimulated by the great interest shown to me by the large American audience, which was composed of psychiatrists, psychologists, social workers, and psychoanalysts. I was given over one hour to deliver my paper, which was followed by a lively discussion. I was also asked to lecture on "Problems in the Treatment of Psychosis" to other hospitals, and a seminar for members of the Psychoanalytic Society of Boston was arranged. The Maclean Hospital which was looking after 150 schizophrenic in- and out-patients asked me to talk talk about "Problems of Dealing with the Erotic Transference in Schizophrenic Patients." The choice of the title for this lecture showed that the psychotherapeutic approach to psychotic patients was obviously quite well established in the hospital, but it was not possible at that time to contact individual therapists to offer supervisory work. Therefore, I could not judge the general standard or skill of the therapeutic work that was going on. It is, however, clear to me that the interest in the psychological approach to psychosis is very much wider in the United States than in England. The opposition to the psychological approach to psychosis in England is mainly related to the continuing emphasis on the organic factors in schizophrenic and manic-depressive states. This has discouraged and still discourages any psychotherapeutic interest. In the United States, this is rather different. Probably through the influence of Adolf Meyer, Harry Stack Sullivan, Robert Knight, Frieda Fromm Reichmann, Harold Searles, and possibly John Rosen, there is a general awareness that psychotic illness is largely determined by psychogenic factors and that awareness encourages many psychiatrists to treat psychotic patients psychotherapeutically.

Such an atmosphere brings with it some other problems, which I discussed in a recent lecture for the Westwood Hospital in Los Angeles on the "Treatment of Psychoses." I emphasized that while it was encouraging and interesting to see so many young doctors and residents attempting to treat, sometimes successfully, very ill psychotic patients in hospital or on an out-patient basis, a personal analysis of the doctor was nevertheless absolutely essential for anyone interested in the treatment of psychosis. Only a personal analysis will bring the therapist into contact with his own hidden psychotic areas, which could very easily become activated during the treatment of psychotic patients, thereby creating anxieties or even confusion if they are not thoroughly dealt with through psychoanalytic therapy. The severe strain that some analysts encounter in the treatment of psychotic patients is first of all related to their own psychotic anxieties, which are stimulated through the contact with psychotic patients and which they have to control and defend against, causing the therapy to become a strain. As it is essential in the treatment of psychotic patients to be receptive and quite open to the communications of the patient who projects his feelings and problems often quite violently, it is obvious that any analyst who is afraid of contact with his patient might himself become severely depressed in attempting to treat psychotics. The most frequent anxiety is the fear of being driven mad by the patient. It is for this reason that the analysis of the analyst should be particularly thorough, and this, of course, includes an exposure of the psychotic areas in the analyst so that the psychotic anxieties and defenses can be worked through sufficiently during the training period. Occasionally a second analysis might be necessary. Even if the analyst feels consciously quite well but has split off or suppressed psychotic conflicts, he will tend to be insensitive or defensive to the psychotic patient's behavior, and it is inevitable that the patient, consciously or unconsciously, will perceive the disturbances in the analyst and react or interact with them. There is also the danger that the latent conflict of the analyst may become stimulated and activated in contact with psychotic patients. For example, the tendencies to omnipotent and omniscient function can become greatly increased. We have to realize that in treating psychotic patients, the analyst's personality, not only his intellect, is a tool in the treatment, and therefore his mental health is an extremely important factor. Only in this way can he respond to the patient with empathy, but without too much involvement, and with sensitivity and receptiveness, but without being overwhelmed by the patient's projection.

One of the most important aspects of the treatment of psychotic patients is the recognition that they communicate with the analyst in very primitive ways—not only by verbal but also by nonverbal means. Nonverbal communication takes place in a great number of ways, for example, through simple behavior, posture, and other actions, such as bodily movements and facial expressions. In addition to the tone of voice, expressions of different feelings or lack of feelings often come through quite clearly. There are, however, a number of nonverbal communications that are conveyed by the patient's projection of his own feelings onto the analyst or the analytic setting. These are often difficult to define or to observe by visual or auditory means. For instance, there is the power of the patient to create an emotional atmosphere which can be clearly noticed. Some of the projections of the patient are accompanied by fantasies that have strong dynamic force. In the psychotic patient, these fantasies are often experienced by him to be so real that they acquire a delusional character. These delusional projections often seem to exert a strong hypnotic influence on the analyst, which may interfere with his functions and may lead to collusion and acting out by the analyst or to the analyst feeling intruded on and overwhelmed by the projection. In other words, not only the patient but also the analyst feels that the projection has a realistic element, such as the experience that something is actually being forced onto him by the patient. The disturbing experiences created by the patient in the analyst should disappear as soon as the analyst becomes able to realize what has been going on. Lasting disturbances in the analyst only take place if his own feelings become inextricably entangled with those of the patient. I feel that it is fortunate that over the years, probably through development of my own inner self and personality and a great deal of experience, feelings of entanglement with my patients have become rare. Patients often fear that by their projection they can damage the analyst, and these fears become true if the analyst is not able to cope well with the patient's projections.

In receiving the nonverbal communications, particularly those feelings communicated by projection, the analyst has to be fairly certain that he can differentiate between his own feelings and the patient's projected emotions and experiences. It often takes some time to diagnose the situation. At first, the analyst may only be aware of an inner tension, and then he notices that something is going on internally that is difficult to understand. At such moments, he may have to remain quiet and allow himself to open further so that the projection of the patient does not get blocked by his personal defensive reaction. The analyst may then become aware, for example, that he feels small, hurt, helpless, and quite powerless to deal with any situation. Outwardly, the patient may have been talking in an aggressive or assertive voice accompanied by similar behavior while in fact he was projecting an infantile helpless part onto the analyst, and the only way the analyst notices this is through a *sudden experience of this emotional situation* representing an aspect of the patient *in himself.* The capacity to pick up the patient's nonverbal projections is, of course, quite essential in the treatment of psychotic patients.

The analyst must also consider how much of his perceptive experience should be communicated to the patient and in which form and at what time. If the analyst interprets the patient's projected feelings too quickly, the patient, because of this too-rapid explanation, may often experience a sense of rejection. So the analyst must contain the feelings that the patient creates in him for a considerable time before he can verbalize them to the patient. But it is, of course, important to be able to identify the patient's projections and to verbalize them to oneself as quickly as possible in order to follow the details of the patient's communication. Some analysts, such as Searles, have studied this interaction with the patient in very great detail.[15] Searles has gone so far as to act out and play the role of another person whom he feels has been projected onto him in order to make the relationship more vivid. I, myself, do not feel that it is useful either for me or for the patient to act out any particular role that has been assigned to me by the patient. Rather, I try to understand that he wants to project something specific. I attempt to bring a number of different aspects or parts of the patient's personality meaningfully together, for these often exist in a split-off form which prevents the patient from understanding himself and thinking about himself. This integrative form of interpretation seems both to help the patient to regain his mental functioning and to strengthen his ego, whereas a piecemeal interpretation of the various aspects that are projected onto the analyst by an enactment of them can be experienced by the patient as an attack or rejection by the analyst, for it can produce states of disintegration that are often experienced by the patient or anxiety that he will fall to pieces.

The anxieties and sensations of falling or of falling to pieces are probably related to the earliest infantile anxiety experiences of the birth situation, where the infant has to relinquish the state of being held safely in the mother's womb. It is therefore understandable that the early mother/infant relationship must be looked upon as a situation that is dominated by the infant's need to be treated by the mother in a way that resembles as much as possible, the prebirth experience. Winnicott's[16] work on the holding environment and Bion's[17] work on the mother as a container of the infant, to be protected from the overwhelming anxieties of falling, from being dropped, and the feelings of helpless rage, are related to these experiences. Most psychotic patients either experience overwhelming anxiety or defend themselves in many different ways against the emergence of overwhelming anxieties. It is therefore understandable that in the treatment of psychotic patients, the analyst's attitude and empathy towards his patient must play a particularly significant role, and as I have pointed out, the psychotic patient communicates his anxieties and needs predominantly in a nonverbal or preverbal form to which the analyst must be receptive. Many analysts, such as Searles,[15] Fromm Reichmann,[18] Winnicott,[16] and others, feel that the needs of the psychotic patient have often to be satisfied by the analyst's behavior, and they feel that verbal interpretations are often contraindicated. For example, Searles stresses the importance of recognizing the infant's symbiotic needs by creating a long period of symbiotic oneness with the patient where the analyst's capacity to remain silent with the patient is of central importance. Nacht's[19] emphasis on the analyst's silence has similar implications as the analyst's attempt to recreate for the patient a situation of an ideal mother/infant experience, where all aggression is eliminated.

I agree that most patients, particularly psychotic ones, often experience the use of words as a situation that makes them acutely aware of being separate from the analyst. Sometimes it is the persistent silence of the patient that draws attention to his resentment of verbal communication, and similarly the analyst's verbal interpretations may be experienced by the patient as a rejection of the patient's wish for nonverbal oneness with the analyst/mother. I have, however, found that most psychotic patients understand and value verbal communications from the analyst when the analyst succeeds in conveying to the patient what he has understood. In this way the analyst's intuitive and receptive empathy is being expressed in a verbal form, which has the advantage that the patient is not infantilized, that is, treated as if he were, in fact, an infant. The analyst should acknowledge fully what the patient feels and needs, but he should not leave out from the analytic relationship the equally important fact that the patient is also a separate being and an adult. Of course, tact and sensitivity must be employed in these interpretations so that the patient feels helped and held together through the analyst's words. I have sometimes been told by a patient that my interpretations fit so well into their own experience that they actually feel a kind of physical contact and holding conveyed by my interpretations. This has convinced me that verbal interpretations can create a holding experience, and this has always been my aim. In my own experience, psychotic patients rarely view correct verbal interpretations as rejection, particularly if the analyst's whole attitude and behavior and way of communicating also conveys to the patient acceptance and understanding.

I have tried in this paper to share some of my experiences with psychotic patients with the reader. I have also attempted to communicate my own understanding of the essential factors in the patient/analyst relationship that makes the analysis of psychotic patients possible. I am fully aware that not all psychotherapists are able or want to treat psychotic patients, and we should be perceptive in accepting our own limitations. However, in my wide experience of supervising students and analysts in many different countries, I have come across very gifted young therapists who show exceptional talent even at the early stages of their psychotherapeutic or analytic training. These people should have all the help that is now available to train them in the treatment of borderline and psychotic patients. Such help would accelerate progress of the psychoanalytic treatment of psychosis, for despite the advances, it is still rather limited.

REFERENCES

1. Bumke O: Handbuch der Geisteskrankleiten, 1928
2. Kraepelin: Psychiatrie, 8th ed. 1913
3. Henderson DK, Gillespie RD: A Textbook of Psychiatry. London, Oxford Medical Publications, 1936.
4. Tausk V: Origins of the influencing machine in schizophrenia (1919). Reprinted in Psychoanal Q 2:1933.
5. Rosenfeld HA: Analysis of a schizophrenic state with depersonalization

(1947). *In:* Psychotic States: A Psychoanalytical Approach. London, Hogarth Press, 1964.

6. Money-Kyrle R: Normal counter transference and some of its deviations. Int J Psychoanal 37:1956.

7. Klein M: Notes on some schizoid mechanisms. *In:* The Writings of Melanie Klein, vol. 2. London, Hogarth Press, 1946.

8. Klein M: A contribution to the psychogenesis of manic-depressive states. *In:* The Writings of Melanie Klein, vol 1. London, Hogarth Press, 1935.

9. Rosenfeld HA: Remarks on the relation of male homosexuality to paranoia, paranoid anxiety and narcissism (1949). *In:* Psychotic States: A Psychoanalytical Approach. London, Hogarth Press, 1964.

10. Rosenfeld HA: Note on the psychopathology of confusional states in chronic schizophrenics. Int J Psychoanal 33:132–137, 1950.

11. Rosenfeld HA: Notes on the psychoanalysis of the superego conflict of an acute schizophrenic patient. Int J Psychoanal 33:111–131, 1952.

12. ————: Notes on the psychopathology and psychoanalytical treatment of depressive and manic-depressive patients. Research Reports of the American Psychiatric Association. November 1963.

13. ————: Notes on the psychopathology and psychoanalytical treatment of schizophrenia. Research Reports of the American Psychiatric Association. November 1963.

14. ————: Object relationship in the acute schizophrenic patient in the transference situation. Research Reports of the American Psychiatric Association. December 1964.

15. Searles HF: Transference psychosis in the psychotherapy of chronic schizophrenia. Int J Psychoanal 44:1963.

16. Winnicott DW: The Maturational Process and the Facilitating Environment. London, Hogarth Press, 1965.

17. Bion WR: Notes on the Theory of Schizophrenia: Second Thoughts. London, Heinemann, 1954.

18. Fromm-Reichmann F: Psychotherapy of schizophrenia. *In:* Bullard DM (ed): Psychoanalysis and Psychotherapy. Chicago, University of Chicago Press, 1959.

19. Nacht S: Curative factors in psychoanalysis. Int J Psychoanal 43:1962.

Harry Guntrip, Ph.D.

My Experience of Analysis With Fairbairn and Winnicott [How Complete a Result Does Psychoanalytic Therapy Achieve?]

It does not seem to me useful to attempt a purely theoretical answer to the question forming the sub-title. Theory does not seem to me to be the major concern. It is a useful servant but a bad master, liable to produce orthodox defenders of every variety of the faith. We ought always to sit light to theory and be on the look-out for ways of improving it in the light of therapeutic practice. It is therapeutic practice that is the real heart of the matter. In the last resort good therapists are born not trained, and they make the best use of training. Maybe the question "How complete a result can psycho-analytic therapy produce?" raises the question "How complete a result did our own training analysis produce?" Analysts are advised to be open to post-analytic improvements, so presumably we do not expect "an analysis" to do a "total" once for all job. We must know about post-analytic developments if we are to assess the actual results of the primary analysis. We cannot deal with this question purely on the basis of our patients' records. They must be incomplete for the primary analysis and non-existent afterwards. As this question had unexpected and urgent relevance in my case, I was compelled to grapple with it; so I shall risk offering an account of my own analysis with Fairbairn and Winnicott, and its after-effects: especially as this is the only way I can present a realistic picture of what I take to be the relationship between the respective contributions of these two outstanding analysts, and what I owe to them.

The question "How complete a result is possible?" had compelling importance for me because it is bound up with an unusual factor; a total

amnesia for a severe trauma at the age of three and a half years, over
the death of a younger brother. Two analyses failed to break through
that amnesia, but it was resolved unexpectedly after they had ended, certainly only because of what they had achieved in "softening up" the major
repression. I hope this may have both a theoretical and a human interest.
The long quest for a solution to that problem has been too introverted
an interest to be wholly welcomed, but I had no option, could not ignore
it and so turned it into a vocation through which I might help others.
Both Fairbairn and Winnicott thought that but for that trauma, I might
not have become a psychotherapist. Fairbairn once said: "I can't think
what could motivate any of us to become psychotherapists, if we hadn't
got problems of our own." He was no super-optimist and once said to
me: "The basic pattern of personality once fixed in early childhood, can't
be altered. Emotion can be drained out of the old patterns by new experience, but water can always flow again in the old dried up water courses."
You cannot give anyone a different history. On another occasion he said:
"You can go on analyzing forever and get nowhere. It's the personal
relation that is therapeutic. Science has no values except scientific values,
the schizoid values of the investigator who stands outside of life and
watches. It is purely instrumental, useful for a time but then you have
to get back to living." That was his view of the "mirror analyst," a non-
relating observer simply interpreting. Thus he held that psychoanalytic
interpretation is not therapeutic *per se,* but only as it expresses a personal
relationship of genuine understanding. My own view is that science is
not necessarily schizoid, but is really practically motivated, and often becomes schizoid because it offers such an obvious retreat for schizoid intellec-
tuals. There is no place for this in psychotherapy of any kind.

I already held the view that psychoanalytic therapy is not a purely
theoretical but a truly understanding personal relationship, and had published it in my first book before I had heard of Fairbairn; after reading
his papers in 1949, I went to him because we stood philosophically on
the same ground and no actual intellectual disagreements would interfere
with the analysis. But the capacity for forming a relationship does not
depend solely on our theory. Not everyone has the same facility for forming
personal relationships, and we can all form a relationship more easily
with some people than with others. The unpredictable factor of "natural
fit" enters in. Thus, in spite of his conviction Fairbairn did not have the
same capacity for natural, spontaneous "personal relating" that Winnicott
had. With me he was more of a "technical interpreter" than he thought
he was, or than I expected: but that needs qualification. I went to him
in the 1950s when he was past the peak of his creative powers of the
1940s, and his health was slowly failing. He told me that in the 1930s
and 1940s he had treated a number of schizophrenic and regressed patients

with success. That lay behind his "theoretical revision" in the 1940s. He felt he had made a mistake in publishing his theory before the clinical evidence. From 1927 to 1935 he was psychiatrist at The University Psychological Clinic for Children, and did a lot of work for the N.S.P.C.C. One cannot be impersonal with children. He asked one child whose mother thrashed her cruelly: "Would you like me to find you a new kind Mummy?" She said: "No. I want my own Mummy," showing the intensity of the libidinal tie to the bad object. The devil you know is better than the devil you do not, and better than no devil at all. Out of such experience with psychotic, regressed and child patients, his theoretical revision grew, based on the *quality* of parent-child relations, rather than the *stages* of biological growth, a "personality-theory" not an impersonal "energy-control theory." He summed it up in saying that "the cause of trouble is that parents somehow fail to get it across to the child that he is loved for his own sake, as a person in his own right." By the 1950s, when I was with him, he wisely declined to take the strains of severely regressing patients. To my surprise I found him gradually falling back on the "classical analyst" with an "interpretive technique," when I felt I needed to regress to the level of that severe infancy trauma.

Stephen Morse,[1] in his study of "structure" in the writings of Winnicott and Balint, concluded that they discovered new data but did not develop structural theory in a way that could explain them; which, however, he felt could be done by what he called the "Fairbairn-Guntrip metaphor." Having had the benefit of analysis with both these outstanding analysts, I feel the position is somewhat more complex than that. The relation between Fairbairn and Winnicott is both theoretically important and very intriguing. Superficially they were quite unlike each other in type of mind and method of working, which prevented their knowing how basically close they were in the end. Both had deep roots in classic Freudian theory and therapy, and both outgrew it in their own different ways. Fairbairn saw that intellectually more clearly than Winnicott. Yet in the 1950s, Fairbairn was more orthodox in clinical practice than Winnicott. I had just over 1000 sessions with Fairbairn in the 1950s and just over 150 with Winnicott in the 1960s. For my own benefit I kept detailed records of every session with both of them, and all their correspondence. Winnicott said, "I've never had anyone who could tell me so exactly what I said last time." Morse's article suggested a restudy of those records last year, and I was intrigued to find the light they cast on why my *two analyses failed to resolve my amnesia for that trauma at three and a half years, and yet each in different ways prepared for its resolution as a post-analytic development.* I had to ask afresh, "What is the analytic therapeutic process?"

In general I found Fairbairn becoming more *orthodox in practice* than in theory while Winnicott was more *revolutionary in practice* than in theory. They were complementary opposites. Sutherland in his obituary notice[2] wrote:

> Fairbairn had a slightly formal air about him—notably aristocratic, but in talking to him I found he was not at all formal or remote. Art and religion were for him profound expressions of man's needs, for which he felt a deep respect, but his interests revealed his rather unusual conservatism.

I found him formal in sessions, the intellectually precise interpreting analyst, but after sessions we discussed theory and he would unbend, and I found the human Fairbairn as we talked face to face. Realistically, he was my understanding good father after sessions, and in sessions in the transference he was my dominating bad mother imposing exact interpretations. After his experimental creative 1940s, I feel his conservatism slowly pushed through into his work in the 1950s. The shock of his wife's sudden death in 1952 created obvious domestic problems. Early in the 1950s he had the first attack of viral influenza, and these became more virulent as the decade advanced. For two years after his wife's death he worked hard on his fine paper, "Observations on the nature of hysterical states,"[3] which finalized his original thinking. He clarified his views on "psychoanalysis and science" in two papers.[4,5] But there was a subtle change in his next paper, "Considerations arising out of the Schreber case."[6] Here he fell back from his "ego and object relations" psychology, explaining everything as due to "primal scene" libidinal excitations and fears. Finally, in his last paper, "On the nature and aims of psycho-analytical treatment"[7] his entire emphasis was on the "internal closed system" of broadly oedipal analysis, not in terms of instincts, but of internalized libidinized and antilibidinized bad-object relations. I went to him to break through the amnesia for that trauma of my brother's death, to whatever lay behind it in the infancy period. There, I felt, lay the cause of my vague background experiences of schizoid isolation and unreality, and I knew that they had to do with my earliest relations with mother, though only because of information she had given me.

After brother Percy's death I entered on four years of active battle with mother to force her "to relate," and then gave it up and grew away from her. I will call that, for convenience, the oedipal internalized bad-object relations period: it filled my dreams, but repeatedly sudden, clear schizoid experiences would erupt into this, and Fairbairn steadily interpreted them as "withdrawal" in the sense of "escapes" from internalized bad-object relations. He repeatedly brought me back to oedipal three-person libidinal and anti-libidinal conflicts in my "inner world," Kleinian "object splits" and Fairbairnian "ego splits" in the sense of oedipal libidinal excitations. In 1956 I wrote to ask him to say exactly what he thought about the Oedipus complex, and he replied: "The Oedipus complex is central for therapy but not for theory." I replied that I could not accept that: for me theory *was* the theory of *therapy*, and what was true for one must be true for both. I developed a double resistance to him consciously, partly feeling he was my bad mother forcing her views on me, and partly openly disagreeing with him on genuine grounds. I began to insist that my real problem was not the bad relationships of the post-Percy period, but mother's basic "failure to relate at all" right from the start. I said that I felt oedipal analysis kept me marking time on the same spot, making me use bad relations as better than none at all, keeping them operative in my inner world as *a defence against the deeper schizoid problem.* He saw that as a defensive character trait of "withdrawness."[8] I felt it as a problem in its own right, not just a defence against his closed-system "internal world of bad-object relations."

But my oedipal analysis with Fairbairn was not a waste of time. Defences have to be analyzed and it brought home to me that I had actually repressed the trauma of Percy's death and all that lay behind it, by building over it a complex experience of sustained struggle in bad-object relations with mother, which in turn I had also to repress. It was the basis of my spate of dreams, and intermittent production of conversion symptoms. Fairbairn for long insisted that it was the *real core* of my psychopathology. He was certainly wrong, but it did have to be radically analyzed to open the way to the deeper depths. That happened. Steadily regressive and negative schizoid phenomena thrust into the material I brought to him, and at last he began to accept in theory what he no longer had the health to cope with in practice. He generously accepted my concept of a "regressed ego" split off from his "libidinal ego" and giving up as hopeless the struggle to get a response from mother. When I published that idea, Winnicott wrote to ask: "Is your Regressed Ego withdrawn or repressed?" I replied: "Both. First withdrawn and then kept repressed." Fairbairn wrote to say:

This is your own idea, not mine, original, and it explains what I have never been able to account for in my theory, Regression. Your emphasis on ego-weakness yields better therapeutic results than interpretation in terms of libidinal and antilibidinal tensions.

When in 1960 I wrote "Ego-weakness, the hard core of the problem of psychotherapy" he wrote to say: "If I could write now, that is what I would write about." I knew my theory was broadly right for it conceptualized what I could not yet get analysed. With I think great courage, he accepted that.

I shall complete my account of Fairbairn as analyst and man by illustrating the difference in "human type" between him and Winnicott, a factor that plays a big part in therapy. The set-up of the consulting room itself creates an atmosphere which has meaning. Fairbairn lived in the country and saw patients in the old Fairbairn family house in Edinburgh. I entered a large drawing room as waiting room, furnished with beautiful valuable antiques, and proceeded to the study as consulting room, also large with a big antique bookcase filling most of one wall. Fairbairn sat behind a large flat-topped desk, I used to think "in state" in a high-backed plush-covered armchair. The patient's couch had its head to the front of the desk. At times I thought he could reach over the desk and hit me on the head. It struck me as odd for an analyst who did not believe in the "mirror-analyst" theory. Not for a long time did I realize that I had "chosen" that couch position, and there was a small settee at the side of his desk at which I could sit if I wished, and ultimately I did. That this imposing situation at once had an unconscious transference meaning for me became clear in a dream in the first month. I must explain that my father had been a Methodist Local Preacher of outstanding eloquence as a public speaker, and from 1885 built up and led a Mission Hall which grew into a Church which still exists. In all my years of dreaming he never appeared as other than a supportive figure *vis-à-vis* mother, and in actual fact she *never* lost her temper in his presence. I wanted Fairbairn in transference as the protective father, helping me to stand up to my aggressive mother, but unconsciously I felt otherwise, for I dreamed:

I was in father's Mission Hall. Fairbairn was on the platform but he had mother's hard face. I lay passive on a couch on the floor of the Hall, with the couch head to the front of the platform. He came down and said: 'Do you know the door is open?' I said: 'I didn't leave it open,' and was pleased I had stood up to him. He went back to the platform.

It was a thinly disguised version of his consulting room set-up, and showed that I wanted him to be my supportive father, but that wish was overpowered by a clear negative transference from my severe dominating mother. That remained by and large Fairbairn's transference role "in sessions." He interpreted it as the "one up and the other down" bad parent-child "see-saw" relation. It can only be altered by turning the tables. I found that very illuminating, containing all the ingredients of unmet needs, smothered rage, inhibited spontaneity. It was the dominant transference relationship in sessions. After sessions Fairbairn could unbend in our theory and therapy discussion, the good human father.

This negative transference in sessions was, I feel, fostered by his *very intellectually precise interpretations.* Once he interpreted: "Something forecloses on the active process in the course of its development." I would have said: "Your mother squashed your naturally active self." But he accurately analyzed my emotional struggle to force mother to mother me after Percy died, and showed how I had internalized it. That had to be done first, but he held it to be the central oedipal problem, and could not accept till it was too late that this masked a far deeper and more serious problem. Later Winnicott twice remarked: "You show no signs of ever having had an Oedipus complex." My family pattern was not oedipal. It was always the same in dreams and is shown by the most striking one of them.

I was being besieged and was sitting in a room discussing it with father. It was mother who was besieging me and I said to him, "You know I'll never give in to her. It doesn't matter what happens. I'll never surrender." He said, "Yes. I know that. I'll go and tell her" and he went and said to her, "You'd better give it up. You'll never make him submit," and she did give up.

Fairbairn's persistence in oedipal interpretations I could not accept as final, cast him in the role of dominating mother. It came to our ears that Winnicott and Hoffer thought my adherence to his theory was due to its not allowing him to analyse my aggression in the transference. But they didn't see me knock over his pedestal ashtray, and kick his glass door-stopper, "accidentally" of course, and we know what that means in sessions, as he was not slow to point out. They did not see me once strew some of his books out of that huge bookcase over the floor, symbolic of "tearing a response out of mother," and then putting them back tidily to make a reparation *à la* Melanie Klein. But after sessions we could discuss and I could find the natural warm-hearted human being behind the exact interpreting analyst.

I can best make this clear by comparison with Winnicott. His consulting room was simple, restful in colours and furniture, unostentatious, carefully planned, so Mrs. Winnicott told me, by both of them, to make the patient feel at ease. I would knock and walk in, and presently Winnicott would stroll in with a cup of tea in his hand and a cheery "Hallo," and sit on a small wooden chair by the couch. I would sit on the couch sideways or lie down as I felt inclined, and change position freely according to how I felt or what I was saying. Always at the end, as I departed he held out his hand for a friendly handshake. As I was finally leaving Fairbairn after the last session, I suddenly realized that in all that long period we had never once shaken hands, and he was letting me leave without that friendly gesture. I put out my hand and at once he took it, and I suddenly saw a few tears trickle down his face. *I saw the warm heart of this man with a fine mind and a shy nature.* He invited my wife and me to tea whenever we visited her mother in Perthshire.

To make the ending of my analysis with Fairbairn meaningful, I must give a brief sketch of my family history. My mother was an overburdened "little mother" before she married, the eldest daughter of eleven children and saw four siblings die. Her mother was a feather-brained beauty queen, who left my mother to manage everything even as a schoolgirl. She ran away from home at the age of twelve because she was so unhappy, but was brought back. Her best characteristic was her strong sense of duty and responsibility to her widowed mother and three younger siblings, which impressed my father when they all joined his Mission Hall. They married in 1898 but he did not know that she had had her fill of mothering babies and did not want any more. In my teens she occasionally became confidential and told me the salient facts of family history, including that she breast-fed me because she believed it would prevent another pregnancy; she refused to breast-feed Percy and he died, after which she refused further intimacy. My father was the youngest son of a High-Church and high Tory family, the politically left-wing and religiously Nonconformist rebel; and anti-imperialist who nearly lost his position in the City by refusing to sign his firm's pro-Boer War petition. That passing anxiety gave my mother the chance to wean me suddenly and start a business of her own. We moved when I was one year old. She chose a bad site and lost money steadily for seven years, though everything was more than retrieved by the next move. *That first seven years of my life, six of them at the first shop, was the grossly disturbed period for me.* I was left to the care of an invalid aunt who lived with us. Percy was born when I was two years old and died when I was three and a half. Mother told me father said he would have lived if she had breast-fed him, and she got angry. It was a disturbed time. In her old age, living in our home, she would say some revealing things. "I ought never to have married and had children. Nature did not make me to be a wife and mother, but a business woman," and "I don't think I ever understood children. I could never be bothered with them."

She told me that at three and a half years I walked into a room and saw Percy lying naked and dead on her lap. I rushed up and grabbed him and said: "Don't let him go. You'll never get him back!" She sent me out of the room and I fell mysteriously ill and was thought to be dying. Her doctor said: "He's dying of grief for his brother. If your mother wit can't save him, I can't," so she took me to a maternal aunt who had a family, and there I recovered. Both Fairbairn and Winnicott thought I would have died if she had not sent me away from herself. All memory of that was totally repressed. The amnesia held through all the rest of my life and two analyses, till I was seventy, three years ago. But it remained alive in me, to be triggered off unrecognized by widely spaced analogous events. At the age of twenty-six, at the University, I formed a good friendship with a fellow student who was a brother figure to me. When he left and I went home on vacation to mother, I fell ill of a mysterious exhaustion illness, which disappeared immediately (sic) I left home and returned to college. I had no idea that it was equivalent to that aunt's family. In 1938, aged thirty-seven, I became minister of a highly organized Church in Leeds, with a Sunday afternoon meeting of 1,000 men, an evening congregation of 800, and well organized educational, social and recreational activities. It was too large for one minister and I had a colleague who became another Percy-substitute. He left as war clouds loomed up. Again I suddenly fell ill of the same mysterious illness. It was put down to overwork, but by then I was psychoanalytically knowledgeable, had studied classical theory under Flugel, knew the stock literature, had an uncompleted M.A. thesis under supervision of Professor John Macmurray, seeking to translate Freud's psychobiology, or rather clinical data, into terms of "personal relations" philosophy, and had studied my own dreams for two years. So I was alerted when this illness brought a big dream.

I went down into a tomb and saw a man buried alive. He tried to get out, but I threatened him with illness, locked him in and got away quick.

Next morning I was better. For the first time I recognized the re-eruption of my illness after Percy's death, and saw that I lived permanently over the top of its repression. I knew then I could not rest till that problem was solved.

I was drawn into war-time emergency psychotherapy by the Leeds Professor of Medicine, appointed to a lectureship in the Medical School, and went on studying my own dreams. I recently re-read the record and found I had only made forced text-bookish oedipal interpretations. Of more importance was that three dominant types of dream stood out: (1) a savage woman attacking me, (2) a quiet, firm, friendly father-figure supporting me, and (3) a mysterious death-threat dream, the clearest example based on the memory of mother taking me at the age of six into the bedroom of my invalid aunt, thought to be dying of rheumatic fever, lying white and silent. In one dream:

I was working downstairs at my desk and suddenly an invisible band of ectoplasm tying me to a dying invalid upstairs, was pulling me steadily out of the room. I knew I would be absorbed into her. I fought and suddenly the band snapped and I knew I was free.

I knew enough to guess that the memory of my dying aunt was a screen memory for the repressed dead Percy, which still exercised on me an unconscious pull out of life into collapse and apparent dying. I knew that somehow sometime I must get an analysis. In 1946 Professor Dicks appointed me as the first staff member of the new Department of Psychiatry, and said that with my views I must read Fairbairn. I did so and at the end of 1949 I sought analysis with him.

For the first few years, his broadly oedipal analysis of my "internalized bad-object relations" world did correspond to an actual period of my childhood. After Percy's death and my return home, from the age of three and a half to five, I fought to coerce mother into mothering me by repeated petty psychosomatic ills, tummy-aches, heat spots, loss of appetite, constipation and dramatic, sudden high temperatures, for which she would make me a tent-bed on the kitchen couch and be in and out from the shop to see me. She told me the doctor said: "I'll never come to that child again. He frightens the life out of me with these sudden high temperatures and next morning he's perfectly well." But it was all to no purpose. Around five years I changed tactics. A new bigger school gave me more independence, and mother said: "You began not to do what I told you." She would fly into violent rages and beat me, from about the time I was five to the age of seven. When canes got broken I was sent to buy a new one. At the age of seven I went to a still larger school and steadily developed a life of my own outside the home. We moved when I was eight to another shop where mother's business was an outstanding success. She became less depressed, gave me all the money · I needed for hobbies and outdoor activities, scouting, sport, and gradually I forgot not quite all the memories of the first seven bad years. It was all the fears, rages, guilts, psychosomatic transient symptoms, disturbed dreams, venting the conflicts of those years from three and a half to seven, that Fairbairn's analysis dealt with. In mother's old age she said: "When your father and Aunt Mary died and I was alone, I tried keeping a dog but I had to give it up. I couldn't stop beating it." That's what happened to me. No wonder I had an inner world of internalized libidinally excited bad-object relations, and I owe much to Fairbairn's radical analysis of it.

But after the first three or four years I became convinced that this was keeping me marking time in a sadomasochistic inner world of *bad-object relations* with a mother, as a defense against quite different problems of the period before Percy's death. This deeper material kept pushing through. The crunch came in December 1957 when my old friend whose departure from College caused the first eruption of that Percy illness in 1927, suddenly died. For the third time exhaustion seized me. I kept going enough to work and travel to Edinburgh for analysis, feeling I would now get to the bottom of it. Then, just as I felt some progress was being made, Fairbairn fell ill with a serious viral influenza of which he nearly died, and was off work six months. I had to reinstate repression, but at once began to "intellectualize" the problem I could not work through with him in person. It was not pure intellectualization by deliberate thinking. Spontaneous insights kept welling up at all sorts of times, and I jotted them down as they flowed with compelling intensity. Out of all that I wrote three papers; they became the basis of my book *Schizoid Phenomena, Object-Relations and the Self.*[9] "Ego-weakness, the core of the problem of psycho-therapy," written in 1960 (chapter 6), "The schizoid problem, regression and the struggle to preserve an ego" (chapter 2) written in 1961, and "The manic-depressive problem in the light of the schizoid process" (chapter 5) written in 1962. In two years they took me right beyond Fairbairn's halting point. He generously accepted this as a valid and necessary extension of his theory.

When he returned to work in 1959, I discussed my friend's death and Fairbairn's illness and he made a crucial interpretaion: "I think since my illness I am no longer your good father or bad mother, but your brother dying on you." I suddenly saw the analytical situation in an extraordinary light, and wrote him a letter which I still have, but did not send. I knew it would put a bigger strain on him then he could stand in his precarious health. I suddenly saw that I could never solve my problem *with* an analyst. I wrote: "I am in a dilemma. I have got to end my analysis to get a chance to finish it, but then I do not have you to help me with it." Once Fairbairn had become my brother in transference, *losing him* either by ending analysis myself, or by staying with him till he died, would represent the death of Percy, and I would be left with a full scale eruption of that traumatic event, and no one to help me with it. Could Fairbairn have helped me with that in transference analysis? Not in his frail state of health and I phased out my analysis in that year. I have much cause to be grateful to him for staying with me, in his increasingly weak state of health, till I had reached that critical insight. The driving force behind my theory writing in 1959–1962 was the reactivation of the Percy-trauma, causing a compelling spate of spontaneous ideas. I could contain it and use it for constructive research, partly because I was giving Fairbairn up gradually, partly because he accepted the validity of my ideas, and partly because I had resolved to seek analysis with Winnicott before Fairbairn died.

Fairbairn first introduced me to Winnicott in 1954 by asking him to send a copy of his paper, "Regression Within the Psycho-Analytical Set-Up."[10] He sent it and, rather to my surprise, a letter saying: "I do invite you to look into the matter of your relation to Freud, so that you may have your own relation and not Fairbairn's. He spoils his good work by wanting to knock down Freud." We exchanged three long letters on each side. I stated that my relation to Freud had been settled years before I had heard of Fairbairn, when studying under Flugel at University College, London. I rejected Freud's psychobiology of instincts, but saw the great importance of his discoveries in psychopathology. Regarding that correspondence, I now find I anticipated Morse's[1] conclusion almost in his words, eighteen years earlier: that Winnicott's "true self" has no place in Freud's theory. It could only be found in the id, but that is impossible because the id is only impersonal energy. In fact I felt that Winnicott had left Freud as far behind in therapy as Fairbairn had done in theory. In 1961 I sent him a copy of my book *Personality Structure and Human Interaction*,[11] and he replied that he had already purchased a copy. I was reading his papers as they were published, as also was Fairbairn who described him as "clinically brilliant." By 1962 I had no doubt that he was the only man I could turn to for further help. I was by then only free to visit London once a month for a couple of sessions, but the analysis I had had made it easier to profit by that. From 1962 to 1968 I had 150 sessions and their value was out of all proportion to their number. Winnicott said he was surprised that so much could be worked through in such widely spaced sessions, due I think in the first place to all the preliminary clearing that had been done by Fairbairn and to the fact that I could keep the analysis alive between visits; but most of all to *Winnicott's profound intuitive insights into the very infancy period I so needed to get down to.* He enabled me to reach extraordinarily clear evidence that my mother had almost certainly had an initial period of natural maternalism with me as her first baby, for perhaps a couple of months, before her personality problems robbed me of that "good mother." I had quite forgotten that letter I did not send to Fairbairn about the dilemma of not being able either to end analysis or go on with it, once my analyst became Percy in the transference. Ending it would be equivalent to Percy dying and I would have no one to help me with the aftermath. If I did not end it, I would be using my analyst to prevent the eruption of the trauma and so get no help with it, and risk his dying on me. My amnesia for that early trauma was not broken through with Winnicott either. Only recently have I realized that in fact, unwittingly, he altered the whole nature of the problem by enabling me to reach right back to *an ulimate good mother, and to find her recreated in him in the transference.* I discovered later that he had put me in a position to face what was a double trauma of both Percy's death and mother's failing me.

As I re-read my records I am astonished at the rapidity with which he went to the heart of the matter. At the first session I mentioned the amnesia for the trauma of Percy's death, and felt I had had a radical analysis with Fairbairn of the "internalized bad-object defenses" I had built up against that, but we had not got down to what I felt was my basic problem, not the actively bad-object mother of later childhood, *but the earlier mother who failed to relate at all.* Near the end of the session he said: "I've nothing particular to say yet, but if I don't say something, you may begin to feel I'm not here." At the second session he said:

You know about me but I'm not a person to you yet. You may go away feeling alone and that I'm not real. You must have had an earlier illness before Percy was born, and felt mother left you to look after yourself. You accepted Percy as your infant self that needed looking after. When he died, you had nothing and collapsed.

That was a perfect object-relations interpretation, but from Winnicott, not Fairbairn. Much later I said that I occasionally felt a "static, unchanging, lifeless state somewhere deep in me, feeling I can't move." Winnicott said:

If 100 per cent of you felt like that, you probably couldn't move and someone would have to wake you. After Percy died, you collapsed bewildered, but managed to salvage enough of yourself to go on living, very energetically, and put the rest in a cocoon, repressed, unconscious.

I wish there were time to illustrate his penetrating insight in more detail, but I must give another example. I said that people often commented on my ceaseless activity and energy, and that in sessions I did not like gaps of silence and at times talked hard. Fairbairn interpreted that I was trying to take the analysis out of his hands and do his job; steal father's penis, oedipal rivalry. Winnicott threw a dramatic new light on this talking hard. He said:

Your problem is that that illness of collapse was never resolved. You had to keep yourself alive in spite of it. You can't take your ongoing being for granted. You have to work hard to keep yourself in existence. You're afraid to stop acting, talking or keeping awake. You feel you might die in a gap like Percy, because if you stop acting mother can't do anything. She couldn't save Percy or you. You're bound to fear I can't keep you alive, so you link up monthly sessions for me by your records. No gaps. You can't feel that you are a going concern to me, because mother couldn't save you. You know about "being active" but not about "just growing, just breathing" while you sleep, without your having to do anything about it.

I began to be able to allow for some silences, and once, feeling a bit anxious, I was relieved to hear Winnicott move. I said nothing, but with uncanny intuition he said:

You began to feel afraid I'd abandoned you. You feel silence is abandonment. The gap is not you forgetting mother, but mother forgetting you, and now you've relived it with me. You're finding an earlier trauma which you might never recover without the help of the Percy trauma repeating it. You have to remember mother abandoning you by transference on to me.

I can hardly convey the powerful impression it made on me to find Winnicott coming right into the emptiness of my "object relations situation" in infancy with a nonrelating mother.

Right at the end of my analysis I had a sudden return of hard talking in session. This time he made a different and extraordinary statement. He said:

It's like you giving birth to a baby with my help. You gave me half an hour of concentrated talk, rich in content. I felt strained in listening and holding the situation for you. You had to know that I could stand your talking hard at me and my not being destroyed. I had to stand it while you were in labour being creative, not destructive, producing something rich in content. You are talking about "object relating," "using the object" and finding you don't destroy it. I couldn't have made that interpretation five years ago.

Later he gave his paper on "The use of an object"[12] in America and met, not surprisingly I think, with much criticism. Only an exceptional man could have reached that kind of insight. He became a good breast mother to my infant self in my deep unconscious, at the point where my actual mother had lost her maternalism and could not stand me as a live baby any more. It was not then apparent, as it later became to me, that he had transformed my whole understanding of the trauma of Percy's death, particularly when he added:

You too have a good breast. You've always been able to give more than take. I'm good for you but you're good for me. Doing your analysis is almost the most reassuring thing that happens to me. The chap before you makes me feel I'm no good at all. You don't have to be good for me. I don't need it and can cope without it, but in fact you are good for me.

Here at last I had a mother who could value her child, so that I could cope with what was to come. It hardly seems worth mentioning that the only point at which I felt I disagreed with Winnicott was when he talked occasionally about "getting at your primitive sadism, the baby's ruthlessness and cruelty, your aggression," in a way that suggested not my angry fight to extract a response from my cold mother, but Freud's and Klein's "instinct theory," the id, innate aggression. For I knew he rejected the "death instinct" and had moved far beyond Freud when I went to him. He once said to me: "We differ from Freud. He was for curing symptoms. We are concerned with living persons, whole living and loving." By 1967 he wrote, and gave me a copy of his paper, "The location of cultural experience,"[12] in which he said: "I see that I am in the territory of Fairbairn: 'object-seeking' as opposed to 'satisfaction-seeking'." I felt then that Winnicott and Fairbairn had joined forces to neutralize my earliest traumatic years.

I must complete this account with the one thing I could not foresee. Winnicott becoming the good mother, freeing me to be alive and creative, transformed the significance of Percy's death in a way that was to enable me to resolve that trauma, and my dilemma about how to end my analysis. Winnicott, relating to me in my deep unconscious, enabled me to stand seeing that it was not just the loss of Percy, but being left alone with the mother who could not keep me alive, that caused my collapse into apparent dying. But thanks to his profound intuitive insight, I was not now alone with a non-relating mother. I last saw him in July 1969. In February 1970 I was told medically that I was seriously overworked, and if I did not retire "Nature would make me." I must have felt unconsciously that that was a threat that "Mother Nature" would at last crush my active self. Every time I rested I found myself under a compulsion to go back to the past, in the form of rehearsing the details of my ministerial "brother-figure's" leaving in 1938, and my reacting with an exhaustion illness. I soon saw that this was significant and it led on to an urge to write up my whole life-story, as if I had to find out all that had happened to me. By October I developed pneumonia and spent five weeks in hospital. The consultant said: "Relax. You're too overactive." I still did not realize that I was fighting against an unconscious compulsive regression. I had never linked the idea of "retirement" with the deep fear of losing my battle with mother to keep my active self alive, in the end. After a slow winter recuperation, I heard in the New Year 1971 that Winnicott had a flu attack. Presently I enquired of Masud Khan how Winnicott was, and he replied that he was about again and liked to hear from his friends, so I dropped him a line. A little later the phone rang, and the familiar voice said: "Hallo. Thanks for your letter" and we chatted a bit. About two weeks later the phone rang again and *his secretary told me he had passed away. That very night I had a startling dream. I saw my mother,* black, immobilized, staring fixedly into space, *totally ignoring me* as I stood at one side staring at her and feeling myself frozen into immobility: the first time I had ever seen her in a dream like that. Before she had always been attacking me. My first thought was: "I've lost Winnicott and am left alone with mother, sunk in depression, ignoring me. That's how I felt when Percy died." I thought I must have taken the loss of Winnicott as a repetition of the Percy trauma. Only recently have I become quite clear that it was not that at all. I did not dream of mother like

that when my college friend died or my ministerial colleague left. Then
I felt ill, as after Percy's death. This time it was quite different. That
dream started a compelling dream-sequence which went on night after
night, taking me back in chronological order through every house I had
lived in, in Leeds, Ipswich, College, and the second Dulwich shop, and
finally the first shop and house of the bad first seven years. Family figures,
my wife, daughter, Aunt Mary, father and mother kept recurring; father
always supportive, mother always hostile, but no sign of Percy. I was
trying to stay in the post-Percy period of battles with mother. Then after
some two months two dreams at last broke that amnesia for Percy's life
and death. I was astonished to see myself in a dream clearly aged about
three, recognizably me, holding a pram in which was my brother aged
about a year old. I was strained, looking anxiously over to the left at
mother, to see if she would take any notice of us. But she was staring
fixedly into the distance, ignoring us, as in the first dream of that series.
The next night the dream was even more startling.

I was standing with another man, the double of myself, both reaching out to get
hold of a dead object. Suddenly the other man collapsed in a heap. Immediately
the dream changed to a lighted room, where I saw Percy again. I knew it was
him, sitting on the lap of a woman who had no face, arms or breasts. She was
merely a lap to sit on, not a person. He looked deeply depressed, with the corners
of his mouth turned down, and I was trying to make him smile.

I had recovered in that dream the memory of collapsing when I saw
him as a dead object and reached out to grab him. But I had done more.
I had actually gone back in both dreams to the earlier time before he
died, to see the "faceless" depersonalized mother, and the black depressed
mother, who totally failed to relate to both of us. Winnicott had said:
"You accepted Percy as your infant self that needed looking after. When
he died, you had nothing and collapsed." Why did I dream of "collapsing"
first, and then of going back to look after Percy? My feeling is that my
collapse was my first reaction of terrified hopelessness at the shock of
finding Percy dead on mother's lap, but in that aunt's family I quickly
seized the change of staying alive by finding others to live for.
    That dream series made me bring out and restudy all my analysis
records, till I realized that, though Winnicott's death had reminded me
of Percy's, the situation was entirely different. That process of compelling
regression had not started with Winnicott's death, but with the threat of
"retirement" as if mother would undermine me at last. I did not dream
of Winnicott's death, but of Percy's death and mother's total failure to
relate to us. What better dream-evidence could one have of Winnicott's
view that "There is no such thing as a baby:" i.e. there must be a "mother

and baby," and what better evidence for Fairbairn's view that the basic psychic reality is the "personal object relation"? What gave me strength in my deep unconscious to face again that basic trauma? It must have been because Winnicott was not, and could not be, dead for me, nor certainly for many others. I have never felt that my father was dead, but in a deep way alive in me, enabling me to resist mother's later active paralyzing inhibiting influence. Now Winnicott had come into living relation with precisely that earlier lost part of me that fell ill because mother failed me. *He has taken her place and made it possible and safe to remember her in an actual dream-reliving of her paralyzing schizoid aloofness.* Slowly that became a firm conviction growing in me, and I recovered from the volcanic upheavel of that autonomously regressing compelling dream-series, feeling that I had at last reaped the gains I had sought in analysis over some twenty years. After all the detailed memories, dreams, symptoms of traumatic events, people, and specific emotional tensions had been worked through, one thing remained: *the quality of the over-all atmosphere of the personal relations that made up our family life in those first seven years.* It lingers as a mood of sadness for my mother who was so damaged in childhood that she could neither be, nor enable me to be, our "true selves." I cannot have a different set of memories. But that is offset by my discovery in analysis of how deeply my father became a secure mental possession in me, supporting my struggle to find and be my "true self;" and by Fairbairn's resolving my negative transference of my dominating mother on to him, till he became another good father who had faith in me, and finally by Winnicott entering into the emptiness left by my non-relating mother, so that I could experience the security of being myself. I must add that without my wife's understanding and support I could not have had those analyses or reached this result. What is psycho-analytic psychotherapy? It is, as I see it, the provision of a reliable and understanding human relationship of a kind that makes contact with the deeply repressed traumatized child in a way that enables one to become steadily more able to live, in the security of a new real relationship, with the traumatic legacy of the earliest formative years, as it seeps through or erupts into consciousness.

Psychoanalytic therapy is not like a "technique" of the experimental sciences, an objective "thing-in-itself" working automatically. It is a process of interaction, a function of two variables, the personalities of two people working together towards free spontaneous growth. The analyst grows as well as the analysand. There must be something wrong if an analyst is static when he deals with such dynamic personal experiences. For me, Fairbairn built as a person on what my father did for me, and as an analyst enabled me to discover in great detail how my battles for independence of mother from three and a half to seven years had grown into my personality make-up. Without that I could have deteriorated in old age into as awkward a person as my mother. Winnicott, a totally different type of personality, understood and filled the emptiness my mother left in the first three and a half years. I needed them both and had the supreme good forture to find both. Their very differences have been a stimulus to different sides of my make-up. Fairbairn's ideas were "exact logical concepts" which clarified issues. Winnicott's ideas were "imaginative hypotheses" that challenged one to explore further. As examples, compare Fairbairn's concepts of the libidinal, antilibidinal and central egos as a theory of endopsychic structure, with Winnicott's "true and false selves" as intuitive insights into the confused psychic reality of actual persons. Perhaps no single analyst can do all that an analysand needs, and we must be content to let patients make as much use of us as they can. We dare not pose as omniscient and omnipotent because we have a theory. Also Fairbairn once said: "You get out of analysis what you put into it," and I think that is true for both analyst and analysand. I would think that the development of clear conscious insight represents having taken full possession of the gains already made emotionally, putting one in a position to risk further emotional strains to make more emotional growth. It represents not just conscious understanding but a strengthening of the inner core of "selfhood" and capacity for "relating." So far as psychopathological material is concerned, dreaming expresses our endopsychic structure. It is a way of experiencing on the fringes of consciousness, our internalized conflicts, our memories of struggles originally in our outer world and then as memories and fantasies of conflicts that have become our inner reality, to keep "object relations" alive, even if only "bad-object relations," because we need them to retain possession of our "ego." It was my experience that the deeper that final spate of dreams delved into my unconscious, the more dreaming slowly faded out and was replaced by "waking up in a mood." I found I was not fantasying or thinking but simply feeling, consciously in the grip of a state of mind that I began to realize I had been in consciously long ago, and had been in unconsciously deep down ever since: a dull mechanical lifeless mood, no interest in anything, silent, shut in to myself, going through routine motions with a sense of loss of all meaning in existence. I experienced this for a number of consecutive mornings till I began to find that it was fading out into a normal interest in life: which after all seems to be what one would expect.

There is a natural order peculiar to each individual and determined by his history, in which (1) problems can become conscious and (2) interpretations can be relevant and mutative. We cannot decide that but only watch the course of the individual's development. Finally, on the difficult question of the sources of theory, it seems that our theory must be rooted in our psychopathology. That was implied in Freud's courageous self-analysis at a time when all was obscure. The idea that we could think out a theory of the structure and functioning of the personality without its having any relation to the structure and functioning of our own personality, should be a self-evident impossibility. If our theory is too rigid, it is likely to conceptualize our ego defenses. If it is flexible and progressive it is possible for it to conceptualize our ongoing growth processes, and throw light on others' problems and on therapeutic possibilities. Balint's "basic fault" and Winnicott's "incommunicado core," since they regard these phenomena as universal, must be their ways of "intuitively sensing" their own basic reality, and therefore other people's. By contrast with Fairbairn's exactly intellectually defined theoretical constructs which state logically progressive developments in existing theory, they open the way to profounder exploration of the infancy period, where, whatever a baby's genetic endowment, the mother's ability or failure to "relate" is the *sine qua non* of psychic health for the infant. To find a good parent at the start is the basis of psychic health. In its lack, to find a genuine "good object" in one's analyst is both a transference experience and a real-life experience. In analysis as in real life, all relationships have a subtly dual nature. All through life we take into ourselves both good and bad figures who either strengthen or disturb us, and it is the same in psychoanalytic therapy: it is the meeting and interacting of two real people in all its complex possibilities.

REFERENCES

1. Morse SJ: Structure and reconstruction: a critical comparison of Michael Balint and D. W. Winnicott. Int J Psychoanal 53:487–500, 1972.
2. Sutherland J: Obituary. W. R. D. Fairbairn. Int J Psychoanal 46:245–247, 1965.
3. Fairbairn WRD: Observations of the nature of hysterical states. Br J Med Psychol 27:106–125, 1954.
4. Fairbairn WRD: Theoretical and experimental aspects of psycho-analysis. Br J Med Psychol 25:122–127, 1952.
5. Fairbairn WRD: Observations in defence of the object-relations theory of the personality. Br J Med Psychol 28:144–156, 1955.
6. Fairbairn WRD: Considerations arising out of the Schreber case. Br J Med Psychol 29:113–127, 1956.
7. Fairbairn WRD: On the nature and aims of psychoanalytical treatment. Int J Psychoanal 39:374–385, 1958.

8. Fairbairn WRD: Psychoanalytic Studies of the Personality. London, Tavistock Publications, 1952.
9. Guntrip H: Schizoid Phenomena, Object-Relations and the Self. London, Hogarth Press, 1968.
10. Winnicott DW: Collected Papers. Through Paediatrics to Psycho-Analysis. London, Tavistock Publications, 1958.
11. Guntrip H: Personality Structure and Human Interaction. London, Hogarth Press, 1961.
12. Winnicott DW: Playing and Reality. London, Tavistock Publications, 1971.

Harold Kelman, M.D., D.Md. Sc.

My Philosophy of Psychotherapy

My life experience determined my philosophy of psychotherapy. I was
born in 1906 in a small Connecticut town "on the other side of the tracks."
An older sister was born there too. Six older sisters and brothers came
from Russia. Being the youngest of eight gained me problems, not privileges. My father left my mother when I was three months old. My play-
mates were from multi-, second- and first-generation Yankee, Irish, German, Polish, Italian, Hungarian, and French families.

Four languages were spoken in my family. As a youth I spoke and
wrote two well, two poorly, and spoke a smattering of three others. I
later studied Latin, French, and German. A facility with language inflections and basics such as kitchen Spanish fortified my aversion to grammar.

I had two unusual teachers of world history in high school and college.
They fostered an historical consciousness. My interest in China began at
age thirteen. In my thirties my interest in the Orient, its histories, religions,
philosophies, languages, and art expanded, leading to many visits, from
1956 on, to the Near and Far East, New Zealand, and Australia.

Before age eight, I began wondering why people were so hurting to
one another. In college, I took psychology courses and had decided on
psychiatry. In medical school, I learned three things: the physiology of
the psyche (before I quite knew what I meant by it)—my professor was
Walter B. Cannon; the clinical investigative attitude; and how to use a
library. In a class of 145, I alone elected psychiatry.

I graduated in the depression (1931) with debts. I needed a paying
job and got one at Kings Park State Hospital. My historical sense told

me the depression would last for some years, that this was no time to go into private practice, but a good time to get the best education possible. After a rotating internship, I took another residency in psychiatry. My contact with Kurt Goldstein, begun in 1934 at Montefiore Hospital where I was a resident in neuropathology and neurology and thereafter a Fellow in psychiatry and neurology, was maintained until his death in 1964. His organismic approach greatly influenced my thinking.

I had no other analyst in mind when I began my personal analysis with Abram Kardiner in December, 1935. Quite accidentally, Karen Horney was my first supervisor, although she became the major influence in my psychoanalytic career and in my life. L. L. Whyte's[1] focus on form, pattern, process, and hierarchy, and Angyal's[2] on holism were two other major influences and, of course, there was Freud. I first published in 1932.[3] More articles followed in clinical medicine, neuropathology, clinical and traumatic neurology, psychiatry, and psychoanalysis.[4-21]

This brief biographical sketch forecasts my personal philosophy of psychotherapy. "Helping people"[17] in pain is central. The "therapist's person" I see as the essential medicine and "the instrument"[19] for conveying it. "Communing and relating"[7] are the vehicles for doing so, as are theories and techniques that define and utilize the structure of the experiencing process.[17]

The therapist must learn the many languages his patient speaks—individual, familial, regional, cultural, national and cosmic—through his symptoms, syndromes, the patterns of his neurosis, psychopathy, psychosis, and somatic responses, his associations, fantasies, and dreams. Prerequisite is a theory of the symbolizing process integral to my ideas on form, pattern, process, hierarchy, and system.[5,17] My therapeutic objective is to help the patient experience himself moment to moment in the here and now so that he learns the meaning of his existence as he creates it. This becomes possible as we support processes that resolve defenses, neurotic solutions, and blockages and enhance the realizing of that person's potentialities as the individual and generic human being he is.[22]

Every patient comes seeking help with the multidimensional feeling "nobody-was-there-for-me." They communicate it implicitly or explicitly as a statement, as wondering, as accusation, and as self-derogation. It all comes to "nobody was there for me, there where I was when I needed them." This encompassing feeling consists of a host of feelings that define how a person experiences the world and themselves in it. "Nobody looked at me and if they did they didn't see me." "Nobody listened to me and if they did they didn't hear me." These expressions may be communicated as verbalizations, as felt states, or may exist as nonverbalizable organizations.

During the first year of life the human bond between infant and *care* takers (mother and others) is productive of social relationships that are crucial for subsequent interpersonal relationship and personality structure. Parents' hopes and expectations will determine how they evaluate their infant's progress and themselves as "good" parents. Participant will be their responsiveness to the uniqueness of their infant's reactivity and temperament. There is more than analogy here with the major transference and countertransference elements. Involved are the needs in becoming a therapist, the therapist's fit with his patient, and the working through of mutual needs.

Schechter feels there "is probably not a single dimension" of the developmental interaction between infant and family that does not occur in psychotherapy with any age group.[23] I agree and redefine transference as an aspect of communing and relating being guided by the experience and phenomenon of blocking[17,22] rather than of resistance. Patients convey that their suffering is a consequence of distortions of their organic modalities during infantile development and wish them responded to in the therapeutic situation. It is the therapist's task to help his patient experience them and while doing so be experiencing him in all the caretaker modes, as mothering and fathering, brothering and sistering, namely in the modes of all concerned, caretaking persons.

This means that every patient is communicating, "Nobody allowed me to suck on them. They did not give me succor. Nobody was there to cling to, to give me support. Nobody remained present so I could look at and follow them with my eyes and body. Nobody heard my crying and responded to it. Nobody saw my smile and beamed, was there to touch me and to be touched by me, to press up against and be hugged in response, to warm me and feel warmed by me, smell me and find me sweet. Nobody was there to hold me, to carry me, to rock me, to swing me, and to feel pleasure in doing so."

Every patient should feel that his therapist has been responsive to his needs. This does not require sexual intimacy nor inviting your patients to dinner in your home, both of which express more of acting out than therapeutically feeling in and through. To many patients, awareness of organic modalities is alien or anathema. They must be identified and helped to come alive. Opportunities for doing so may come from dreams or from charged emotional situations occurring during therapy. Patients can be helped to a greater experiencing of them through actual and fantasied situations which would involve the range of organic modalities participant during infantile development. The therapist's task, to work through the developmental distortions of general and special needs and the defenses built up around them, as well as the consequences of the infantile anxieties, has been regularly mentioned. I have written about the attendant tensioning process.[12,17]

Schechter asserts that *"social stimulation and reciprocal interaction, often playful and not necessarily drive connected or tension reducing constitute a basis for the development of specific social attachments between the infant and others."* He adds that *"mutual playfulness is a model of freedom and spontaneity in human relatedness."*[24] I agree with both positions. I see the mode of playfulness which is tension producing and tension reducing as an integral aspect of creative psychotherapy in all age groups.[11]

Therapy solely focused on working through can be experienced as burdensome, thus limiting its creative possibilities. I could not work for the hours I do and the years I have with the difficult problems I confront for extended periods if I did not find what I was doing as challenging, exciting, filled with novelty and the unexpected.[16] I have yet to fall asleep through having been "bored to death," although I have been accused of both. Creative psychotherapy requires a spirit of playfulness, in which patient and therapist have some good laughs with and at each other. Humor, anecdote, metaphor, paraphrasing, storytelling, tonal inflections, facial expressions, and gestures are essential modalities in such a therapy.

Satisfying play between infant and caretaker in an atmosphere of freedom helps a child work through destructive character formations. This development enhances mutual trust and increases self-esteem and self-confidence, freeing him to "be alone in the presence of the mother."[25] This prepares him for the longer separation from his mother and leads to the development of greater autonomy.

These are integral to the therapeutic process at whatever age and pertinent to the effective use of the analytic couch. These positions regarding tension, anxiety, and play are at variance with our current cultural ethos and lead to reconsideration of many classical concepts, including the repetition compulsion and regression.[14,15]

Caring has deep roots in all Western religions and philosophies: the Greek *Eros;* St. Augustine's *Caritas;* modern Protestantism's *Agape;* the Jewish *Mitzvah;* and Existentialism's *Sorge.* When a patient says "Nobody cared" he is saying "Nobody was on my side, there for me against those who were not for me." He is referring to the caring of all significant others since he was born. That person is also saying, "I did not exist for anybody," hence "I did not know that I could have an existence, and that my existence could have a meaning."

All mentioned aspects of "Nobody-was-there-for-me" say, "Nobody was present for me, to me, with me, physically in space and time and emotionally responsive to me." This means "nobody was present as a presence for me, nobody who had substance, carried weight, had an identity and personhood." To be a presence means to have been touched by the spiritual, which is prerequisite to being present to another who is groping, reaching out for, and struggling toward a clarification of the big questions regarding the meaning of existence.

A sensitive therapist is aware that through the many forms of "Nobody-was-there-for-me," a patient is asking "Will-you-be-there-for-me?" Even as the caring one's response is affirmative, the patient is immediately confronted by a paradox. He must have faith before he has a basis for that faith. He must trust before he has had any experience that this helper is trustworthy and will be responsive to his suffering. He is asking "Are you the kind of person who can commit himself to my challenge and grow in the process?"

The therapist is the most important medicament and nurturant in the caring process. He is the instrumentality for dispensing those vital ingredients at the proper time and in the correct dosage. He must do so with an economy of time and with the minimum of unnecessary pain. Therefore, more is required of him from his personal analysis, his reanalysis, and additional supervision. He should maintain contact with developments in his field by attendance at meetings, through teaching, writing, and ongoing self-analysis. A therapist who does not learn from each success and failure and grow through them is limited.

I have attempted to define the phenomenological structure of the person of the therapist as an instrument by identifying seven of his attributes expressive of eleven modes of his being.

1. He reflects the *nonteleologic* attitude which focuses on the what rather than on the why, on sequences of patternings leading to deeper and wider contact with "direct referents" and thereby the "self-propellent feeling of process."[26]
2. His attitude of *unconventionality* implies noninvolvement in the conventional amenities, the patient's questions, the cultural prejudices, and the compulsive patterns to which he adheres, blocking more spontaneous "freer associating."[9]
3. The therapist's *unobtrusiveness* allows his patient free rein to express his projections, externalizations, and fantasies and whatever in him that is compulsive, spontaneous, and contradictory.
4. Through his *incorruptibility* the therapist remains uninvolved with the patient's attempts at seducing or intimidating him into compulsive patterns of relating. He does not get caught in his patient's system of claims and counterclaims, reward and punishment, submission and domination strategies.
5. Being *respectfully vigilant,* he is open and responsive as he listens to

the whole person of the patient, as he is driven, anxious, conflicted, hostile, contemplative, and receptive.

6. Being *threshold conscious* means the therapist is alert to the whole spectrum of processes available for emergence. This includes those as yet subliminal, taking shape and ready to break through.

7. *Choiceless awareness* means awareness of everything: feelings, perceptions, sensations, thoughts, behaviors both experienceable and observable, as they emerge into awareness without assumption or preconception, without choosing which causes conflict.

These seven attributes are expressions of eleven modes of the therapist's being. They are formulated as paradoxes, that ancient door to wisdom via the illuminations following their resolution through the tensioning process.

1. *Passionate objectivity* concomitant with *dispassionate subjectivity* describes the first mode.

2. Simultaneously the therapist is and moves toward the *ultimate of personal,* which is the *ultimate of the impersonal* as the *ultimate of the impersonal* is the *ultimate of the personal.*

3. The therapist is *action in nonaction* as he is *nonaction in action.*

4. Thereby he is and becomes more open and able to contain *tension-producing* and *tension-reducing* processes and to experience the *natural oscillations in the tensioning process.*

5. This means being open to and aware of *conflicting* and *cooperating processes* expressive of hierarchies of systems in process, from the most autonomous to the most subordinate.

6. The *willpower of desirelessness* pervades the foregoing. The therapist will be free of the compulsion to do, of the *furor sanandi,* of being ambitious for his patient. He will be able to go with him at his pace, in his ways, in his struggle toward self-realization.

7. He will be *morally tough,* which requires *moral compassion* as *moral compassion* requires *moral toughness,* both integral to and prerequisite for *moral courage,* which is inherent in the previous six modes described.

8. The therapist will know his patient as *phenomenon* and directly as *noumenon,* at moments, as both are transcended in a condition of secondlessness. This is the precondition for freer associating[9] in its progression to its ultimate forms.

9. Concomitant with the foregoing is the mode of being characterized by that *sound which is silence,* that *motion which is stillness,* that *passion which is serenity,* all leading to and expressing *pure lucidity* which is the *form of nonform.*

10. As these modes obtain, the therapist, at the same moment, paradoxically can be *at his own core and at that of his patient* and freely move between both. In such movement, all available forms of caring can be conveyed.
11. Expression of these modes of being are the therapist's *knowing, reacting, responding, resonating, containing,* and *being effective* with *dualistic* and *nondualistic theories* and *techniques* regarding the nature of man.

The developmental process and the therapist's person define the model of him and his patient's being, and being there for each other as communing, relating, and communicating. These models, in turn, follow from the model of the universe of which they are aspects. All these models are describable in terms of form. A universal forming process is postulated,[10] the symbolizing process of which is an aspect. The moment there is awareness of being and any of its attributes, they have emerged into and take form through the forming process. The forms become organized into sequential hierarchies that are denotable and connotable. The model of symbolizing defines hierarchical ways that patients and therapists as whole persons can be there for each other in therapy seen as a developmental process— as emerging and resorbing aspects of a continuous and connected universe. The widest and deepest ground for communicating with each other is through communing. To reach communing, we must go the way of relating.

Communing and relating contain what is subsumed in the concepts of the doctor-patient relationship and of transference and countertransference.[17,22] The models of the therapeutic process of the person of the therapist as instrument and communing and relating require a psychoanalysis of the experiencing process. This I attempted to formulate, including the theories and techniques appropriate to such a therapy in which feelings have primacy.[17,20]

Our feelings are at our core and emanate from it. Through them, we are in continuing connectedness with the unitary processes: feeling-thinking, feeling-willing, feeling-perceiving, and feeling-sensing. Through our feelings, we influence and are influenced by the whole. The whole is constituted of organism-environment as an aspect of cosmos. In contact with the flowing interconnectednesses of our feelings, thoughts, wishes, sensations, and perceptions, the possibilities for more communing, better communicating, and fuller relating are greater.

In the light of my ideas on symbolizing, the primacy I give to feeling questions becomes evident. I ask implicit, open-ended "what feeling" questions.[20] Although I may ask for information and discuss practicalities, I rarely make a statement because it is often experienced as a demand

and coercion and responded to with closure and defensiveness. Open-endedness allows for the widest play of freer associating. More open spaces obtain for the emergence of the unexpected, the novel, and the creative. The focus on what directs the patient's attention to the "whatness" and "whating" of his feeling processes and thereby the "how," "howness," and "howing" of them. Sequences of what, whatness, and whating are sequences of how, howness, and howing. This focus confronts and resolves that ancient paradox of form versus function and transforms it into forming is functioning as functioning is forming.

The focus on feelings leads to freer associating involving sensing, conating, and cognizing because of their interconnectedness. It may take weeks and months of asking "What are you *feeling?*" about this or that before the patient hears you. He will be unaware that he constantly reacts with "I *think.*" Only in time does he open to responding and resonating to feeling questions that reverberate through all dimensions of his being.

When I ask, "What are you feeling?" I am guiding the patient's attention to the lower end of the rationative levels of the symbolic spiral. As his attending process is focused, there is more contacting of prerationative levels of the spiral. As the patient becomes more able to move down the metaphorical symbolic spiral, he also becomes freer in moving up and down, from foreground to background, from the manifest to the latent and back again.

The use of feeling questions is a technique. The question, "what is technique?" raises questions regarding techniques of research and therapy which Freud said "at a certain point" diverge.[27] I have reformulated Freud's position. "Being guided . . . by the pure research viewpoint . . . that is observing by introspection and inspection the forms as they arise in awareness, and experiencing them—is therapeutic. Formulating these emerging forms into patternings of different orders of abstraction is theorizing. What we name therapy (healing, helping, technique) and theory (systematizing . . .) are both rooted in . . . the experiencing and conceptualizing aspects of . . . the universal forming process."[12]

As the therapist is guided by the seven attributes and eleven modes of his being, the point of divergence recedes, the gap between research and therapy narrows, the mutual enrichment of both increases, and ultimately they become identical. Therapy is research as research is therapy, each being abstractions of a unitary process.

What is technique? More accurately, what is techniquing? It becomes a continuum of processes. On one end are moments of techniqueless therapy, as in moments of communing, when there is pure lucidity and formlessness and secondlessness, to the impossible of pure technique. The latter would imply form without content, the mind facing itself in pure abstraction. This is saying that there are hierarchies of interconnected kinds of techniquing between the two extremes of absolute subjectifying and absolute objectifying.

What then is an interpretation? As usually understood, it is a discrete, concrete intervention premised on a theory to effect a confrontation that points at surface conscious content to reach unconscious material and the genetic antecedents of what is happening in the transference. This is a telling, according to concepts, that focuses on, Why did who do what to whom where and when?

My notion of interpreting is to focus attending on feelings that will bring associations to those feelings and to interconnected conations, cognitions, sensings, and perceptions and hence to total bodily sets maintaining character attitudes. My objective in pointing is showing, not telling, so that experiencing is fostered. Thereby compulsive patternings are identified and resolved and spontaneous ones identified and enhanced. Rather than interpretation, I therefore prefer the holistic term *illuminator*. I see my questions as guiding patients to look in areas less illuminated and into the dark so that they may come to light, thus effecting change.

The notion of illuminators is congruent with my ideas on insight. The concepts of intellectual and emotional insight are limited. Illuminating emerging forms while focusing on the experiencing process produces greater awareness of the spectrum of dimensions in paradox forming and paradox resolving, tension producing and tension reducing, conflict and cooperation, forming and resolving processes. Thereby the person creates and miscreates himself and his world. Through feeling questions, a patient is guided to experiencing; to the unity of insight and outsight, in feeling—sensing—perceiving—conating—thinking as an interconnected matrix in holistic seeing; to the interconnectedness and continuity of all levels of the symbolic spiral. In such experiencing he is creating his own meaning. I therefore feel that a more appropriate term for what is called insight, the insight and outsight of holistic seeing, is *creative vision*.

My views on symbolizing, experiencing, process, illuminators, and creative vision are basic to my ideas regarding dreaming. Our noun-oriented language, subject-predicate in form, forces us to hypostatize a process and abstract from it a dreamer who dreams a dream. What obtains is a unitary process (organism-environment) from which emerge forms reflecting a process we call dreaming.

Trapped into a noun-oriented language, I must start with a dream and describe how I work with it. After a patient has related a dream, if he hasn't associated to the dream, I may ask, "What comes about the dream?" to evoke all that follows from "what" questions and to introduce the feel of processes, coming and emerging, with the implication from below and from within. The patient is introduced to the feel of moving from surface to depth, from the manifest to latent, to the feeling of levels and into the notion of the symbolic spiral. The question is open-ended. It asks for and welcomes everything. It is implicit, not explicit. The latter narrows the focus of the patient's evenly hovering attention.

I may ask, "What feelings come about the dream?" Once he hears "feel" not "think," he may find he cannot contact his feelings. This can be very frightening. Finally, he may find that he is scared of feeling, because so often feelings stand for what is unconscious, unknown, and uncontrollable.

"What feelings did you have as you were dreaming? About your dream since you dreamt or as you're telling it to me now?" Such questions may help him open to a wider range of feelings and more dimensions of them. It is educating him in experiencing process—educate in the root meaning of *educare,* to lead out. It introduces him to the multidimensionality of feelings and the dreaming process. Both are enhanced as he experiences the continuity and interconnectedness of the various levels of the symbolic spiral.

"What feelings do you have about" particular parts of the dream? His selection tells us what symbols have importance for him and are available to be explored. After some associations to a sequence of symbols, we note what he has not talked about. In a wondering tone I may say, "There are some parts of the dream you haven't commented on" or I may ask, "What feelings do you have about repeating the dream?" adding at times, "Some parts weren't clear to me." In repeating the dream, aspects not previously mentioned will be brought up, those previously mentioned might be related with a different emphasis, and other parts will be omitted. Asking about these changes fosters a feeling for process.

"Do you recall the dreams you had in the past month or months?" Ones recalled and not recalled and how they are recalled are revelatory. If the patient doesn't allude to the fact, I might ask, "Do you recall having dreamt about your father and your mother several times in the past week or past months?" And "What do you feel about the way your father and your mother come up in the dreams you had about them in the past week or month?" This is using the methods of sequence and comparison as well as the method of similarity and difference to help the patient experience change, process, and transformation. To underscore all these, I might ask, "What feelings do you have that you see your father this way in Dream 1," and/or "Dream 2," and/or "Dream 3?"

To help a patient experience that this is his dream and his creation, I might ask, "What do you feel if you see all the people in the dream as aspects of yourself?" This is asking him to experience his dream as self and object presentation. "What do you feel you're trying to say to yourself?" will help the patient feel into whatever self-confrontation he is attempting, what problems he is trying to define, what solutions he is searching for, what stands he is attempting to take with regard to certain positions and the values invested in them. Feeling questions with regard to fear, anger, joy, sorrow, and anxiety dreams help a patient feel into what positions invested with what values have been confronted that evoke such feeling responses.

I do not interpret dreams. By illuminating, through feeling questions, I guide the dreaming process so that wider and deeper experiencing of its manifold patternings takes place. Each patient creates his dreaming. He knows its meaning idiosyncratically and authentically. Through our mutual work he experiences the dreaming process and arrives at and creates his meaning as it emerges, which ultimately is the meaning of his dreaming.

These are some of my views on psychoanalysis as an experiencing process, some of the techniques used in such an effort, and the theories that guide me, the dualistic ones like Freud's, the process, system, and holistic ones, like Horney's. I have also been moved by what existentialism and phenomenology can contribute, as well as by what the philosophies and religions of the East can offer. I have asserted[8] that psychoanalysis, while it has been Western in its theorizing, is more Eastern in its techniques. Therefore, I have attempted also to make use of the nondualistic theories that would harmonize more with that fact.

This way of working can be taught. I have been doing so since 1941.[15,17,18] In the process, certain problems must be dealt with. Universally prevalent in the West and increasingly in the East is the overemphasis on intellect, theory, compulsive intellectualizing, flight from feelings and organicity, blocking of feelings, and alienation. Understanding such difficulties, we see how they interfere with teaching a psychoanalysis that focuses on the experiencing process.

Although many candidates-in-training may have come from other countries, visited them, had friends from many different groups, and studied sociology, anthropology, and history, the blocks to sociological, cultural, historical, and cosmic consciousness can be formidable. What was natural to me because of my life history was alien to most, often even on an intellectual level. A life history that should have given them some mutually commensurable experiential referents with other groups was minimal or lacking. Their early emotional blocking contributed to this state of affairs. Often they were amazed when I pointed out the number of cultures in the United States, the many different ways America was spoken, and our diverse cultural, societal, and generational value systems. However, they all became, in different measures, proficient in working with the experiencing process.

My philosophy of psychotherapy is the outcome of intensive and extensive work with patients. I have worked with many consecutively for over ten years, quite a few for over fifteen, and four for over twenty years.[16] I have many follow-ups on patients of fifteen years, quite a few of twenty, a number of over twenty-five, a dozen over thirty, and at least five over thirty-five years. From about 1945, I saw patients for sixty sessions weekly, fifty minutes each. In 1965 I began slowly to cut down to fifty, expecting to reach thirty by the age of seventy-three.

Since 1939, I have been involved with the psychoanalytic movement, as founder of organizations and institutes, as dean and president of several, as teacher, and as training and supervising analyst. In 1946, I worked with sixteen psychiatrists who were in analytic training. I have analyzed about seventy-five and participated in over 300 supervisory analyses. All of these activities have involved long hours of work made possible by my interest and energy and also by the fact I have never married.

Through my contacts, writing, and interests, I have lectured throughout the United States, Europe, Near, Middle, and Far East, Australia, and New Zealand. All of this has been possible through limiting my working year to thirty-six weeks, since 1950, having started with forty-eight in 1936. During my free time I played, wrote, and traveled. The latter contributed to a number of publications, particularly regarding the Orient.

Since I am involved with the psychoanalytic movement, many of my friends are psychoanalysts. Continuing contact with my family and friends outside the field, particularly those I have met during my travels abroad, who often visit me in New York, has given a necessary balance to my psychoanalytic relationships, as has an interest in the performing arts, literature, athletics, and of course travel.

While engaged therapeutically with my patients, I have been socially involved with none. Because so many of my colleagues were people who I had analyzed and with whom I had worked closely in training institutes and organizations, I have limited my socializing with them to functions associated with organizational activities. I feel this was necessary for my sanity and survival. I have lived through phases of the psychoanalytic movement where key figures became socially and personally involved with analysands. I have seen what pain it caused and the disruptive consequences for all concerned and the organizations in which they participated.

I feel fortunate to have come into psychiatry and psychoanalysis at a great time. I felt some of that excitement in the seminar Kardiner[28,29] gave in the mid-1930s on the relation of psychoanalysis and anthropology and in those that Rado conducted during that same era when he was in his most creative period. I had the experience of having been a participant in the founding and fostering of the Association for the Advancement of Psychoanalysis (1941), the American Academy of Psychoanalysis (1956), of which I later became president, and the program in Psychoanalytic Medicine at the Postgraduate Center for Mental Health (1969). To have participated in the training of many young people, with the pleasures and pains, the successes and failures, I regard as among my most enjoyable experiences. Psychoanalysis has been for me a great adventure. It has been challenging. It has been exciting. It has been fun. It has been my life since I was thirty-three years old. I have been fortunate.

Dr. Kelman passed away, while this volume was in press, March 30, 1977.

REFERENCES

1. Whyte LL: The Next Development in Man. New York, The New American Library of World Literature, 1950.
2. Angyal A: Foundation for a Science of Personality. New York, Commonwealth Fund, 1941.
3. Kelman H: Observations in catatonia with mixtures of carbon dioxide and oxygen. Psychiatric Q 6:513–522, 1932.
4. Kelman H: The doctor-patient relationship. A round table discussion. Am J Psychoanal 15:16–19, 1955.
5. Kelman H: Life history as therapy. III. The symbolizing process. Am J Psychoanal 16:145–166, 1956.
6. Kelman H: A unitary theory of anxiety. Am J Psychoanal 16:127–152, 1956.
7. Kelman H: Communing and relating. Am J Psychoanal 18:77–98, 1958; ibid. 18:158–170, 1958; ibid. 19:73–105, 1959; ibid. 19:188–214, 1959.
8. Kelman H: Psychoanalytic thought and eastern wisdom: *In* Masserman JH (ed): Science and Psychoanalysis, vol 3. New York, Grune & Stratton, 1960.
9. Kelman H: Freer associating: Its phenomenology and inherent paradoxes. Am J Psychoanal 22:176–200, 1962.
10. Kelman H: Toward a definition of mind. *In* Scher JM (ed): Theories of the Mind. New York, The Free Press of Glencoe, 1962, p. 243.
11. Kelman H: Creative talent and creative passion as therapy. Am J Psychoanal 22:133–141, 1963.
12. Kelman H: Tension is not stress. *In:* Advances in Psychosomatic Medicine, vol 3. New York, Karger, 1963.
13. Kelman H: Psychoanalysis and the study of etiology: a definition of terms: *In* Marin JH (ed): The Etiology of Neuroses. Palo Alto, Science and Behavior Books, 1966.

14. Kelman H: Psychoanalysis in cosmology. Compr Psychiatry 9:581–607, 1968.
15. Kelman H: The Process in Psychoanalysis. New York, Postgraduate Center for Mental Health, 1969.
16. Kelman H: The chronic analyst: *In* Masserman JH (ed): Science and Psychoanalysis, vol 16. New York, Grune & Stratton, 1970.
17. Kelman H: Helping People: Karen Horney's Psychoanalytic Approach. New York, Science House, 1971.
18. Kelman H: Teaching process psychotherapy. Psychother Psychosom 20:56–69, 1972.
19. Kelman H: Chronic analysts and chronic patients: The therapist's person as instrument. J Am Acad Psychoanal 1:193–207, 1973.
20. Kelman H: Irrational feelings: A therapeutic approach. Compr Psychiatry 14:217–225, 1973.
21. Kelman H: Altered states of consciousness in therapy. J Am Acad Psychoanal 3:187–204, 1975.
22. Horney K: Neurosis and Human Growth. New York, Norton, 1950.
23. Schechter DE: Infant development. *In* Arieti S. (ed): American Handbook of Psychiatry (ed 2), vol 1. New York, Basic Books, 1974, chap 12.
24. Schechter DE: On the emergence of human relatedness: *In* Witenberg E. (ed): Interpersonal Explorations in Psychoanalysis. New York, Basic Books, 1973, pp. 21, 25.
25. Winnicott D: The capacity to be alone. *In:* The Maturational Processes and the Facilitating Environment. New York, International Universities Press, 1965.
26. Gendlin E: A theory of personality change. *In* Worchel P, Byrne D (eds): Personality Change. New York, Wiley, 1964.
27. Freud S: Recommendations for physicians on the psychoanalytic method of treatment, 1912. *In:* Collected Papers, vol 2. London, Hogarth Press, 1933.
28. Kardiner A: The Individual and His Society. New York, Columbia University Press, 1939.
29. Kardiner A: The Psychological Frontiers of Society. New York, Columbia University Press, 1945.

Hilde Bruch, M.D.

The Tyranny of Fear

In recent years, I have seen in consultation many patients with anorexia nervosa who were referred for evaluation because they were not making progress or were getting worse, although they were in treatment with experienced psychiatrists. What is so difficult about these particular patients and why do things miscarry with them though their therapists are success-ful in treating other patients? There are, of course, many different reasons for such treatment failures, and various aspects need to be clarified in each individual case. I wish to focus here on one factor only, because it is observed rather frequently, namely that these patients intimidate people that try to help them, not only their families but also their therapists. If I have been able to establish rapport with some of these patients, I relate it to the fact that being aware of this possibility, I acknowledge its presence, communicate it to the patient and family, and thus convey that I refuse to be intimidated but that I want to look at how and why they use or need this method of relating to the people with whom they are involved.

A therapist may experience uneasiness, even outright anxiety, for many different reasons. The actual situation may be dangerous, and it would be foolhardy or negligent not to be concerned. The patient's behav-ior may be so aggressive or provocative that it arouses anger which, if not admitted to oneself, is experienced as tension. The patient's behavior may also touch on old, often unacknowledged problems of the therapist and provoke a countertransference reaction. It is my feeling that we are so aware of this latter possibility that we are apt to turn away from the direct anxiety-arousing behavior and do not identify it correctly. The pa-

83

tients I am concerned with had often been seen by many different therapists who had in common that they had not only not clarified these anxiety arousing issues but had avoided them.

CASE 1

How to handle a patient's unbridled aggression applies of course to other situations, too. Some time ago, a friend, also a psychiatrist, was visiting when I received a phone call; it was the father of a seventeen-year-old young man whom I had seen in consultation the day before and whom I was to see again the next day. He sounded excited; he wanted me to talk to his son because things had gotten out of hand, the son was breaking up the house. To my amazement the son came to the phone and explained that they had had an argument and he had gotten upset; it was correct, he was breaking things. My response was brief, "Stop it. We'll talk about it tomorrow."

My friend broke out laughing, saying that this was the shortest psychiatric consultation ever. I agreed that it was short, but what else was there to do? My friend knew the family, as a matter of fact, she shared office space with the referring psychiatrist. Such emergency calls had come with increasing frequency, and the therapist had responded with long explanations in his efforts to help the young man understand the underlying conflicts that resulted in these uncontrollable outbursts.

I explained my position; I simply didn't know enough about the situation to say anything that made sense; even if I knew more, I doubted that I would engage in a long telephone conversation under these circumstances. Several things were clear. The father was upset by the outbursts but had also recognized that the son was not completely out of control; otherwise he would have contacted the police, not a psychiatrist. On the other hand, if the son was upset enough to mess up the house, then he was not in a state of mind to listen to some long-winded psychodynamic explanation. At best, it might convey to him that I considered him helpless, under the influence of unconscious and uncontrollable forces or something like that. I had wanted to convey the opposite, that he was not helpless, that even if he had destructive impulses, nevertheless he was in a position to control them.

As an aside, I should like to add that the long-range outcome was good. The consultation had focused on the question of whether the young man needed to go to a psychotherapeutic treatment center, and this was the decision that was agreed on. However, there was a waiting period before admission, and there were many upsets and shouting matches; nevertheless, there was no other outburst where he became physically violent or destructive.

In anorexia nervosa, the behavior that provokes uneasiness and concern is rarely as readily recognized as aggressive or as being directed against others. Anorexia nervosa is an illness where the patient achieves the dominant position through weakness. One might express it as a paradox, that the anorexic's low weight, her frightening skeletonlike appearance, carries a lot of "weight" in the family and that she thus controls the home and quite often also, the therapist's office or a hospital service. The manipulative weakness that requires psychotherapeutic intervention needs to be differentiated from the physiological deterioration that may require immediate treatment as a medical emergency. Not to react to such a realistic need with alarm and appropriate action may lead to unnecessary delay of treatment and, unfortunately, not uncommonly to death of the patient.

CASE 2

Bianca had been anorexic for nearly three years when she was referred for treatment at age eighteen. She had finished high school in a foreign country where there were no treatment facilities. She was now enrolled in college where she had her own room in the dormitory. She was happy about this arrangement because she felt free from the constant supervision by her mother whom she blamed for her weight being so low, around seventy pounds, because the constant fighting had kept her from eating. She was sure that now when she was under her own direction she would eat the proper amounts.

It turned out that she did—but with dramatic and nearly fatal result. After two weeks, she looked definitely better and she noted that she had gained five pounds. She became panicky about this, feeling "fat," and took enormous amounts of laxatives and diuretics, something she had taken before in smaller amounts and had promised to discontinue. She looked like a ghost when she appeared for her next office appointment, so pale and with such sunken features that I could only gasp, "What happened?" After learning the facts, I took her to the emergency room. She was severely dehydrated and her circulation was poor, having lost at least eight pounds during the last forty-eight hours, and the electrolyte level, in particular that of potassium, was dangerously low. She was admitted to the hospital for intravenous infusion of electrolyte and glucose solutions. She was kept at bed rest and was given normal hospital food from which she ate sparingly, with much protest. Her internist advised, actually ordered, that she should stay in the hospital until her weight was safely above eighty pounds. She was outraged when I actively supported this prescription. She reacted with enormous anxiety and angry protest, "Do you want me to hate myself?"

Until then, her attitude toward psychiatric treatment had been somewhat condescending; she felt she did not really need it. Even she could see that a person who experienced intense self-hatred for gaining a few pounds, and who had nearly killed herself to undo this weight gain, must be very unsure and have a low opinion of herself, and she agreed that she needed help for that. Bianca made a complete recovery; after reevaluating her unrealistic aspirations and distorted self-image, her weight returned to normal. Throughout treatment, a worried glance at the door through which she had stumbled in near collapse served as a nonverbal message that she was driving herself too hard or that in other ways she was denying herself due respect for her needs.

For me this episode was an important learning experience. I had felt uneasy about this new patient with such a low weight who promised to take care of herself in a strange and new setting. It seems that the appeal not to be like the overcontrolling mother made me put my better judgment aside, and I "trusted" her to do it. The anxiety and guilt about having not anticipated this turn of events caused me to take a realistic look at the need to integrate medical and psychiatric management of an anorexic patient. The severe malnutrition is a real and dangerous illness, and to make meaningful psychotherapy possible the worst malnutrition needs to be corrected. I will not now accept an anorexic patient for ambulatory treatment unless the weight has been brought up to at least eighty-five to ninety pounds, depending on the height of the patient. Usually this can be done in several weeks of medical hospitalization, while being in psychotherapy. Below this level of weight, all psychological reactions are influenced by the toxic effects of the severe nutritional deficiency; the ghastly appearance interferes with any prospect of social relations; most of all, the danger to the patient's physical safety makes me uneasy, and I function better as a therapist when I am not worried about a patient's immediate health. Patients will accept such a statement if it is given with an adequate explanation about the underlying causes of the illness, that though it looks like an illness of weight and appetite the real illness has to do with problems of self-esteem, the fear of not being outstanding enough, and that these are the difficulties for which they need help.

To insist on weight correction seems to be the area that many psychiatrists find difficult to handle. Many patients I see in consultation have been in treatment for several years, but the weight has remained at a dangerously low level. A twenty-year-old girl had been anorexic and in treatment since age thirteen, the last four years with the same therapist, whom she quoted as saying, "When the cause is corrected the effect will correct itself." Her weight was sixty-two pounds and she vigorously protested against my insistence on improving her nutrition before I would make a psychiatric evaluation, that the secondary effects of the starvation had nothing to do with the underlying "causative" psychological problems. This knowledge, that the starvation has a distinct and disturbing psychological picture of its own, is slowly gaining ground. Until now, many psychiatrists honestly felt that resolution of the underlying conflicts would bring about normal eating behavior. This it does not. Many cling to this theoretical assumption because in this way they avoid a head-on collision with the patient's attitude of not wanting to gain weight, and they will not be confronted with the manipulative and intimidating behavior of the anorexic. Most patients who come for consultation have been exposed to a variety of usually inconsistent treatment approaches and have developed an endless variety of tricks to defeat them all.

CASE 3

A characteristic example is Minna who was twenty-two years old when she was referred for consultation. The anorexia had begun at age sixteen when she had been a beautiful and tall girl, five feet nine inches, and weighing 135 pounds. She began dieting with a plump friend who soon gave it up, but Minna stuck to it, losing way beyond what was pretty. The more she lost, the more she wanted to lose, and her weight dropped to sixty-nine pounds. At age eighteen, at a psychiatric hospital, she was given electroshock treatment, large doses of psychotropic drugs, and tube feedings. On discharge, she weighed 120 pounds, but she lost weight again until she weighed about ninety pounds. Her parents and Minna herself insisted on repeated medical examinations in the hope of finding an organic reason for the illness, but none was ever found. Some effort at psychotherapy was made in the local mental health clinic. Eventually she finished high school and tried to attend college but dropped out on several occasions due to her weakness and nervousness. She remained constantly preoccupied with her weight, was depressed at times, and cried a lot. The consultation was arranged by the therapist at the mental health clinic who felt that no progress was being made.

Minna was an only child, not only of her parents but of a large group of childless relatives. She had been raised with much indulgence but also with great expectations. The great disappointment of her life was that the family did not permit her to go to New York to become a ballerina when she was sixteen. "My true ambition was to become a prima ballerina. With this ambition came an obsessive body awareness with the desire to be thin. I had never dieted before and found the task almost impossible. To achieve my goal I made myself feel guilty and whenever I ate I conjured mental images of obese people who would never dance. Food soon became so repulsive to me that I could hardly stand to eat." The low point of her life was the hospital experience, of which she spoke as "the snake pit." "After six months I was discharged—a drugged zombie; my problems were only worse. Today I hate to eat, because of the guilty feelings, but I can no longer run at a hysterical pace without food as I once did. I often cry after I eat, attempt to vomit, and take large doses of laxatives, and I have thought of suicide." The whole consultation was dominated by the enormous display Minna made of her many symptoms and many pains, to which I reacted with cool and polite objectivity. I tried to focus on the family constellation and found mother and daughter allied against the father, whose drinking they blamed as the cause of all problems, though it had developed only after Minna's illness.

An attempt was made to focus on other difficulties, but Minna would not participate. She had a severe hysterical outburst afterwards. When the mother finally reached me by phone, after having tried all afternoon, she wanted her daughter to be hospitalized; she could not stand her screaming and complaints; the anxieties were intolerable. Since nothing had been touched on that would justify such an outburst, I advised them to go on to the emergency room of the hospital if she truly was unmanageable, otherwise to wait until her appointment the next day. It seems that my attitude that the problem could wait had a sobering effect, and the family went to sleep.

During the exploration on the following day, Minna was rather aggressive, attacking me as well as the referring doctor, saying that we wanted to put her on trial, that she was being accused of being sick in order to punish her parents, that nobody considered that she was punishing herself more than others. I agreed that this illness involved always a self-punishing element, but we had not yet learned anything about her own role, and therefore I could not have spoken of her punishing her parents. She became defensive and evasive, saying that people could not expect much from her because she was sick, that they blamed her sickness for manipulating others. I agreed that I had thought of her as someone who could lead a more active and independent life, who could look with a certain objectivity at her own problems and what they contributed to her illness. From the way she behaved here, it would be difficult to find out what had brought it on, but when the focus shifted to her, she had a fit of anxieties and complaints. Minna complained, "I want somebody who says 'gaining weight won't make it all right—I will help you with the depression,' but nobody listens." It was pointed out that the exact opposite was true, that the moment the focus was on her and the underlying problems, she objected and would not even take the chance of telling her own story. She accused her present psychiatrist of not being interested enough in her weight. By now, even she could recognize that the moment things didn't go her way, when the focus wasn't entirely on blaming others, she stopped communicating or would cry accusingly, "I am here on trial," or "It makes me so anxious." I summarized her behavior as, "You intimidate people with your crying fits and then when an effort is made to look at what needs to be clarified, you withdraw behind your panic attacks or not eating."

Minna began to talk more openly about what really troubled her, how isolated she felt, how shy she was with people, how easily her feelings were hurt, and how she would withdraw when things did not go her way. She had made keeping isolated a way of life, by offering herself as so breakable that her whole behavior was an open message, "Don't touch me!" or "I am so anxious—I can't approach anything." She summarized it as "I push the panic button" whenever something didn't go according to her plan, and she admitted that this had interfered with her making progress in therapy. We now explored together why treatment had been unsuccessful for these many years, how her dramatic display of hypersensitivities had kept her therapists, who were less experienced with such problems, from discussing any painful issues. Her deeper anxieties concerned her fear of not feeling anything emotionally, of feeling frozen and unable to love anybody. She could now talk in realistic terms about her illness, how it had interfered with her taking positive steps toward pursuing her own life. She felt vengeful toward her parents and, at the same time, demanded continuous care from them. As a child she had felt it was her task to keep them together, and now she often feels that it is her illness that keeps them together. She is aware that if she wants to live her own life she must leave home but is afraid to do so. She seems to demand, "They must change first," even though in this way she denies herself the chance of recovery. She openly discusses the many situations where she feels, "I can't cope," becomes frightened and then, "I push the panic button." When at the college she develops new symptoms whenever she encounters difficulties, such as stomach cramps, coughing fits, headaches, back pain, and so forth, and always renewed weight loss because she would refuse to eat.

She now is interested in the question of how to find alternatives to her present way of life. It makes sense to her to stop using weakness as a weapon and being sick as an embodiment of her whole power and strength but to pursue instead a career of her own liking. She had been aware of the seriousness of the underlying problems but had not believed that anybody could understand this.

The status quo was shaken up sufficiently that she carried through on the plan to move away from home and to become involved in intensive therapy. A year later, I received a report from her psychiatrist that she had taken these steps and was making progress in treatment. My own contribution had been mainly my not reacting to the dramatic and demanding display of suffering but offering warm and sensitive help in exploring her real problems.

CASE 4

The display of anxiety and guilt was much less dramatic in the following case but just as severe in its coercive effects. Tina was twenty-one years old, weighed seventy-five pounds, and was five feet, one inch tall when seen in consultation after seven years of anorexic illness. She continued to be plagued by the fear of gaining weight and suffered from severe sleep disturbances, spending the nights eating compulsively followed by vomiting, and sleeping all day. She had finished high school but did not feel well enough to attend college or to develop her considerable artistic talents.

She was an only child of middle-aged parents and had always been extremely close to them. She was a healthy child, tall for her age, but stopped growing when she was twelve years old and became a short adult. She had always envied children who were smaller and thinner than she was. The anorexia nervosa began when, at age fourteen, she changed from grade school to high school; she experienced this transition as being "pushed out of the nest." Her weight decreased from 110 pounds to nearly 70 pounds and menarche did not occur. It was also noticed that she became less communicative and withdrawn. She and her parents have been in some form of treatment for all the ensuing years.

She was in treatment with a psychoanalyst but was twice hospitalized for weight loss. The second time, she was admitted much against her wishes to an adolescent service, with a weight as low as fifty-nine pounds. She gained to ninety pounds in five months on a behavioristic program whereby all pleasurable activities were restricted unless she gained a prescribed amount of weight. The outcome was reported as a great success by the hospital, but Tina felt that "everybody was happy but me. I was absolutely desperate and miserable." She had always been somewhat irregular in her sleeping habits. In the hospital, she began to spend days in bed in an effort to check her compulsive eating; or she would eat huge amounts and secretly throw up. The persistent sleep disturbance and compulsive eating with vomiting appeared to be directly related to this program. After her return home, family therapy was instituted. Tina felt that the new therapist was against her, that he tried to force her into different behavior and activities. She made a serious suicide attempt which required lengthy medical and surgical hospitalizations. Her weight increased to nearly 100 pounds; after discharge, she brought it down again through vomiting after binge eating.

As in other cases, extensive information was obtained ahead of time so that plans could be made accordingly. I wrote that it was fortunate that Tina's sleep disturbance could be studied at the Baylor sleep laboratory. The father responded with an immediate telephone call, requesting to postpone such a study because Tina was afraid of it. This little episode was like a warning signal of the extent to which Tina's anxiety dominated the picture, so that the parents had become intimidated. During the consultation, other problems came into the open. Tina was in poor nutrition, but she emphasized that the low weight was the least of her problems, that she needed help with her severe tension. Someone had told her that alcohol relieved tension, and she felt that she now was an alcoholic. At first, she resisted the idea of hospitalization to improve her nutrition; when she decided to enter the hospital, she directly blackmailed her parents to provide her with alcohol to get over the shock. This was not permitted, and she had no withdrawal symptoms when alcohol was stopped.

During the first few sessions, Tina was so anxious, hostile, and uncommunicative that I became affected with the same timidity that her parents showed. One of her accusations was that I made her feel guilty, that I put blame on her, and that that made her just more tense and anxious. Once I clearly recognized what was happening, I raised the question of what Tina did to stop the grownups from functioning. "Feeling accused" and "being made to feel guilty" were made the focus of direct exploration. This question seemed to hit an important spot because she actively cooperated with this approach. I confronted her, that I had gained the impression that she, in fact, did feel guilty, not because I or anybody else *made* her feel this way, but because she truly felt guilty about the way she had conducted her life during the last six or seven years. It was she who had deprived herself of many experiences that would have been constructive, exciting, and rewarding if she had permitted herself to live her own life and had pursued the development of her personality and talents. "You feel guilty for not having pursued the promise of your own development. If you think of this as accusing, though it is not meant as accusing, it can mean only that you misunderstand what I try to say as simply as possible." Later we dealt with her fear of acting and behaving like a well person. We also explored her refusal to cooperate with the sleep study, though at this moment the sleep disturbance was the most handicapping symptom. I explained that her behavior suggested to me that she was afraid of being unmasked, that she feared that there might not be anything wrong with her sleep pattern, and that it all would be revealed as a big act. Her readiness to feel tense and frustrated and to use this as a weapon was also openly examined. She also learned that in her the threshold of feeling hurt and frustrated or discouraged was exceedingly low, and this acted like a brake against her doing the things that everybody needs to do. It stopped her from even trying or permitting her to find out how things would go. It could also be recognized that her continuous talk about enormous anxiety was related to the fear of not doing as well as she expected, that she would feel immediately discouraged and then withdraw. Then she would get angry for having given up; the true anxiety was her reaction to her own anger.

At the end of the consultation, it came into the open that she spoke of "feeling guilty" whenever something realistic about the future was discussed; in other words, her real fear was that she had to face the fact that she no longer was a true invalid. She finally agreed to a study in the sleep laboratory. To her amazement and relief, some abnormalities in her sleep patterns were discovered, and she received useful instruction on how to handle this. She felt relieved that she was vindicated, that it had not been an act.

These patients, and many others, experience the exploration of their anxiety-arousing behavior as something positive, namely reassuring them that they are effective in some way, though their method was prolonging the illness. Amazingly, it had not occurred to them that anything they did was effective. By speaking of the consequences of a patient's behavior, the message is conveyed that he is not a helpless victim of inner forces and motivations, that he has methods of exercising control, that he can function differently. Treatment being unsuccessful for so long convinces them that nobody can help them or that they are truly inadequate.

It is important that this inquiry is not carried out in an accusing way or with the intent of conveying to a patient that he is hostile or aggressive. The important point is to convey that he is not helpless, that he has many abilities or potentials that are undeveloped. This, in turn, is based on the theoretical assumption that the important issue in treatment is to let a patient feel more competent, less the result of what other people do to him, but somebody capable to develop his capacities.

Even this formulation may lead to difficulties, namely when dealing with patients who cannot tolerate the idea that there are things they do not know and need to learn, who cannot admit evidence of something wrong with their thinking and reasoning, and whose anxiety and anger are aroused by the very fact that something new comes up.

CASE 5

This was dramatically expressed during the treatment of Irma who had become anorexic at age fifteen and who came for consultation after having been in treatment for three years. She had been hospitalized twice, and her weight had been brought up in behavior modification programs. She had reacted with enormous depression and renewed weight loss, brought about by vomiting after binge eating. Several physicians and psychiatrists had been involved, with repeated sudden changes, because the father was dissatisfied with the progress. Several of the previous therapists spoke in their reports of strong paranoid tendencies.

Actually, Irma had been trained for this. An only child, born when her parents were middle-aged, the father had devoted his full love, efforts, devotion, and intelligence to raising this girl into something of a superbeing. As a financier, he held a high administrative position, and effective speaking skills were part of his profession. He literally raised his daughter as an expert in the adversary process through long debates with her on whatever topic came up. She experienced losing in these debates as the ultimate failure. She was intelligent and articulate in developing elaborate debating techniques. The father described this in critical terms, that she had developed the habits of a shyster lawyer who would distort the truth by careful minute arguments which added up to intellectual dishonesty. It was impossible for Irma to accept anything that she had not known previously or to even consider that there might be something that was unknown to her. Any effort to focus on definite aspects of her behavior and its effects aroused enormous anxiety and aggression. Once she got involved in an argument, it was nearly impossible to stop or interrupt it and to focus her attention on what had aroused it, because no argument was finished unless her adversary was reduced to the role of admitting that she, Irma, had been right and her opponent, (in her case, myself) had been wrong.

The first big area of disagreement was her weight. She knew that I was in disagreement with the behavior modification programs. I had expressed clearly that successful treatment was not possible with a starving organism and that it was her task gradually to correct her weight. After three years of treatment, her weight on arrival was seventy-two pounds, her height, five feet six inches. She was in such a miserable state that she accepted hospitalization although at that time would not admit her weakness; much later she described in moving terms the torture it had been even to move around. Since she was eighty-five pounds when ambulatory treatment began, and when she enrolled in college, she absolutely refused to weigh more, that no one had the right to fix a "correct" weight for her, that she was not the victim of statistics, that her own taste and desires were the only things that mattered.

To anticipate results: her weight gradually went up and she would describe now how different she felt, how she could enjoy activities and socializing, how she was now able to concentrate, how it had been nearly impossible to study when her weight was so low because she had been continuously hungry and preoccupied with food.

As long as it was a matter of debate, there was no way of stopping her from attacking me and reducing me to the point of helplessness. Actually, her method of debating was rather primitive, in spite of the enormous elaborations. She simply took whatever point was under discussion and extended it to the extreme, thereby forcing her opponent to agree that it was *not* "always" or "never" the case; ending up with the demanding question, "Don't you agree, don't you agree—you have to admit that you were wrong."

As time went on the attacks became more and more personal, and I became the object of her constant discussions with her friends and associates, and also with other patients. It became a systematic process of character assassination, that I was ignorant, senile, unethical, contradictory, not up to date in my knowledge, not remembering everything she told me, disliked by all my patients, and altogether unfit to be a therapist. Efforts to clarify and come to an understanding of her unbridled aggression were always sidestepped by the declaration, "You are rigid, you just don't want to admit that you were wrong, that you made a mistake." Whenever there was a problem that upset her, she could glibly say, "I want to talk about something else today because I need you. You know, of course, it is all negative transference."

For quite some time, efforts to help her recognize the background of the aggressive behavior were futile. She considered my calling her behavior "aggressive" an attack on her and would burst out with a new attack. Her repeated counterargument was "I get along so well with everybody else; they all like me and think I am nice. Only you have to attack me and tell me I am wrong because you are unable to recognize my real problems." Gradually things changed; suddenly she was having outbursts of anger against some of her friends, or she would get involved in destructive relationships; she found herself unable to maintain her friendships or to be happy in any relationship. Some of the underlying problems gradually became clear: Whenever somebody she cared for did not show positive outgoing interest in her, she felt devastated and hurt and became counteraggressive, or she would withdraw into binge eating and vomiting. It became apparent that my focus on her contradictions and misconceptions represented my not being "positive" in relation to her, admiring her intelligence and wide range of interests, but being fault-finding instead. It was only then that some constructive work could be done, that there were other ways of relating to people than by diminishing them to the status of nincompoops. She also learned that there were a wide range of feelings. Until then, whenever feelings were aroused in her, she would translate them immediately into aggressive action.

Work with such a patient is exhausting and taxes one's equanimity. I developed several techniques of handling her attacks. After having been truly angry a few times and controlling these feelings, I developed sort of an act, interrupting her with an angry loud voice, while being in reality quite calm when she attacked me for having become angry. I felt this display was necessary, because any comments made in a quiet tone of voice were not listened to or were treated as if nothing had been said. The angry tone was necessary to interrupt her monotonous accusations.

In this way, she could be confronted with the fact that her technique, obviously intended to arouse anger or to show my weakness, represented at the same time a method of blocking treatment progress, because an angry therapist could not possibly be tuned in on her real needs. When she got completely caught up in her arguments and her aggression was out of control, paralyzing all efforts at constructive work, I felt forced to withdraw to a defensive position and explain to her that she was a voluntary patient, that nobody forced her to stay in treatment with such an incompetent person, and she might prefer to look for a therapist who fulfilled her requirements. This statement, that she had the right to seek another therapist, was effective because that was what her father had done repeatedly; she knew from bitter experience that changing the therapist was not the solution but would only lead to further delay in her treatment and recovery. This approach usually led to a brief period of more relaxed work, saying that she had come to Houston to work with me, that she had felt for the first time somebody understood her condition, that she truly trusted me or she could not tell me all these negative things. This lasted until the next time when something else came up that she had not recognized ahead of time and that aroused her anger. But gradually, point by point, issues were clarified and she learned to accept herself as she was, not as she pretended to be.

Things were complicated by the fact that her parents, too, operated in a similar way with constant attacks. Whenever things seemed to be going well, there came messages from her parents that they didn't believe in psychiatry, or didn't trust me, or felt treatment was not progressing fast enough, or that father wanted a report on how long this whole thing would last, or some long story about having had some terrible experience with a physician in their home community. I know of no other woman as often "nearly killed" by a physician as Irma's mother. It was not always clear whether these were truly messages from the parents, or whether she was accumulating ammunition for a renewed attack on me.

That something constructive was accomplished in spite of all these interrupting and delaying maneuvers seems to be related to the fact that, basically, Irma was convinced that she wanted and needed help and that she had experienced that her condition could be understood and treated. In addition, there was my absolute refusal to be drawn into her attacking arguments, or to apologize for so-called errors or to admit to any of the defects she had compiled for me while at the same time I was open about any misunderstandings that had actually occurred. I readily admitted to one mistake, namely that I had permitted her to go on with her ranting too long before I found a way of using it in the treatment process. I told her frankly that her behavior was annoying and unconstructive, but if that was the best she could do, then that was what we had to work with.

Not all patients are ready or capable of going along with this approach, which focuses on how their behavior and symptoms influence others. Though most react as if it were a relief to speak openly about the effect of their behavior, giving them the status and respect of being considered effective, some, like Irma, use all their energy in an effort to maintain their assumed status of absolute superiority by being constantly on the attack. Still others object to such inquiry and withdraw from it.

CASE 6

Recently I saw in consultation a young woman whose domination of the environment through her anxiety and threats was extreme. She would repeatedly phone her mother at night asking for help because she was on the point of slashing her wrists or committing suicide in another form. The presenting complaints were uncontrollable eating binges, compulsive vomiting, and excessive use of laxatives. She spoke of these symptoms as "my anorexia" and wanted someone to help her get rid of this terrible illness. Otherwise she felt her life was going perfectly; she had friends, was doing well in her career, and had a boyfriend who offered only one difficulty—he must not learn of her dreadful symptoms. Her constant preoccupation with suicide, and her repeated attempts, were cited as expression of her despair about her abnormal eating behavior. She saw no relationship to something disturbing in her self-concept or in her attitude toward others. When an effort was made to focus on those aspects of life which she said had nothing to do with the eating and vomiting, she became indignant, maintaining that she would not want anything touched there, that everything was perfect. She did not keep her next appointment, and her parents brought the message that she refused to continue the consultation. In reviewing this course of events with the referring psychiatrist, it became apparent that the mother's unwillingness to let go of her role as the great protector had as much to do with the interruption as the girl's fear of becoming independent of her.

COMMENT

Much has been said that the way an individual therapist uses and modifies the techniques he has been taught is related to his personality. I am inclined to go one step further, namely, that the theoretical formulation one prefers as meaningful is closely related to his personality and experiences. Theories with the basic assumption that treatment aims at stimulating patients to become more competent in coping with life by developing their own resources and capacities have much more appeal to me than those in which an individual appears as a helpless object on whom a psychological operation is performed. Whatever I have been taught, I have developed it in the direction of evoking initiative and autonomy as necessary steps for more effective and satisfying living. In the patients with whom I am concerned, previous therapists had explored the symbolic and unconscious meaning of their various dramatic symptoms in the expectation that insight would lead to their resolution.

In my experience, symptoms lose their original meaning in such a long-standing illness and need to be understood in operational terms, what functions they have in the ongoing life of a patient. Furthermore, the malnutrition itself has a disturbing influence on their psychic functioning. Deeply convinced of their ineffectiveness, these youngsters experience a sense of power and being in control, of getting attention and consideration, by arousing fear in those responsible for their care, while at the same time becoming more and more imprisoned in an invalid way of life. The therapeutic task is to cut through this enmeshment and to help them develop their own inner capacities for true independence, so that they no longer need to exercise power through weakness and the tyranny of fear.

There is no doubt in my mind that in my approach to treatment I am relatively little impressed by or sympathetic to a patient's display of dramatic helplessness. In some form or another, I always recognize and focus on his potential for independence and self-expression, and I communicate this as soon as possible. I have the feeling that certain features of my own background and development have something to do with this preference for being active and self-assertive. I was born a third child out of seven, with a much admired older sister and brother. The great concern of my early life was the possibility of being relegated to the status of a little one. I learned early that for status and recognition I had to rely on my own efforts and certainly for achieving and getting what I wanted. There was nothing more deplorable than a hand-me-down. I learned early how to make things fit me, whether it was something concrete like a dress or something in the line of knowledge and ideas. An outer expression of this capacity to carry through on what I recognized as my individual need is the pursuit of an academic career, something unheard of at that time for a girl of my small town background. The same determination to be independent, not to compromise, is expressed in my leaving Germany within a few months after the Nazis came to power. It is also expressed in changing my medical specialty from pediatrics to psychiatry when I had recognized the importance of psychological factors. If I wanted to pursue this interest I felt I had to become a full-fledged psychiatrist and psychoanalyst, not a pediatrician who was interested in psychology.

All these decisions were steps into something unknown, without any role model. I had never known, or even heard of, a woman physician, and I had no contacts when I came to the United States. Yet I recall little hesitation or anxiety in taking any of these steps. It may well be that my refusal to be intimidated by these patients who have everyone else stymied is related to my remaining calm when confronted with life situations that arouse anxiety in others. I have a peculiar memory for my school years; I envied the girls who were afraid of examinations; they were so happy when they had passed. I just wrote the examination paper, and passing was a matter of fact. In a similar way these difficult patients do not arouse anxiety in me; they offer difficult problems that need to be solved, something that requires alert interest but freedom from anxiety.

The fact that I had been a pediatrician greatly influenced the way I reacted to psychiatric and psychoanalytic theory and teaching of the early 1940s. Having observed parents and children in interaction, in sickness and in health, it was impossible for me to accept a theory in which the "vicissitude of the libido" or what-have-you determines the development of a child. My pediatric observation had left me convinced that even a newborn infant is an active participant in his development, that the way he interacts with his parents and others is important, and that he is more than a helpless creature dominated by instincts.

It was fortunate that at the time of my training the orthodox psychoanalytic model was beginning to be revised and alternative formulations offered. I was impressed by Sullivan's approach and his efforts to reconstruct what really had gone on during an individual's development, how the child's "mode of experience" influenced the way he assimilated and reacted to what happened to him. This was more in agreement with what I knew about children than a formulation in which he appeared more or less passive in his own development.

Sullivan's definition of the therapist as "participant observer" was more congenial to me than the orthodox image of the therapist as a "blank mirror" who only reflected what the patient transferred onto him. It is essential for a "participant observer" to pay attention to his own feelings and reactions, in particular to be alert to any situation or process that arouses uneasiness or fear in him. Alert attention to one's own feelings is a helpful guide to further inquiry (incidentally, also to one's own self-understanding) and thus to successful resolution of a patient's problems. This stands in contrast to the image of the uninvolved analyst who interprets a patient's problems on the basis of some special secret knowledge.

This overall attitude was supported by, or in agreement with, my experiences in the treatment of obese and anorexic individuals. I had become increasingly dissatisfied with the results of interpretative, insight-giving psychotherapy and recognized gradually that such patients, in spite of their good intelligence, needed help with developing thus far deficient mental tools and guideposts for orienting themselves about their own needs and their relationships with others. Formerly, psychotherapy had been nearly exclusively preoccupied with unconscious conflicts and motivations; the importance of disturbances in the perceptual and conceptual area had been comparatively neglected. These patients misuse the eating function in their efforts to solve problems in various areas of living that have nothing to do with nutritional need. A frequent reason for such misuse of a function is the organism's failure to differentiate between hunger and other sensations and feeling states; the brain is continually making mistakes in its effort to discriminate between bodily and psychological needs. Pursuit of this question leads to the deduction that the awareness of hunger is not innate knowledge but one that contains elements of learning. Incorrect or confusing early experiences interfere with an individual's learning to differentiate "hunger," as the need to eat, from other reasons of discomfort that have nothing to do with food deprivation.

Misuse of the eating function is not an isolated symptom but is always associated with other problems in the area of active or passive self-awareness. Passivity has always been considered a characteristic of obese people; it was surprising to discover that anorexics, too, suffer from a deep-seated fear of not being in control, of being helpless under the domination and powers of others, in spite of the vigorous and stubborn surface behavior. A common deficit was recognized in the background of such patients, namely absence or paucity of confirming responses to a child's expressions of his needs. Though well-cared for in the physical sense, this had been superimposed according to the mother's conviction, not the child's clues. A child growing up this way may acquire the facade of adequate functioning by robotlike cooperation with the environmental demands. The gross deficit in initiative and active self-awareness becomes manifest when he is confronted with new situations and demands for which the distorted early life experiences have left him unprepared. It is at this point that the anorexic picture develops. Such patients need assistance in acquiring the heretofore undeveloped tools for orienting themselves about their own "self," body and competence. Helping them become aware that their behavior and attitude has an effect on people around them is a first step in this direction.

REFERENCES

Bruch, H., Sullivan's interpersonal theory of personality. *In* Burton A (ed): Theories of Personality: An Operational Viewpoint. New York, Brunner Mazel, pp. 143–160, 1974.
Bruch, H., Learning Psychotherapy. Cambridge, Harvard University Press, 1974.
Bruch, H., The constructive use of ignorance. *In* Anthony EJ (ed): Exploration in Child Psychiatry. New York and London, Plenum, pp. 247–264, 1975.

Ralph R. Greenson, M.D.

That "Impossible" Profession

The title for this talk occurred to me at the end of one of those working days when all my clever insights turned out to be wrong, when I discovered the right interpretation only after the patient had left, when what I considered profound insight was revealed as complicated confusion, and when my kindly passivity was felt by my patients merely as inattentiveness. On such days I have attempted to reassure myself by recalling that such feelings pass and that I might be exaggerating the difficulties in practicing psychoanalysis. But even sober reflection leaves no doubt that the practice of psychoanalysis makes arduous demands on the psychoanalyst. I should like to address myself to the following questions: What are the extraordinary difficulties that seem to be inherent in the profession? Are there any factors that might play a mitigating role?

Freud himself seemed to be of a pessimistic frame of mind in this regard and I want to quote part of a paragraph from "Analysis Terminable and Interminable"[1]

Here let us pause for a moment to assure the analyst that he has our sincere sympathy in the very exacting demands he has to fulfil in carrying out his activities. It almost looks as if analysis were the third of those 'impossible' professions in which one can be sure beforehand of achieving unsatisfying results. The other two, which we have known much longer, are education and government. Obviously we cannot demand that the prospective analyst should be a perfect being before he takes up analysis, in other words that only persons of such high and rare perfection should enter the profession. But where and how is the poor wretch [Freud's words] to acquire the ideal qualifications which he will need in his profession? The answer is, in an analysis of himself, with which his preparation for his future activity begins. For practical reasons this analysis can only be short and incomplete [p. 248].

Today, I believe, we would modify the last sentence and say that for practical reasons the analysis can only be long and incomplete.

In order to pursue the question: what makes the practice of psychoanalysis so arduous? we have to examine the various skills that the analytic situation demands of the psychoanalyst. Facility in gaining insight into the mind of another human being is inextricably tied up with the analyst's unconscious mind and the degree to which it is accessible for use by his conscious ego. The analyst's personal analysis has the ultimate aim of increasing the analyst's ability to utilize his insight into the important drives, defenses, fantasies, and conflicts of his own infantile life and their later derivatives. The psychological processes that the analyst has to employ in his technical procedures are also decisively involved in the formation of his own character and personality. Even his knowledge and intelligence are influenced by the degree and kind of resolution of his neurotic conflicts. I would go still further and add that the motivations that have led him into the field of psychoanalysis also play a role in how he works with patients.

Skills, traits, and motivations are the crucial elements in the analyst's armamentarium. They are interdependent and interrelated and bound up with the conscious and unconscious emotions, drives, defenses, fantasies, attitudes, and values of the analyst. Nevertheless, for purposes of clarification I shall artificially separate these factors—skills, traits, and motivations—in order to highlight those factors which cause the most difficulty. (Limitations of space will reduce this inquiry to an outline.)

SKILLS

The primary task of the psychoanalyst is to gain a detailed understanding of the patient's emotions, attitudes, and actions. The most difficult part of this job is to comprehend the unconscious processes which go on in his patient's mind. This depends on his skill in being able to translate the patient's conscious material into its unconscious and preconscious antecedents. While he listens to the patient precisely and carefully, he also has to sense what lies behind the various subjects the patient is expounding. While he listens to the melody, he must also listen to the hidden themes, the "left hand," the counterpart. This is possible only if he listens with the so-called evenly suspended attention that Freud[2] described. He listens consciously, intellectually, and detachedly, and at the same time from the inside as a participant. This kind of listening requires that the analyst have the capacity to shift from participant to observer, from introspection to empathy, from intuition to problem-solving thinking, from a more involved to a more detached position. It is necessary for him to oscillate, make transitions and blendings of these different positions.[3-7]

The ability to empathize with the patient is an absolute prerequisite for psychoanalytic practice. It is our best method for comprehending the complex, subtle, and hidden emotions in another human being.[7-9] Empathy means to share, to experience partially and temporarily the emotions of another person. It is essentially a preconscious phenomenon. It can be consciously instigated or interrupted, and it can occur silently and automatically, alternating with other forms of relating to people. The essential mechanism in empathy is a partial and temporary identification with the patient. In order to accomplish this it is necessary to regress from the position of detached, intellectual observer to a more primitive kind of relationship in which the analyst becomes one with the person he is listening to. It requires the capacity for controlled and reversible regressions.[10]

Empathy is a special variety of intimacy with another human being. In order to empathize the analyst must be willing to become emotionally involved with his patient. He cannot empathize coldly; he can only empathize out of some wish or willingness to become close. Then he must be able to give this up and become the observer, the thinker, and the analyzer again. Empathy is most likely to come into play when the analyst feels lost or out of touch. Empathy becomes a means of regaining contact with the un-understood patient. It resembles other identificatory processes which occur when one is attempting to reestablish contact with a lost love object. One must be able to do this again and again and yet retain the ability to return to the detached an uninvolved position of analyzer. This is one of the important antithetical, bipolar demands of psychoanalytic practice.

Another skill of vital importance to the analyst is the ability to communicate meaningfully to the patient. He gathers the data from the patient by detached or involved listening and understanding. Then he is faced with what to say, how to say it, and when to say it. This again depends to a great extent on his capacity to feel in empathic contact with the patient. He must be in intimate touch and yet not so close that he loses his independent judgment. He must be clear and precise, and the words he uses should usually be from the living language of the patient and not from his own private vocabulary. If his language is too distant, what he says will seem unreal. If his language is too much like the patient's, then there is the danger of having too much impact, which may be traumatic. Intonation, tone, force, rhythm are often more important than the precise words one uses, because the tone of what one says indicates the nonverbal, the preverbal relationship one has to the patient and is apt to stir up reactions derived from the early mother-child relationship.[11-16]

Matters become more complicated because the analyst has to be skillful in communicating not only with words and with tone but also with silence, which is very different. He has to know when to be silent and how to be silent, and he has to understand the many meanings of silence to the patient—when it is comforting and reassuring and when it is distant and hostile. He must sense when silence is warm and when it is cold; when it is probing, questioning, and demanding; and when it is apt to be felt as a terrible stress and a criticism. The analyst cannot perform these delicate deliberations only with his conscious intellect. He has to do this also preconsciously, unconsciously, with empathy. And again this has to be reversible. One must be able to make oscillations, transitions, and combinations of these various methods of communicating. These skills also have complicated antithetical properties and are a severe demand on the psychoanalyst.

The psychoanalytic situation demands of the psychoanalyst that he possess the ability to relate to his patient in such a way that the patient will develop a transference neurosis and also a working alliance. This is another instance when the analyst is required to have proficiency in maintaining two conflicting positions, for the attitudes and techniques which further the transference neurosis are often in opposition to those which facilitate the working alliance.[16-18]

Stated in condensed form, in order to facilitate the development of a transference neurosis, one must frustrate the patient's search for neurotic gratifications and reassurance. Only in this way does the analyst induce the patient to regress in his quest for satisfaction and security. Furthermore, the analyst must try to comport himself so as to present himself to the patient as a relatively blank screen for the latter's fantasies, displacements, and projections.[2,19]

On the other hand, one must work with the patient in such a way that he can also become one's co-worker part of the time, working along on understanding and integrating his insights. One must induce him to mobilize his relatively nonneurotic capacity for object relationships and to partially and temporarily identify with the analyst's point of view. In order to promote the working alliance the analyst must demonstrate to the patient unwavering pursuit of insight and understanding in the daily work. No matter what the patient presents to him, be it ugly or beautiful, delicate or brutal, sensitive or crude, loving or hateful—the analyst is concerned only with why, how, when, and with whom did this happen. To the analyst each hour is important, and he is willing to devote years in his attempt to understand the patient.

The analyst must also safeguard the rights of the patient if he hopes to maintain a working alliance. The patient is in a relatively helpless position when he comes for help and will therefore tend to accept uncritically and submissively what one offers him. This forms part of the uneven and tilted relationship Greenacre[19] has described. The analyst must be sure not to demean him unwittingly and to take advantage of his helplessness by treating him with imperious attitudes. The procedures of psychoanalysis are strange, unique, and artificial, and the patient has a right to know, at the proper time, why one asks him to use the couch, to do free association, why one refuses to answer his questions, etc. By protecting his rights as an adult one nurtures his self-esteem, so that one day he can become a truly independent human being and not just a submissive, masochistic patient.

Again we have two sets of demands on the analyst which are in opposition to each other—the deprivational incognito required of the transference neurosis and the reasonable co-worker of the working alliance. These two positions should not nullify or neutralize each other. Each has to exist at the proper time, and there must be oscillations, transitions, and blendings of them. Only a strong and consistent therapeutic commitment to the patient (within limits that are controllable) makes this contradictory combination of attitudes possible. It is for this reason that I consider the therapeutic commitment mandatory and not optional, even in the case of training analysis.[16,18]

TRAITS

To perform the complex, subtle, and conflicting skills I have outlined requires persons of unusual sensitivity, personality, and character. Yet all that is not sufficient. No one is a born psychoanalyst or suddenly blossoms into one. The psychoanalytic situation makes such arduous demands that the talents and abilities a person brings with him to the field have to be supported by an analyzed character structure. And here I want to quote Freud[1] again:

But where and how is the poor wretch to acquire the ideal qualifications which he will need in his profession? The answer is, in an analysis of himself, with which his preparation for his future activity begins. . . . This alone would not suffice for his instruction; but we reckon on the stimuli that he had received in his own analysis not ceasing when it ends and on the processes of remodelling the ego continuing spontaneously in the analysed subject and making use of all subsequent experiences in this newly-acquired sense [pp. 248–249].

The experience of having undergone a therapeutic psychoanalysis (as well as a continuing self-analysis) is a prerequisite for the practice of psychoanalysis. However, certain traits of personality and character are necessary for reaching a high level of professional competence in the field. I realize that the selection of only a few qualities as being of special importance for psychoanalysts is apt to be highly subjective. I therefore recommend the works of Ella Sharpe[5], Chap. II; 20, Ernest Jones,[21] and Leo Stone,[16] who have written more extensively on this subject.

The relationship between analytic skills and personality traits is a complex one, and the origins of skills and traits vary from individual to individual. Here I shall pick out only what I consider to be the major faculties and outline the most typical antecedents. A single source may be the fountainhead for many traits and skills; although they share the same source, the traits or skills may be uneven in quality. On the other hand, a single trait or skill may have multiple origins.

The analyst should possess a lively interest in people, their ways of life, emotions, fantasies, and thoughts. He should have an impelling but benevolent curiosity. Too little curiosity makes for a bored analyst. Too harsh a curiosity will cause the patient to suffer unnecessary pain. There should be pleasure in discovering things and in bringing insight to the patient; yet this should not be a scoptophilic or sadistic gratification. This is possible only when curiosity has become a relatively deinstinctualized and neutralized activity. I want to stress the term relatively, because sublimations are rarely absolute and final. Partially and occasionally such activities do become reinstinctualized, and one has to be aware of this occurrence. Hartmann's[22] ideas on sublimation are valuable for understanding this problem.

An analyst should meet the unknown in the patient, the strange and the bizarre, with an open mind and not with aversion or anxiety. One has to be free of the usual restricting conventionality of society and relatively indifferent to the superficialities of everyday life. In order to be initially receptive and accepting, it is necessary for the analyst to let himself be credulous and gullible. Only in this way is it possible to do full justice to what the patient might be feeling. With yet another appeal for the necessity of antithetical requirements, the analyst must also be somewhat skeptical, knowing how people distort, twist, and change things to make themselves appear virtuous or innocent. On the other hand, a hawklike, detectivelike suspiciousness about everything the patient says may make the analyst appear clever but may estrange him forever from the patient, because an analyst cannot empathize properly with a patient when he is trying to entrap him.

I have already mentioned the central importance of empathy, and I want to add that I believe that the capacity to empathize requires a willingness temporarily and partially to give up one's own identity. People with a rather narrow sense of identity, rigid and fixed, are unwilling or unable to empathize; the analyst's self-image has to be flexible and loose. Yet he may not lose his identity. At the end of the hour, he has to end up being the analyst. Furthermore, I am not referring to consciously playing a role, which implies conscious deception. When I talk about empathizing and letting oneself be carried away temporarily by the patient, I have in mind something similar to what Beres[23] and Rosen[24] have described about what happens when one lets oneself be carried away temporarily by a piece of music or art. This is also what is required in empathizing. But one cannot have multiple identities. Empathy—and I dwell on it because it is so crucial—is a special kind of nonverbal, preverbal closeness which has a feminine cast; it comes from one's motherliness, and men (and women too) must have made peace with their motherliness in order to be willing to empathize. This is derived from the mental bisexuality of the analyst, a trait Jones[21] pointed out in Freud. People who are empathizers are always trying to re-establish contact, like people who are depressed. I believe that analysts who have been depressed and have overcome their depression make the best empathizers.[9] One must be able to regress to empathic contact with the patient and then be able to rebound from it in order to check on the validity of the data so gathered.

The skill in communicating to a patient is very different from ordinary social talking, history-taking, cross-examination, or lecturing. Eloquence, erudition, and logic are not of primary importance in the art of talking to a patient. The essential element is a therapeutic attitude with an empathic undertone. I want to stress the point about the therapeutic attitude because I know it is controversial. The commitment to help the patient should be manifest or latent in all interactions with him from the first interview to the last. I want to state my position about this clearly and emphatically. I believe only sick people—patients who suffer from neurotic miseries— can be successfully treated by psychoanalysis. Candidates, research workers, investigators cannot undergo a deep analytic experience unless they are able and willing to become patients. And parallel to that statement I believe that deep psychoanalysis is first and foremost a method of treatment and therefore can be carried out effectively only by therapists— people trained and dedicated to helping or curing the emotionally ill. A medical degree does not automatically make one a therapist, nor does lack of it prevent a therapeutic attitude. It is my conviction that the analyst's commitment to help the patient—ever present but under control—is an essential ingredient which enables the former to develop the subtle skill of communicating meaningfully and effectively with the latter.[5,16,21,25]

Other skills play a role in communicating but are secondary. Literary skill is of little value. Verbal dexterity can be the difference between a more deft therapist and a more clumsy one, but I do not believe that it is ever of decisive importance. Analysts who tend to remember the brilliant things they say to their patients may sound good at meetings, but I sometimes wonder how it felt to the patient. What appears brilliant to the patient usually comes from the patient's dynamics at the moment and not from the analyst's cerebration.

I want to return to another skill in communicating—the silent part—which requires a very different set of traits: patience, the ability to wait, to suspend judgment. Here too one must be careful, because what looks like a virtue may turn out to be something quite different. Patience—or what looks like patience—in the very silent analyst may really be hidden passive, sadistic, aggressive impulses. Or patience may be a screen for professional indecisiveness or timidity. Here too the important question is whether the capacity to wait and be patient is or is not a relatively conflict-free ego function.

I stated earlier that to facilitate the development of a transference neurosis in the patient, the analyst has to maintain attitudes suggested in the term "deprivational incognito." In order to achieve this the analyst must be able to stand aloof from his patient, restrain his therapeutic intentions, and blanket his normal, humane responses. In part, this stems from the analyst's ability to control his loving and reparative tendencies. Partially, however, it is derived from the analyst's ability to inflict pain on his patient, which in turn stems from some aspect of hatred for his patient. I realize this may be a shocking way of putting it—hating one's patient—but I see no reason to camouflage reality. Just as the analyst must be able to love his patient, within limits, so must he be able to hate his patient, also within limits. Inflicting pain, be it in the form of aloofness, silence, making interpretations or charging fees, are ultimately all derived from hatred. It is important that the analyst be able to do this without unconscious anxiety or guilt and for the patient's therapeutic benefit.[26]

On the other hand, the working alliance requires an ever-ready willingness on the analyst's part, no matter how offensive a façade the patient may be presenting, to keep in mind that this is a sick and relatively helpless human being, a child. This brings with it the danger that one becomes overly concerned and then tends to overprotect and indulge the patient.

And yet one may not remain wooden and untouched. The analyst has to be reliable in human terms, not rigid and predictable by starting every hour exactly on the hour and ending every hour exactly in fifty minutes, come hell or high water. This kind of reliability is valueless. The patient needs the knowledge that his analyst is a human being who is both concerned and expert, who is trying to help him by providing an atmosphere where he can gain insight and understanding. The corollary danger is that of showing sympathy and loving kindness too early and too copiously. The analyst who does so is as bad as the one with the wooden face. Instant warmth has no place in psychoanalysis, which cannot be done in a hale and hearty manner, cheerfully or lightheartedly. Neither can it be effective if it is essentially grim, gloomy, or agonizing. The analyst must be able to feel a genuine liking, compassion, and acceptance for his patient while establishing an atmosphere in which the latter can develop the necessary transference reactions. Then he must be able to communicate insights within the patient's ability to bear them.

The wish to cure the patient should be apparent not in zealousness but in the analyst's seriousness of purpose, his rigorous pursuit of insight, his nonritualistic respect for the various instrumentalities of his profession, and his willingness to struggle for years toward the long-range goals. The analyst's ability to administer painful insights is as much a sign of his therapeutic intent as his concern for the patient's dignity and self-respect. Bearing the hostile and humiliating outbursts of his patients without retaliation is as important as remaining unperturbed by their sexual provocations. This does not mean that the analyst should not have feelings and fantasies in response to his patients, but their degree and quantity ought to be within limits that enable him to control his responses—so that what comes into the open is only as much as the patient requires.

The analyst must permit the patient's transference feelings to reach their optimal intensity without intervening. This calls for his ability to endure stress, anxiety, or depression quietly and patiently. The analyst is the bearer of insight which is usually painful, and which must be conveyed in an atmosphere of straightforwardness, compassion, and concern. How to resolve the conflict between creating an atmosphere of deprivation and concern and maintaining closeness to the patient and also distance is an extremely personal matter and I do not think there is a single, exact prescription. However, I do maintain that despite individual variations, analysts who do deep psychoanalysis for therapeutic purposes must be able to reconcile these two antithetical tasks, and they must have the character traits which enable them to make this possible.

MOTIVATIONS

At this point I should like to turn to the psychoanalyst's motivations that lie behind the skills and character traits I have been describing. They are the most difficult to dissect, because some of the motivations originate in the most primitive unconscious instinctual drives related to the earliest forms of object relations. This makes them hard to verbalize and almost impossible to verify. I also want to make the point that later maturational processes in the ego, id, and superego—as well as experiential factors—modify these motivations so that an early motivation may then be transformed into newer forms of motivation. Furthermore, there are complex hierarchies of instinct and defense which may present a similar surface, so that it is hard to judge from the external appearance what the motives are. I shall limit this discussion of motives to the three main tasks of the analyst: (1) the analyst as the gatherer and transmitter of insight and understanding; (2) the analyst as the target of the transference neurosis; and (3) the analyst as the treater of the sick and the suffering.

The origin of the urge to understand a patient can be traced back to the propensity to get inside another human being.[5] This is related to the infantile wish and need to get inside the mind and body of another human being and has primitive libidinal and aggressive beginnings. It seems to start with the urge for symbiotic fusion with the mother. Secondly, it may also be derived from the strivings for omnipotence and the overcoming of fear toward the stranger. Later libidinal and aggressive strivings may also play a role. For example, gathering, acquiring, and gaining insight may indicate anal components; curiosity about sexual matters may be derived from oedipal peeping, etc.

The transmitting of insight, the giving of an interpretation may stem from impulses of feeding, nurturing, teaching, protecting, mothering, fertilizing, and impregnating. It can also be used as a means of reparation for past unconscious guilt feelings and counterphobic activities. Nor should we forget that every analysis we do also serves in some way or another as a continuation of our own analysis. I believe that the analyst will always learn something about himself from every patient he helps, because if he helps them, it means that he has made mistakes with them that they were able to bring to his attention. He learns about himself from the mistakes because they derive in part from unconscious feelings within himself.

However, I believe that the point of origin of a given motivation is not the decisive factor in determining its value or harm. What is significant is the relative degree of deinstinctualization and neutralization that has taken place. The gradations of neutralization will decide to what extent the function of serving as the bearer of understanding has become relatively conflict free and an autonomous, reliable ego function. I do not believe it matters, for example, whether giving a patient insight means feeding, nurturing, protecting, or teaching. What is important is that the feeding, nurturing, protecting, or teaching should be free of its sexual or aggressive undertones and is therefore neither unduly exciting or guilt-producing to the analyst.

Similarly the fantasies associated with getting inside the patient in order to obtain insight are not the crucial factor; the real issue is whether this activity is still associated with anxiety and guilt-producing fantasies. However, it must be borne in mind that this is never established once and for all, since pressures from the id, superego, and the external world do make for regressions and progressions. Another important consideration, therefore, is how readily accessible to the analyst's conscious and reasonable ego are these aggressive and libidinal fantasies. Awareness of the countertransference may set other adaptive measures in motion in the psychoanalyst; these may supplement the safeguarding function which the neutralization has failed to handle.[22,27-29]

It does not do justice to the complexity of the human mind or the arduous demands of the analyst's profession to expect that the obtaining and delivering of insight might be completely or permanently free from conflict, guilt, and anxiety. Yet I would like to go further and suggest that these activities not only should be relatively free from guilt and anxiety but they should be pleasurable. The daily work of therapeutic psychoanalysis is difficult and often painful for the analyst. He needs a certain amount of positive pleasure in the performance of his duties to enable him to sustain a lively interest in and concern for the goings-on in his patients. The pleasure in listening, looking, exploring, imagining, and comprehending is not only permissible but necessary for the optimal efficiency of the analyst.[20,30]

I should now like to turn to the motives for comporting oneself as a relatively nonresponsive blank screen so that the patient can displace and project onto that screen the unresolved, warded-off imagos of his past. What would make someone want to go into a profession where he has to be a blank screen so much of the time? Yet it seems that many analysts find the blank screen requirement very easy. If the ease stems from a tendency to be withdrawn, emotionally isolated, or uninvolved with other human beings, it is a serious drawback. The mature variety of this willingness and readiness to be the blank screen is dependent on one's capacity to be alone. Analysts must be able to be alone, to be quiet, to be contemplative, introspective, to have a sense of privacy about themselves and even about their patients. They work with the most intimate details of another person's life, and yet the patient has a right, even in analysis, to a certain sense of privacy.

Again, the ability to be quiet physically and to play the role of the blank screen must be controllable and reversible. One must have the ability to bear the roles the patient casts on one in his transference reactions, to endure being the hated enemy or rival, or the dearly beloved or the frightening father, or the seductive loving mother, etc. Not only does the analyst have to endure it and allow it to happen, he must also help the patient embellish and refine the character type that he has displaced onto the analyst at the moment so that the patient can better understand what he is experiencing. The analyst becomes in a way a silent actor in a play the patient is creating. The analyst does not act in this drama. He tries to maintain himself as the shadowy figure the patient needs for his fantasies, but he helps the patient work out the details of the character the latter is creating. He becomes in a sense the stage director. Or he is like the conductor of a symphony. He does not write the music, but he clarifies and interprets it. The interpretive work of the analyst as he listens to what the patient fantasies is at best related to the creative process in literature, music, and art.[10]

Finally, let us examine the analyst as the treater of the sick and suffering. Freud was, to say the least, highly ambivalent about this point. I shall quote him because what I want to say is very different. Here is Freud[31]

> After forty-one years of medical activity, my self-knowledge tells me that I have never really been a doctor in the proper sense. . . . I have no knowledge of having had any craving in my early childhood to help suffering humanity. . . . I scarcely think, however, that my lack of a genuine medical temperament has done much damage to my patients. For it is not greatly to the advantage of patients if their doctor's therapeutic interest has too marked an emotional emphasis. They are best helped if he carries out his task coolly and keeping as closely as possible to the rules [pp. 253–254].

I do not believe Freud was accurate in his evaluation of himself on this point, which may be presumptuous of me or perhaps defensive of my ideals. (See also Stone[16] on this issue.) Be that as it may, I do not agree with this point of view because I do feel that the physicianly attitude toward the patient is a basic prerequisite for an analyst. This issue is complicated and also contains several opposing elements. The physician is the activator of highly charged and diverse fantasies in the patient. The physician is the one who comes when the parents are frightened, when the parents are confused, when the parents are worried; he is even stronger than father. It is the physician who may look upon everyone's nakedness, including that of the parents, and that too had been the sole prerogative of the parents. He alone is not afraid or disgusted by vomit, feces, urine, pus, or blood. In some ways he is like a powerful and awesome father, and in others, like a mother. The physician is involved in many aspects of the patient's bodily intimacy and in the nursing care of the sick human being, and both resemble the mother's role.

Furthermore, he is also a scientist; he observes, gathers data, thinks, and remains overtly unmoved. In a sense, he is a researcher. Yet the analyst is neither a researcher nor a parent but a peculiar and unique blend of the two which is the psychoanalytic therapist.

All of this leads us to the analyst's motivations in becoming a therapist. Freud said,[31] "My innate sadistic disposition was not a very strong one, so that I had no need to develop this one of its derivatives. Nor did I ever play the 'doctor game'; my infantile curiosity evidently chose other paths" (p. 253). He indicated that the urge to become a physician originates in sadistic pregenital strivings and sexual curiosity. Ernst Simmel[32] wrote a very remarkable paper on the doctor game and its pregenital antecedents and later derivatives. Such urges as the need to mutilate and inflict pain upon the body of another produce sadistic doctors, whereas reaction formations in this regard make for the indecisive, passive, and inhibited ones. Restitution and reparation phenomena are responsible for the compulsive rescuers and masochists among physicians.

I have already mentioned the urge for fusion blended with destructive aims, the anal-sadistic and phallic strivings which may lie underneath the wish to be a doctor. The physician may unconsciously fantasy himself as the sadistic father torturing the victim-patient; he may be the oedipal father, the impregnating father, or the suckling mother with her infant-patient.[32] On the other hand, defensive maneuvers may decisively color the picture, which may shade into the realm of sublimation and neutralization. The search for knowledge may be a conflict-free derivative of the urge to gain access to the unknown and dangerous body and mind. A feeling of kinship with suffering humanity may lead to the wish to fight against the tyranny of unnecessary sickness and pain. Once again, it is impressive to note the diversity and the antitheses among the different elements that make up the motivations.

CONCLUSION

Perhaps I have now convinced you that psychoanalysis is truly an impossible profession. It seems to spring from such primitive motives; it is related to such infantile object relations. The traits required are so varied and so contradictory, and the skills so complex and antithetical. Yet psychoanalysis cannot be altogether an impossible profession, since it is sometimes practiced with success and even with pleasure. However, certain conditions have to be fulfilled.

I should place in the primary position the fact that the psychoanalyst has experienced a deep personal analytic experience. Preferably, this should include some analysis outside of the confines of a training situation. In addition, he should be able and willing to do a continuing amount of self-analysis. The analyst should be able to recognize that the occurrence within himself of some neurotic conflicts is inevitable and requires constant self-scrutiny. I mean not an obsessive search for perfection, but a willingness to recognize the coming to light of blind spots which he will have the humility to recognize as such and be willing to explore. I believe that if these factors are adhered to, the psychoanalytic work will give pleasure and a sense of accomplishment which will compensate for the many hours of frustration and disappointment.

It is no doubt also true that a good personal life outside one's work is an essential prerequisite for making psychoanalysis a rewarding profession. This means that the psychoanalyst must have the opportunity to stop being a psychoanalyst when he comes home. He should feel free to react as a spontaneous, wholehearted, whole person when he leaves the office. If he has to be right and rational in the analytic hours, he needs a place to be wrong and to be irrational at times. He needs a place where he can expose his frailties and not only not be punished for it, but even have them looked upon as endearing qualities. It is easy to love and admire a bright man, but only a truly loving wife can love one who is a fool at times. And the psychoanalyst needs this. His work takes so much out of him emotionally that if he really is wholehearted in his work, he becomes depleted. The analyst needs some emotional sustenance when he comes home.

With these requirements fulfilled, it is possible to enjoy psychoanalytic work. It is certainly in many ways terribly rewarding. It is one of the few places where science and art and creativity all come together. Analysts work with some of the most interesting people in the world, probably the most creative people in the world, and every patient that one works with offers us a new world to explore. More than that, the analyst's work is needed. He does good for the most part, is respected in the community, and well remunerated. Despite all the difficulties, how fortunate is the psychoanalyst!

REFERENCES

1. Freud S: Analysis terminable and interminable (1937). *In:* The Standard Edition, Vol 23. London, Hogarth Press, 1964.
2. Freud S: The dynamics of transference (1912). *In:* The Standard Edition, vol 12. London, Hogarth Press, 1958.
3. Ferenczi S: The elasticity of psycho-analytic technique (1928). *In:* Ferenczi S: Final Contributions to the Problems and Methods of Psycho-Analysis. New York, Basic Books, 1955.
4. Sterba R: The dynamics of the dissolution of the transference resistance. Psychoanal Q. 9:363–379, 1940.
5. Sharpe E: The technique of psycho-analysis (1930). *In* Sharpe E: Collected Papers on Psycho-Analysis. London, Hogarth Press, 1950.
6. Reik T: Listening With the Third Ear. New York, Farrar, Strauss, 1948.
7. Fliess R: Countertransference and counteridentification. J Am Psychoanal Assoc 1:268–284, 1953.
8. Schafer R: Generative empathy in the treatment situation. Psychoanal Q 28:342–373, 1959.
9. Greenson RR: Empathy and its vicissitudes. Int J Psychoanal 41:418–424, 1960.
10. Kris E: On preconscious mental processes (1950). *In* Kris E: Psychoanalytic Explorations in Art. New York, International Universities Press, 1952.
11. Sharpe E: Psycho-physical problems revealed in language: an examination of metaphor (1940). *In* Sharpe E: Collected Papers on Psycho-Analysis. London, Hogarth Press, 1950.
12. Greenson RR: The mother tongue and the mother. Int J Psychoanal 31:18–23, 1950.
13. Loewenstein RM: Some remarks on the role of speech in psycho-analytic technique. Int J Psychoanal 37:460–468, 1956.
14. Rycroft C: The nature and function of the analyst's communication to the patient. Int J Psychoanal 37:469–472, 1956.
15. Loewald HW: On the therapeutic action of psycho-analysis. Int J Psychoanal 41:16–33, 1960.
16. Stone L: The Psychoanalytic Situation. New York, International Universities Press, 1961.
17. Zetzel E: Current concepts of transference. Int J Psychoanal 37:369–376, 1956.
18. Greenson RR: The working alliance and the transference neurosis. Psychoanal Q 34:155–181, 1965.
19. Greenacre P: The role of transference: practical considerations in relation to psychoanalytic therapy. J Am Psychoanal Assoc 2:671–684, 1954.

20. Sharpe E: The psycho-analyst (1947). *In* Sharpe E: Collected Papers on Psycho-Analysis. London, Hogarth Press, 1950.
21. Jones E: The Life and Work of Sigmund Freud. New York, Basic Books, 1955.
22. Hartmann H: Notes on the theory of sublimation (1955). *In* Hartmann H: Essays on Ego Psychology. New York, International Universities Press, 1964.
23. Beres D: The psychoanalytic psychology of imagination. J Am Psychoanal Assoc 8:252–269, 1960.
24. Rosen VH: Some aspects of the role of imagination in the analytic process. J Am Psychoanal Assoc 8:229–251, 1960.
25. Gill MM, Newman R, Redlich FC: The Initial Interview in Psychiatric Practice. New York, International Universities Press, 1954.
26. Winnicott DW: Hate in the counter-transference. Int J Psychoanal 30:69–74, 1949.
27. Winnicott DW: Metapsychological and clinical aspects of regression within the psycho-analytical set-up (1955). *In* Winnicott DW: Collected Papers. New York, Basic Books, 1958.
28. Spitz RA: Countertransference: comments on its varying role in the analytic situation. J Am Psychoanal Assoc 4:256–265, 1956.
29. Khan MMR: Silence as communication. Bull Menninger Clin 27:300–310, 1963.
30. Szasz TS: On the experiences of the analyst in the psychoanalytic situation: a contribution to the theory of psychoanalytic treatment. J Am Psychoanal Assn 4:197–223, 1956.
31. Freud S: The question of lay analysis (1926). *In* Freud S: The Standard Edition, vol 20. London, Hogarth Press, 1959.
32. Simmel E: The "doctor-game," illness and the profession of medicine. Int J Psychoanal 7:470–483, 1926.

M. Masud R. Khan, B.A. (Hons.), M.A.

From Secretiveness to Shared Living

A vast psychoanalytic literature exists today prescribing how to help a patient make use of the analytic situation and process. On the one hand is the Kleinian approach, insisting that the earlier an analyst interprets and exposes the archaic unconscious fantasy systems of a patient and the corresponding anxieties, the sooner the patient is able to get into analytic process (cf. Segal[1] and Meltzer[2]). On the other hand, there is the classical approach, of gradually analyzing the defense systems of a patient, conscious and preconscious, to establish a working alliance (cf. Greenson[3] and Sadler, Dare, and Holder[4]).

In the British Psycho-Analytical Society, where I have been reared, there is a third tradition: namely that of Winnicott and Balint. Winnicott[5] had emphasized the necessity of *management* in the regressed and borderline cases before interpretations can be mutatively effective. Balint[6] had recommended the creation of an unobtrusive clinical ambience to establish a climate of trust with the patient.

In the clinical work that I shall report now, my emphasis will be how I, as an analyst, *accommodate to* the quirks and the needs of a patient before true interpretative analytic work begins to materialize. Here my style of clinical handling is influenced more by witnessing Winnicott's therapeutic consultations with children over some two decades than by his work with adults.

CASE MATERIAL

It is one of the ambiguous privileges of being a nonmedical psychoanalyst in England that no patient can self-refer himself to me. Either a physician or a psychiatrist refers a patient to me when they think the person concerned can gain from psychoanalytic treatment. One great advantage of this is that we, the lay analysts, do not have to take a case history. We have no choice but to start an analysis straight away, or refuse it, unencumbered by a debris of organized facts and rehearsed events by the patient. We can wait for the person to tell or not tell his facts before he can find that mutuality of trust and privacy that is the essence of the psychoanalytic method.

A distinguished physician had rung me to inquire whether I had a vacancy and could take into analysis a very bright young man. I agreed to it. He asked when Jonathan could come for his first session. I gave the date and time. He asked Jonathan, who was with him in his consultation room at the time, and it was all arranged. The physician then asked me whether I wanted to be sent detailed notes, and I said, "No, please!" However, he insisted on telling me, with Jonathan's permission and demand, that the prospective patient was a youth of twenty-four, of foreign origin, who had made a fabulous success during the past three years in his profession of choice, both economically and socially. But he was in one hell of a mess in himself and in his personal life and needed urgent care and treatment analytically. He had been in and out of psychotherapy with analysts and psychiatrists since the age of nine years! Furthermore, the physician added, "I am allowed to tell you that now he is dangerously near to getting hooked on drugs, but he is a youth of true integrity and honesty." I accepted all that as a frame of reference. I did state one condition to the physician concerned, namely, that he must stand by me all the way, twenty-four hours each day, because the acute and critical moments he will have to handle medically, and not fail to meet the *demand* of that need, no matter how hysterically and deliberately engineered by the patient, and whatever the hour. I further added that this meant that of the total strain and stress of this treatment, the physician shall have to carry 70 percent and I, 30 percent. He agreed to it, and I must categorically confess that I could not have seen this case to its conclusion if this physician had failed the person of the patient even once—which he never did.

Now I shall report from the first three sessions. For his first session, Jonathan arrived 40 minutes late. He was apologetic: "I am sorry, Sir, but my car did not arrive in time." I noticed his use of the word "Sir." It was most atypical and unusual, both for his culture and his generation. But he had spoken it with a sincerity of respect toward an elder and that I could not disregard. Jonathan was not nervous, he was fidgety. He asked me, "Do I lie down or can I sit and talk,?" I responded that most persons find it more private to speak about themselves lying down! He took off his coat and lay down on the couch. I watched his compliance and could not help registering that he did not know what to do with his hands or where to place them once he lay down on the couch. In less than a minute, he was standing and asking whether he could smoke a cigarette. He shuffled through and searched his coat and his trouser pockets and then somewhat sheepishly, but with a distinct note of arrogance, said, "May I borrow a cigarette, Sir, my chauffeur had forgotten to give me some." I smiled with irony and said, "In that case you must sack the chauffeur!" He sat down in the chair and relaxed. He changed the subject and asked, "Have you read all these books?" I replied that cultured persons do not read books, they live with them. He changed the subject again, and said, "I rang my mother last night and she tells me you are very famous." I deadpanned that and told him it was generous of him to let his mother know he was again going to be in treatment, because she must have been very worried. For the first time a curiously earnest look flickered across his face. Of course, I had realized that he had felt insecure and paranoid enough to check on me, but I did not say so. Then he asked anxiously, "Will you take me into treatment?" and I replied, "I cannot tell that today, since I hardly know you, but I am willing to take you in analytic *care.*" At that note the first session ended.

I shall drift away from the clinical material here to make a few comments. Some twenty-six years ago, toward the end of my two years of supervision of my first clinical case as a student, Miss Freud had once remarked, and I quote it as I remember it and not exactly as Miss Freud had said it, "It is important to think about a session afterwards afresh, and not only remember what was actually said in that session by both the parties concerned. Only thus will you build up a personal 'card-index' in your head for future reference!" I shall now use the phrase the "afterimage" for what Miss Freud had insinuated as a necessary task of thinking back about what had clinically transpired. And I never fail to examine and take notes on this "afterimage" after a first session, and all critical sessions with a patient.

Now to return to Jonathan and the "afterimage" of my first clinical encounter with him. I had already surmised that he was incapable of reaching out for unsponsored help, because his physician had made the appointment for him. He had arrived forty minutes late with a snobbish excuse and had learnt the tricks of aristocracy, which is nonexistent in his country of birth and nurture, but he was handling them very clumsily. But what had surprised me most in the afterimage was his relation to his body, especially the disquietude of his hands. He very subtly had touched something all the time: his face, the cigarettes, the chair, his tie, and the like. I deduced that as a child he must have suffered from compulsive tics and recalled Winnicott once remarking about tics: "Tics are a child's way of making sure he *exists* as well as the world around him, by touching all the time. We can say by looking at a person that he exists, but he doesn't know it for himself, necessarily!" I had also noted that his mannerisms of speech and behavior were those of a puppet. And I was really aghast when I recalled what

he looked like: a shabby golliwog impersonating a human being! His hair dishev-
elled, his expensive clothes messy! He was bizarre indeed! But he knew his way
in life. I also realized he had told me nothing about himself and shared nothing.

For his second session, Jonathan turned up punctually. He was dressed this
time in typical hippy style: jeans, a tight sweater, and an open-neck shirt with a
glaring scarf round his neck. He had cigarettes and sat in the chair and told me
he had been *through* many "headshrinkers" since he was nine. I noticed his cheeki-
ness and let him be. He gave me a rather long list of very celebrated people he
had encountered and mixed with since his last session. Suddenly he asked me,
"Does it bore you, Mr. Khan?" I waited while he itched, pinched, and scratched
himself everywhere, and then said, "No, but it does not impress me!" Then he
astonished me with a question, "Do you think, Mr. Khan, I am sick?" I answered
immediately, "I don't think so, but you are all loused up!" He laughed and told
me how his Negress Nanny used to pick lice out of his hair, and it used to
annoy his mother very much, because there were no lice in his hair. Before I
could say anything he asked whether he could use my phone. I said, "Yes!" He
talked to someone and I left the room. He remarked, "Please, Mr. Khan, you
don't have to leave the room." I told him "I don't have to, but I shall, because
I respect privacy." When I returned he was silent for a while and then told me
his reasons for seeking analysis. According to him, he was the "whizz kid" of
the Pop Jet Set in London, and everyone invited him and sought him out, and
he didn't know what to say and felt ridiculous; hence he always took some beautiful
model girl with him. Here I asked my first question: "How many children did
your parents breed?" He said he was one of the only twins; he had a twin sister.
Then he praised a painting on my walls. After this he shuffled around and asked
how long his analysis would last. I said I couldn't tell. He told me of his last
therapist and what a fool he had made of him. I told him that he wouldn't succeed
in that respect with me. He sat fidgeting a little longer and then said he must
leave as he had an appointment with his solicitor. The session had lasted thirty-
five minutes.

Jonathan did not turn up for his next session. His physician rang me when
I was expecting him and said Jonathan was very sorry he had confused the appointments, but he needed to see his physician more urgently than me and would
keep his next appointment. I accommodated to that and he did turn up.

I felt sure that Jonathan had vividly and genuinely demonstrated to me his
style of functioning in life and coping with a diffuse and chronic ailment in him
in these first three sessions. He had also made clear his incapacity to fit or use
the *prescribed* analytic process. He was a youth who had real talent and had
made his way in life by using it. I had to respect that and accommodate to *his
dosage* of the therapeutic relationship and process to himself. All too often, reading
the contemporary analytic literature, I get the impression that diagnosing and
interpreting psychopathology in our patients is our clinical variant of morality.
We pretend not to judge, and yet our interpretative language is normatic and
demands standards of psychic health while it makes out to be helping the patient
to recover from his ill health. Of course, it was not lost on me that Jonathan
had reacted to his first two encounters with me with panic and paranoid anxiety

and taken flight into hyperactive manic proliferation of his professional activities
on the one hand, and dispersion of his being into others—his colleagues, friends,
parents, and his physician—on the other hand. Hence, his physician had sedated
him, shrewdly realizing what had happened. There is now a myth of pure psychoanalysis that actualizes only and exclusively through the transference and the analytic
process. We, the analysts, are the only ones that believe in this myth and persist
in perpetuating it. In lived lives, we and our work call upon others who do all
the dirty work for us and carry its strain from our patients, be it their families,
friends, or physicians. I had sensed a certain authenticity of resourcelessness in
Jonathan and realized that he was manipulative but not devious, cunning but
not dishonest. I also felt I had to work for him to find his trust in me and discover
his being in his own person. Given the support of his physician, I felt sure I
could help Jonathan be his own person. On this conviction I decided to continue
with his analysis, realizing the risks entailed, both for myself and largely for his
physician, who would have to account for any lethal mishaps during our mutual
care of Jonathan. Suicides rarely work when intended, but accidents are the surest
route to suicide, and Jonathan drove supercharged cars recklessly.

I hope I have not given you the mistaken notion that I had any illusions
that Jonathan's care and treatment were going to be easy. For a year and more
he kept up the same pattern: arriving late or leaving early or disappearing abroad
for professional reasons. But during this year I got to know all the maneuvers
of Jonathan in private and professional life. All the same, I was beginning to
get discouraged and felt I was achieving nothing for Jonathan and should give
up. Only his physician's insistence that I was helping Jonathan kept me going.

Then a fortuitous happening changed the whole climate and nature of therapeutic work with Jonathan. One day he arrived beaming, carrying a beautifully
wrapped parcel. He asked me, "Will you accept a gift, Mr. Khan?" I hesitated
because I had learnt that Jonathan was a compulsively generous person and his
gifts were his technique of negating gratitude or belonging. I hedged by asking,
"Depends on what it is." He squashed that, parrying me by saying, "Please open
it and find out." I did, and it was a magnificent backgammon board. He asked
me whether I knew how to play it and I said, "No." "Then let me teach you;
only last night I won over 1500 pounds playing against one of the best players
in London!" There was a joyously naughty gleam in his eyes when he said that.
Then he added, "I will play you ten games to teach you how the game works
and then we play for real." I accommodated to that. While Jonathan was setting
up the board to play, myriad ideas and apprehensions scampered through my
head. Was he intent on asserting his omnipotence and humiliating me? Was he
trying to subvert the whole analytic process by this ruse? Then I recalled that
only a few weeks earlier when he was bemoaning his incapacity to converse with
people, I had interpreted that he always tried to astonish or dominate with what
he spoke, and did not realize that conversation in ordinary social intercourse is
playing. Now he had brought me a game. I had the potential space to change
his gamesmanship into playing. I took that chance, recalling Prince Hamlet's
device: "The Play is the thing wherein I shall catch the conscience of the King!"

In the session in which Jonathan had taught me to play, I noticed two significant facts. He had played only two games and then sat and told me in a coherent narrative how he had won the game last night. Unlike always before, he had not bounced from one thing to another. The second was that he had stayed the full length of a session for the first time. The rhythm of relating that evolved was somewhat as follows. Jonathan now arrived punctually and then would either talk first and then ask to play, or if he was wrought up and nervous, play first and then talk. But he was beginning to talk about himself, even though tangentially. Of course, he slaughtered me in each game and collected his ten pence per game. In one session, I took the opportunity and said, "You realize Jonathan you do not play, you slaughter!" This had a curiously significant effect on him, and he told me how he used to drive his mother, his Nanny, and his therapist crazy when he was about eleven years of age and would build complex structures from Meccano sets, and just as they would begin to get excited that he would complete whatever he was doing, he would smash it all up.

From this point onward, it was possible to show him that he had missed the experience of playing in childhood and had instead taken to asserting his will.

Gradually the backgammon games diminished over a period of some three months. But during this time, I learned a lot about his childhood.

Before I relate that, I must describe one of the last games we played. I was winning, and suddenly he introduced a new rule of which I knew nothing and of course he won. Then he rather sheepishly asked, "Do you think that was dishonest?" I said bluntly, "No, it was not dishonest," since he had also given me a book on how to play backgammon, and if I had read it, I would have known the rule. But that he was *secretive* for sure, and that worried me, because it was out of character with his general behavior. Jonathan, for the first time, began to cry in a session.

Now I shall report the last phase of Jonathan's treatment, which lasted roughly six months. Jonathan asked me whether he could attend three times a week instead of five, and I accepted that because I felt it meant he had grown out of attachment toward dependency and relating in the clinical setting. I had learned a lot during the backgammon games about his childhood. His parents had divorced when he was four years of age, and he was shuttled from grandparents, to living with his mother, to visiting his father: all of whom lived in different cities. Leaving each one always caused him enormous anxiety and terror. His father was very fond of him, but because of his own business preoccupations, he had little personal time to spare, and Jonathan was handed over to his staff to be spoiled and indulged. He was a bedwetter up until the age of eleven and could make no use of psychotherapy, to which he had been submitted from the age of nine. In his private life, he was a very compliant, shy child, riddled with tics. Now it was possible to show him how all his pinching and scratching of his face and body, as well as of objects, was really the same phenomena as tics, and it was his technique of making sure that the world around him did not disappear.

Jonathan was a person of acute intelligence, and I was myself surprised, once he began to change, at how he grew rapidly into an adult youth. He no longer spent his private time ringing everyone all over the world and became very self-sustaining. Toward the end of his treatment, he was able to start a relationship with a woman, which was mutual and nourishing for him. This was also the first time in his life that Jonathan had a home of his own and a private life. He had always lived vagrantly, drifting from friend to friend. In his relationship to me, he also began to be able to use the couch and could tolerate my absence from his sight and therefore be private with himself in my presence. Unfortunately, his treatment had to end for external reasons, as he had to leave the country. He still comes every three to four months for a few sessions and has maintained his growth.

DISCUSSION

I have deliberately eschewed giving a detailed account of the complex psychopathology of this patient, which we had analyzed quite thoroughly. Here my intention is to show how the potential space of the secret for a child, where he can build up and sustain a private tradition of the maturing and growing Self (cf. Khan[7]) can become distorted into secretiveness. The function of secretiveness is not only to protect the Self from impingements that the growing but vulnerable ego cannot cope with but also to protect the significant caretaking persons in the child's familial environment. Jonathan was exposed to and witnessed events and conversations in the lives of his grandparents, father, and mother, which he had been exhorted by each party concerned not to tell and share with others. This splitting of familial coherence of experience he had, at adolescence, turned into his technique of living. As Winnicott[8] has remarked, "In psycho-analysis as we know it there is no trauma that is outside the individual's omnipotence. Everything comes under ego-control, and thus becomes related to secondary processes." Jonathan's life-style shows clearly how his ego had brought under its control the cumulative trauma of being made an accomplice to the secretiveness in his family. But this achievement had turned him into beserk extroverted vagrancy of existing and robbed him of that potential space within which a person can grow in secret and privacy with himself.

This brings me to my second point, namely the clinical tolerance of nonrelating by such patients in the clinical situation and the transference. Our bias is to interpret such nonrelating either as resistance or hostile refutation of the analyst as a persecutory figure. That is and can be often true, but to interpret it is to make a patient feel culpable for a basic incapacity in him. In this area of work with such patients, I find a concept of Winnicott's most helpful. Describing an infant's way of relating to the spatula in the consultation situation, Winnicott[9] describes "a phase of hesitance," that intervenes between the infant's attraction to the spatula and his final acceptance of it. I believe that what we take for resistance in such patients is, in fact, "a phase of hesitance" that must be clinically allowed for and accepted as such.

The last point I wish to make is that Freud's concept of free association entails the capacity in the patient to play. We cannot demand this capacity as a *given* in such patients. We have to enable them to be able to play with their fantasies and inner world experiences before they can free associate. Once that capacity is reached then analysis proper can start and then, as Dr. Lacan says, ". . . when he (the patient) can speak to you of himself, the analysis will be terminated."[10] I would add to it that then the patient can also begin to live from the potential space of the secret and his privacy with himself, as well as sharing life with others.

REFERENCES

1. Segal H: Introduction to the Work of Melanie Klein (1967). London, Hogarth Press, 1973.
2. Meltzer D: The Psychoanalytic Process. London, Heinemann, 1967.
3. Greenson R: The Technique and Practice of Psychoanalysis. New York, International Universities Press, 1967.
4. Sandler J, Dare C, Holder, A: The Patient and the Analyst. New York, International Universities Press, 1973.
5. Winnicott DW: The Maturational Processes and the Facilitating Environment. London, Hogarth Press, 1965.
6. Balint M: The Basic Fault. London, Tavistock, 1968.
7. Khan MMR: The Privacy of the Self. London, Hogarth Press, 1974.
8. Winnicott DW: The theory of the parent-infant relationship (1960). *In:* Maturational Processes and the Facilitating Environment. London, Hogarth Press, 1965.
9. Winnicott DW: The observation of infants in a set situation (1941). *In:* Collected Papers. London, Hogarth Press, 1975.
10. Lacan J: Fonction et champ de la parole et du langage en psychanalyse (1953). *In:* Ecrits. Paris, du Seuil, 1966.

David Shainberg, M.D.

Transforming Transitions in Patients and Therapists

There are moments in most psychoanalytic sessions in which there is a transformation of both patient and analyst.[1] These events signal the awakening of the healing powers available in a human situation, and they express the organic growth functions that are part of all living systems when they act in the face of uncertainty.

In these moments, I am aware that constructive organizing or energy has begun. My patient may alert me that something new is happening in our encounter, or I may perceive it as part of my own cognitive or emotional functioning; it may take the form of memory, image, feeling, thought, or life occurrence.

This energy is there. We are part of it and always in an active relationship with it. In moments in which we actively partake of our intimate connection with each other, we are directly working in this energy. The action of such a moment is different from other times. It contradicts the tendency of energy systems to move toward disorder of equilibrium. It contradicts automatic patterning in that the new associations construct a new way we are together in the universe. They inject solid, substantial ordering that reveals our capacity to make our way in the world as active creatures and that counteracts the entropic process.

Prior to this event, the patient and myself have been involved in a repetitive form of interaction, an habitual way of relating. It may be some form of blind acceptance or pleasure in a set relationship that prevented appreciation of our separateness and aloneness in the universe. Whatever it was, it blocked our work because, up until that point, the need for security forced us to connect in modes that did not allow the challenge of our encounter to emerge. Analysis was a collusion for protection rather than a way of seeing our uncertainties in the world and in our relationship. But at what I call "the healing moment,"[2] I feel my patient and I contact the essence of creativity.

According to myths, the creation of the world was a result of emergence from chaos. This is embodied in many of our current astronomical and biological myths as well. Numerous rituals of slaying the dragon represent periodic repetitions of primal immersion in chaos and subsequent evolutions of a spontaneous world of form. The initiation ceremonies or other tribal customs of primitive man centered around birth, marriage, and death. They were meant to evoke resonances to the beginning of time and provide experience of rebirth and the creation of a new world that begins at that moment.[3] In many such myths, for example, the word for cosmos, meaning world, is also used for year. Each year, the world dies to be reborn again on New Year's Day.[4] More deeply, the people who participated in these rituals identify with the inherent creative powers that are found everywhere in the universe and are manifested articulately in the origination of the world. Every creative event by each one of us, be it the way we conduct our lives or the way we write or paint, involves a similar participation in a chaos of uncertainty. Out of that chaos, form is established, but the important part of the creative action is the process of acting inside the chaos.

At such a transforming moment in psychoanalysis, I feel my patient and I move in conjunction with that primordial process of creation, the way the seed evolves into the plant and the egg moves from fetus to embryo to live, complete organism.[5-9] This similarity is evident in the way this moment of energy transformation of the moment differs from the previous time in the analysis. Associations, memories, or thoughts begin to convey a connection to specific universal principles. There may, for example, be an awareness of some life-expanding aspect of my personal history. Or my patient may remember some part of his life that enlarged his consciousness. In whatever way, one of us experiences a sense of connecting that alerts us to a new beginning articulation in a chaos in which we are always immersed, though perhaps unconsciously. One who is so alerted awakens the other by some communication that tells him of the possibility that is latent in his own or the other's association.

This recognition is distinct from the recognition of blocks to perception: defensive processes, transferences, or other repetitive behavior patterns. Those blocks prevent an open flow of creative participation by not totally engaging the chaos. They shape the relationships and their flow automatically in standard modes and are not part of the attentive process that picks up nuances and ambiguities and runs with them, finding new connections at every turn. So they are deadening, rather than transforming. Identifying such blocks provides the opportunity to move into new dimensions. When they are perceived as blocking me or my patient or both, we immediately move into new action, aware of how we have been ensconced in a mold or mundane pattern.

One man reported that he had wanted to go early one morning to observe the children in the research nursery. But when he arrived, his boss asked him to wait outside so a visitor could observe that morning during the first twenty minutes. He was annoyed and refused to do what he was asked. In his discussion with his boss and with me, he argued that he had been treated poorly. He was angry that he was "being pushed around." As we talked, he saw that he had lost touch with the fact that he had gone early to see how the children arrive. Asked about this interest, he realized he wanted to see the children entering because he wanted to see how the morning "unfolded." He was beginning to get a feel for *unfolding* and the way unfolding takes place everywhere in the universe. In fact, he was beginning to see similarities between himself, nature, the children, and the world. There is a process of increasing awareness of the world's unfolding that was discovered in our flow. The whole way he was living was now becoming an example or an aspect of this general principle of unfolding in the world.

In the beginning of these moments, attention may be focused on forming or growing through such acts. A memory of someone who helped our growing in earlier periods may surface. We are, however, only at the beginning of a two-step process in the transformation. After the first part occurs, spontaneously or after discovering the falseness of the block, my patient or I will begin to move to enlarge the vision. Here we actually work together. This is one of the deepest satisfactions of my work. I sense a cohesive sharing with my patient as we both participate in this creative process. It is like a team coming to the edge of a forest and working its way through each thicket to a clearing and then on to another thicket. The spirit is one of teasing out the brambles and the vines together until there is a clearing through which first one and then the other can walk.

In this context, I recall a patient's dream. He had rented a bus and did not know why he had it or what to do with it. He tried to figure out how to take his children and ex-wife back to the house, stay with the children, whom he loved, and get the bus back. We talked, and I asked him to tell me the dream again. He did, adding that he actually discovered in the dream that he could leave the bus where it was already parked and be rid of it. And further, he could take his wife home and stay with the kids. In our talk, there was movement through the woods into the clearing as we worked together. Hearing him once, I had asked him to repeat himself. Something in the mutual walk together had felt incomplete—when I asked again to hear the dream it was because together we sensed this incompleteness and were working together to clarify it. This action produced the further insight that cut through our thicket. It became clear that his desire was to have all that the bus symbolized but did not know how to extricate himself from his solution. Yet it hit him in the dream that he could simply let it go and begin to deal directly with the problems he wanted to solve. The process of our discussion was just as direct and simple; it met obscurity and let it go.

At these times, we were able to pull together, working for each other's growth and expansion into more of the universe. This kind of unity occurred within (and in some ways was) the mystery of the relationship we came to share. We come to know and realize many relationships in our lives, and many, as well as this one, often seemed arranged for the protection of the participants. So often it is "I will scratch your back if you will scratch mine" or "I won't do anything to make you uncomfortable if you won't do anything to make me so." These are agreements to avoid suffering and amount to people using each other for pleasure that avoids suffering. Such relationships might be "power over another," which makes life easier for oneself and for one who is dependent on power. Or the relationship is based on the ongoing flattery one person offers the image another has of himself. That image had been formed originally to protect the person from pain, and the person who supports the image unwittingly supports that avoidance of confrontation with life; he frustrates growth, though doing it unwittingly under the aegis of friendship (or authority). Most relationships and, more often than not, the analytic ones, are, at their most truthful level, inauthentic processes based on communal deception and the agreement that neither person will really disturb the archaic structures of the other.

In contrast, a moment of transformation in a psychoanalysis takes place when my patient and I give up the protectiveness of our isolation and begin willingly to move toward helping each other toward greater self-articulation and acceptance of human suffering. We stop decorating the rooms of our minds with fantasies of hoped-for pleasure from one another. We face up to the realities of our existence, albeit the simple one here of the unclearness of our discussion. At these moments, I feel myself in the presence of the mystery of human relating; it is often a monumental experience.

My patients express an appreciation of such moments marked by awareness. They can go with the thrust of their energy of movement, which seems to mobilize a capacity they did not think they had. They speak of realizing what they can do for themselves: that they can evaluate the moment-to-moment of being according to the feedback they get from their own actions and the way their minds are flowng with imagery, thoughts, and fantasies. They use awareness of this action of their minds to guide their responses and can be alert and attentive to the action of being alive right there in their present. This is an exhilarating moment; they begin to participate vibrantly in the action of being alive.

In the following pages, I give several detailed examples of the way these moments arise. Perhaps reading them will serve others to come to respect such moments if they do not do so already; for the rest, I cherish this opportunity to share with you our mutual appreciation.

A WEEKEND IN A ZEN MONASTERY

For weeks she had been talking about her plan to spend a weekend at a Zen Monastery. Her husband was clearly against it. She feared a confrontation with him and looked for ways not to go. Her husband could not bear the thought of being without her for three days. Except for his being away at meetings, I do not think they had spent a weekend apart in almost thirty years of marriage. She hated him, she said, and considered him as much like her mother, whom she also hated. It was a cold, implacable hate (which on another level was the fear of differentiation).

She finally went to the monastery. In the next session, she reported that the weekend had had a powerful impact on her, as well as having been enormously difficult for her husband. He had, she said, been nasty and used violent language in his rage about having to be alone. But for both of them, she emphasized, "It was not just any weekend or any way of being away from him for the weekend. I went to a place where I was acting on my own behalf. This really got to him and got to me because it was against everything about our marriage."

Like very subtle partners in the destruction of each other, they lived a life which, on the surface, was committed to the "right things." She was a professional person and he was a lawyer. But at the core of this front, they did not care about anything and went through their lives automatically, avoiding a serious commitment to anything. How they did this is difficult to pinpoint. They spent weekends at their country home, playing paddle tennis and engaging in shallow relationships with everyone with whom they joined in, throwing away their time in meaningless pursuits. Every Thursday night, they went unenthusiastically, almost as a routine, to the theater. Dinners together were a series of her monosyllabic responses to long, talkative remarks and reports by him. Their relationship was a skirting around each other. As nearly as I could tell from her, he is very dependent and needs her support at his professional functions. He resents it when her schedule interferes. As she described their sexual behavior, one could only feel sad. She said, "He calls me from his bed with 'Hey, fatso, come over here.' And I waddle over there. He says, 'I love your fat ass' or something equally distasteful to me, and fucks me. Then it's over for that time until I have to go through it again."

She had been to two analysts who had supported her staying in the marriage. Not, I think, that it makes much difference what they did, because she was as dependent on her husband as he was on her. She hated them both for their inability to help her break this chain. Her dependency on him was based on the need to prevent herself from being on her own. The cold detente that existed between them protected her from facing the rage she felt toward him as himself and as a reminder of her mother, the representative of what she should do and be. If she left him, she felt she would have a kind of undifferentiated relationship to reality which she did not want. (How many people live like this? The relationship is a compromise, a way of not facing the unknown of their loneliness which demands they make structure in their own time. On the positive side, it is a way of moving with the unknowns of a relationship that presents mystery in small doses of the engagement with another. Yet these small doses do not disrupt the inner certainty the way hours of aloneness disrupt a separate person.)

In a dream the night after returning from the monastery, she was walking lightly on water. When she looked back, she saw a man drowning; he had fallen through the ice. She tried to pull him out and then began to yell for help. Her husband stood there, unmoving. Somehow she and another man saved the drowning man.

As the session continued, she talked more about the monastery. For the moment, she seemed to leave the direct subject of the dream. She was at first resistant to the discipline of the place. But as she let go and participated more, she had felt the special tone of "people helping each other." People were supporting the needs of other people toward spiritual development. She had never known this kind of thing was possible; in fact, she felt hopeless that it was possible. In her previous analysis, in her marriage, in her life, and in her early family, self-development was something that no one ever supported. They would help you join symbiotic dependencies in which everyone clung together to make sure no one ever developed on his own. But "they" never helped you with getting free on your own. This is also true in the dream: she calls to her husband, but he does nothing. The real helper is me. She and I rescue the drowning man, who is—herself. This is her first awareness that she has spent her life walking in this fantasy of floating over the water with the image of herself as some Christlike saint, blithely oblivious to her own sense of drowning.

She told me of an incident at the monastery: She was working in the field one day, and they had finished their assigned task; she put down her tools and started back to her room to rest. On the way, she met the director, who asked, "Have you finished work?" She said, "We finished the job we were doing." He remarked, "We usually work until the bong sounds to end the work period." She realized with a jolt that he meant if you finished one job, you go on to the next. She was very moved by this statement and went on to say, "They did not show me any special attention because I was older than most of the residents." To which I repeated, "We work until the bong ends the work period," adding, "and then they lower us six feet down. We do one job and we go on to the next."

As I said this, I was extremely moved. My body trembled as I said what I did about death. It resonated in me that our life is just that, one job and then another. Our search for specialness with petty thrills and our focus on pleasures and desires get in the way of our realization of the simplicity of what this man said. This woman's life had left her in a state of overwhelming sorrow. I was simultaneously awed by the dream and the blank, baldness of the combination of statements that cut through the decadence of living on the surface of being. But she has been part of a whole system, our system, and each of the pieces, her professional husband, her own good education, her job, her theater tickets, their yearly travel experience, their country house, and the paddle tennis all were designed to stuff their time to avoid the emptiness. It all has the right form, but as we see here, it is empty. Sadly she reported how her husband had been cheating ("just a little") on the insurance forms he submits for their medical bills. But she could not dodge the directness of the Zen Master: "We usually work until the bong sounds to end the work period." We united our attention on this simple affirmation and participated in an awareness of the life's energy. Such a moment transforms me.

Look at this from another angle: she often told me how she hated her previous therapist, how he would rather naively praise her husband, a lawyer, an upstanding participant in the community. How grateful or satisfied she should be! I knew this analyst and could well imagine his feeling such things. As we moved through this set of sessions about the trip to the monastery, I found myself verbally supporting her feeling of being separate. I felt a deep gratitude to the monastery and its people for being what it was and what they were, in a world filled with decadence. No question inside of me of this sympathy; I could see that there was a very powerful feeling mobilized in her, and I felt we had at last recognized a real focal distinction in her process. The issue of her growth had been at the periphery of her personal process; she had played with its contingencies for years: three analysts, professional school, group therapy, hypnosis, and many books, meetings, and classes, but meanwhile the shape of her daily life, her husband, her daily activity was a way of not helping herself. She still continued to move into pleasure domains to avoid the deep sorrow and loneliness she felt. She had never confronted her time in the emptiness of life, the emptiness was her world when it was not filled with husband, theater, travel, country house, children, paddle tennis, and work. This fact was there, but untouched.

As we moved in this process, I felt we were onto something very important and very serious. I supposed I knew something of all this in my life as well. Pinpointing the difference between the world of secular disasters and the holiness (wholeness) of the monastery made me clear about my own dilemmas. I moved to support her. She panicked and was afraid. She would say to me, "Thanks for being on the right side, but I will never leave my husband." I wonder about this moment. Often we come to it in our work. It is a sacred time because the patient's life is at stake. So, perhaps, is ours. She focuses on the husband, whether to leave him or not. That is not the question, but she grabs at it. The issue is an example, an instance of the whole self-delusional process. Leaving him would mean nothing more than finding other ways of pleasure or escape from her loneliness. How many times have we seen people leave one spouse for another and reinstitute this same, deep pattern. Sometimes it is an even deeper commitment to the pleasure pattern in the new marriage because the struggle with the emptiness, the contact with the fact of emptiness, was part of the first marriage, which often contains an awareness by both parties that it is an attachment, a known escape, and also a recognition that it can never fill the mutual emptiness. Knowing this is a grappling with the process of attachment; both partners struggle with their emptiness. The first marriage, coming as it does when the person is in direct contact with the unformed chaos and emptiness of earlier life, is still a contact with uncertainty and its constant failure to assuage the pain of psychological dearth is a possibility that a second marriage often seems to bypass in its commitment to a safe "relationship." So often the second marriage gives up on dealing with the emptiness and establishes itself as a belief in "attachment"; the new mate is typically one who joins more thoroughly than the first in a *partnership that avoids emptiness.* Two is safer than one. Accomplices, they structure this into the new agreement.

With this woman, her concern about breaking up her marriage avoided the newfound clarity. She did not want to see this marriage as an example of her general problem. She said she would not leave him and was sweating profusely as I kept emphasizing she did not want to leave her dependency, which was the real issue. She refused to see it. She resisted, fought it off, by saying she could not leave him and be all alone. She made plans in her head: she would move into her office; she checked her bank account, thought of how to get more funds, reviewed the status of their health insurance; she imagined *ad infinitum* what his response would be, recalling that when she called him on return from the monastery, his response had been "Fuck you." She anticipated violence, but it was the violence she felt about separating from her dependency on him and her superficial modes of engaging life.

This is the actual content of her consciousness. Sad as it is, it has a very important connection to the moment of transformation. When I realize the way this woman is moving when faced with the dilemma of her emptiness, I become rather annoyed and convinced of the difficulty of our work. People do move toward these superficialities. She sees her life built on a false structure of escape. She is afraid of the realization and what it truly means: it is awesome to realize she gives up herself to her fear all the time. It is awesome to think how we are all embedded in these patterns—she and I and all of us. It is one of those moments when I find myself boiling in rage at everyone and everything that ever deceived me and asked me, begged me, seduced me, as a child, into believing their games. Because that is what we do; we go along in these communal society games re-creating the blindness and escapes that deny our emptiness, our paltry, secondhand lives. We simply do not look. We dig ourselves into these protective pits. When they are challenged, we find ourselves in deep fear of losing. How will I live alone, she asks. She is alone, isolated, within her whole structure; but now if she loses that, she thinks she will be really alone. She considers the loss of her pettiness isolation because she has never participated in the world as a human organism; she has been in a constant terror or being there empty; the one who lives in escapes never knows the support available for anyone who would live in the world. Instead, she has these fences that she fears losing. As I listen, I feel her cling and fear and believe in the necessity of her husband, her life, and her verbal games. But then, too, there is something new, the possibility of a change; she entertains the possibility of letting it all go and being in her emptiness. It is in itself an awesome awareness that we are alone, and, in the face of all that she has built and has been, there is, in fact, a chance. She has seen this, and together in this religious moment, we share the immensity of this opportunity and work to support her participation. That the bong will sound on us all is clear to her and me and is an ever-present reality. Death is the power of the chaos and confronts us both with our nothingness. Knowing our nothingness together, we create our presence in the universe again.

POWER

The simple fact of a human being struggling in a world of terror commands a *respect*. The meaning of that word "respect" is "to give attention to." To give attention to this struggle, to know, and appreciate how far it goes in our daily life is both inspiring and extremely difficult.

She said she had had to please her father and brother to avoid the terror of her mother. She was like a small country in search of allies in a war-torn world. She did not necessarily like them, but with the suavity of an expert politician, a four-year old knew what she had to do. She had a friend now who was taming her devils, and it reminded her of the same devils she did not know how to exorcise in her relationship with her mother. So she had avoided them by setting up the defensive liaisons with her brother, her father, and everyone else. With the men, though, there were the same problems: they were big, she felt small; she felt compelled to please them while avoiding the violence that existed in her mother and herself. Her devils turned up everywhere. I felt a strong presence in the room as I became aware of her definitive terror. There it is: she is there, standing out as a clear statement of this attempt to master the chaos. Her demons were her forms in that soup. I could think of her sequential statements as causally related, or I could, as I did, see how distinctly this whole situation emerged out of nothingness; she was this fragility of being, creating protective alliances that would protect her.

I know sometimes I feel this way too. Her uncertainty contacted my daily existence. Her mother was an instance of all the powerful sense of change, a transience in the universe that threatens each of us.

The question crept into my consciousness: Why did she feel she had to have power? She could not feel powerless if she did not first put undue faith in power. This circular system veiled the deeper awareness of her relationship to the actual

transience of life. That actuality defined limits and bounded facts that command
us *to understand necessity as well as freedom.* She wanted transcendence without
recognition of constraint. It was awesome to realize how fear was the base of
her superstructure of worry about power and powerlessness.

Our transformation came when she weakened her commitment to escape
into the field of power and powerlessness. She stopped pushing. Then she had a
dream. (I write so easily, "she had a dream." But it is momentous to realize she
suddenly felt desperately uncertain, and this uncertainty was the terror she had
avoided all her life seeking power and certainty. There was tremendous suffering
because she did not have power. Then, the dream. It is truly remarkable that
the dream begins to be a new way of relating to the world. It is beyond power.)

Consider the simplicity of the dream: she wrote her last name "rigidly."
Take that simple fact and watch how it unfolds holographically as she comments
on it: "My last name is what is rigid: that is what is usually changed with marriage;
I am eligible for marriage, except my last name won't change. I am not eligible
to love because that calls for flexibility. I can have the form but not the substance."

When we place power in the form, we do not have the power that is able
to meet the novelty of every moment within the form. She says, "I am afraid
that people see me as aggressive. This is messy. No one can read how afraid I
am." But it is a messy problem. She is caught in a need for power gained through
social relationships she calls friendship; this had been a means to avoid actual
contact with her suffering. Together we see that a change in her family name is
a change in the rigidity of the family's niceties of being nice. The transformation
is underway; she engages the chaos of her uncertain life but so far meets this
uncertainty with rigidity. Yet the old solutions blur into a question about a new
way.

I feel we are really together here as she confronts our mutual presence in
the unknown. The dream is an economical struggle with the dilemma. It is direct—
there is no longer an illusion that there is a way out through total control or
manipulation. I feel this dream works from inside that chaos of uncertainty we
all share.

I say to her, "I think you have resisted or hesitated to get into reading
yourself and reading your real uncertainty that you felt as aggression." She says
the most direct and vital statements so far: "I have not been complaining about
my feeling of emptiness lately. I have discovered that as I do feel the emptiness,
I find I also have tender feelings." We may guess that the feelings called tender
are her recognition of a unity with life and with other organisms that have emerged
out of the nothingness and will soon, too, move back into nothingness.

THE DRUG

I gave him the prescription for Valium when he was again having trouble
sleeping. For several years, he had been getting the drug from his internist and
avoiding asking me or bringing it as a problem to our work; with me, he was

supposed to be tough and do without such crutches. He would tell me about getting it elsewhere but would keep it out of the direct contact with me because he wanted me to think of him as a strong man. I did not press him on the issue, aware as I was of the subtle and sensitive nature of our relationship. He needed to go just at his own pace when it came to how he wished to share.

This event occurred when he talked to me of his insomnia and his need for medication. I was willing to hear his plea. It brought us together or recognized we were together. I acknowledged, as we talked, that it was clear he needed the drug and we had better take cognizance of this need. He could go for weeks with insomnia, reversing his day-night cycle, and eventually be unable to work.

He came to the next session with a glowing smile. He said, "You helped me. I felt you were saying do not get spaced out on insomnia and were taking a stand for me." It was true—my giving the drug at this point was a specific act: it was, I felt, part of our process of self-differentiation, and it reinforced his continuity. I gave the drug so he could go on meeting the tension he was feeling, and I hoped he would not be driven into oblivion by his anxiety. I recognized that he did become anxious as he moved toward more awareness of all he felt in each moment of daily life. He saw my act as a help, because our work shared the value that he be able to see and feel rather than be clouded in consciousness.

His possibility to grow and do things in this world manifested a basic universal process of nature. He saw me as helping him, and this vision was something brand new between us, which was also part of the basic universal growth possibility. He felt we were working together and registered the direction of our work in his extension of his participation in life. To be free and clear about what he wanted was a move into the actual world. He recognized (for the first time) that the instructor at the swimming pool really helps the kids. He had never allowed such consciousness to penetrate his awareness, and I don't think he could until he allowed that he and I were together. He reported this with awe and reverence in his voice—the same awe and reverence I feel together with him. I realize the positive supporting capacities in our working together for greater self-differentiation of each of us. This self is the capacity to move in the flow of uncertainty without becoming fixed or defined.

He began to feel more about help, my help, and was amazed that help actually existed. He had never thought it possible. I detected a softening in both of us, a mutual compassion. This was one of those important moments in my work, our work, and the work of life. It was the kind of event I always remember. It guides future orientation with every patient. I have had patients interrupt and patients terminate. Whenever I remember one of them months or years later, I think of the times we shared this mutual clarity about the possibility of our working together to see the blocks to participation in life. Our shared support binds us together, knowing the unity of being alive to the possibility of greater consciousness of all on this planet.

As we moved into this awareness, he immediately confronted a dilemma. Out of his condition, which included all of his history, he took the prescription to his father's pharmacist so he would not have to pay for the drug. This "dependency" was an attempt to remain in a familiar system, a move to *limit* his participation in life. His actual condition—an open limitedness that we all experience and share—had become clear when he discovered his relationship to me. He had faced his insomnia and my help; these together were instances of being enmeshed in his life within his limits and the responses he had to these limits within which he had acted and moved. Action within the old system with his father avoided the novelty and uncertainty. As expected, the pharmacist yelled that he could not fill the prescription until he consulted his father, who had instructed him never to give this thirty-year-old man anything without first contacting him.

The pharmacist, as agent for his father, was the "cause" of humiliation, proof that he was not strong and tough. This need to be strong presupposes its opposite, that "he is weak." If he did not need to feel strong, he would obviously not feel weak. When I gave him the prescription, I indicated that he did not have to be strong, and that it was not weak to take pills. It was simply a fact that right now in his state, taking the pills was the most economical and proficient act. His faith in me made this a sensible communication. I had for years communicated my awareness of his constructive and inherent strengths which, like all such strengths, had limits. He needed to respect what he could do as well as what he could not do at any one time. The important part of this five-year communication was his awareness of his real capacity in seeing, hearing, and understanding—but he needed to know its parameters. I take great delight and feel very good when I am able to help a patient know that he has capacity and he can use it.

Apparently, this had got through to this man, but he "needed" his strong-weak dichotomy; that field gave him an orientation he could fight, relate to, circumference his life with its values. The condition of recognizing my help initiated a series of open-ended questions that frightened him enough to precipitate a return to the world of "strong-weak" and the conflict in which he fluctuated between one and the other.

I learned something here. *Clear openness between us* was the issue at the heart of our terror. His conflicts about money, about dependency on his father, the pharmacist, all were in some way totally irrelevant. That was illuminating—it was an insight. I saw that those issues had a blocking effect on the moments when he felt I could help him and was dependable, not someone on whom he would be dependent. The difference between these two, dependable and dependent, is so profound that every time it is clarified, I relearn that the petty issues such as dependency and independence, are designed not to permit belief in oneself. I see instantly that I can depend on myself, the patient can depend on himself and, together, our dependableness in this world helps one another be in this world.

As I watched him circle, I felt he knew I was there to help him; I was dependable; I think as we know that together he comes into contact with the first limits in life he will deal with: my dependableness and willingness to be there for him when he is angry, afraid, drunk, and unable to stand up for himself. I often feel an overwhelming terror at the responsibility I have taken on. I have spent many sad hours understanding my failure to carry this trust: the times when I have been unable to be there for someone; when life's circumstances made it necessary for me to make a move they could not tolerate or felt it indicated I was undependable. These moments resonate again at such a time, and I wonder whether I will be able to be there for this person and live through his changes as he fears to face himself living in the world straight and simply, a condition of necessity that has to be lived.

THE FEE

I raised her fee. She told me it bothered her; she really had trouble feeling into this increase and, being unable to allow herself to respond, she simply felt, "Wow, that's a lot." She felt it was too difficult to face allowing herself to get into how "too much it was." She had to dodge this money issue, so she began a series of inner movements, feeling she had no right to object because the other patients had so much harder a time than she did. After all, she did not really feel the money and others did. It meant so much more to them to pay high fees because they gave up so much for coming to see me. She does not work and does not suffer with the fee. They do suffer; therefore she is not equal to them and has no right to feel this is a lot of money to pay for coming here. What could she do anyway: quit, yell at me, or what? But then, as she began to explore some of her actual feelings that it was a lot to pay, she came to sense that "this fee was really too damn much." This was a difficult moment, because she saw that she was very involved with me. She hated to see that. She was trapped by my escalating needs and the escalating costs of a society in a spiraling inflationary economy. This kind of being trapped by the actualities of our world was the very thing she hated and had spent her life avoiding. She did not get involved in her own work as a painter or seem really to care about anything that went on in the world outside of her own apartment. By not participating, she had the illusion that she was unaffected by the transitions of society. The raised fee confronted her with her involvement with me and put this position in jeopardy.

The night after the fee change and the night before this discussion, she had a dream. She felt her life was over. The life, that is, of this illusion. She had lost a tooth, which came out, roots and all, covered with silver paper. There was no blood, and she was less disturbed than usual by this kind of a happening in a dream. However, she was struck by the way the filling of the tooth was on the *outside instead of on the inside*. The inside processes of participation were the very part of her existence she avoided through staying on the periphery of the world. She said, "I do not want anything to cost me anything, so I do not want to feel that this is a very high fee or that I would have to pay you for your services. I do not want to give something of myself." If she did, she would have to "bleed" a little.

But another side of this was a new awareness of our deep connection in the primordial creation of our reality. In her statement, she was exactly right. She is trapped by my growing needs. As she put it, she is trapped by the growing needs of those involved with me as well. I thought of my wife's wishes for new household items, my children's private schools and increased tuition costs. My needs for vacations and for considerable free time. Longer vacations mean I must charge more in the time I am here. Our connections are the responsibility she presents me with. How *do* I spend my time and my money? She states implicitly that if I charge her, I am responsible to us both. Concretely, she says raising my fee asks her to trust my needing this money to make it possible for me to help her and us move along the path of truth. She directly questions whether I need my ways of spending money for our purposes. We are in an intimate communication for our mutual work together in the chaos of our uncertainty. The only issue is whether or not whatever we do and ask of each other is helpful in furthering the work toward the articulation and clarification of the mist that prevents us from seeing the truth. She raises the issue of how this creating is being conducted. Is there integrity in my struggle, or do I take the cheap and self-indulgent way out? This is an awesome responsibility that I share with all my patients who struggle with the blocks to our perception of meaningful connections. I think she had a hard time trusting me to make a responsible move and asking of her no more than was absolutely necessary for sustaining this central issue. It may not have been necessary to charge the high fee and if it isn't, I cannot. Am I sure she can trust me to make this decision for our work? It is true that she does not want anything to cost her in any domain, but is this cost absolutely and clearly one that is part of the given actuality of our process. If it is, we have to deal with what is and work with it. This is a feature of our awesome interresponsibility to each other that we discover in this moment—we deal with our mutual participation in that unlimited energy of empty space.

HOPELESSNESS

Joan's patient writes from Europe that she has discovered hidden strength as a result of their work together. Like Joan, the patient is involved in an entangling, dependent relationship with her husband. The patient's nomadic existence is a commitment to avoiding tension. Whenever difficulty arises, the couple leaves one part of the country or world for another, gathering just enough money to prepare for the next trip.

Telling me about this woman, Joan comes up short when she says, "I really want her to come back." She wants her to return so they can work for these hidden strengths. This is that moment when new possibility enters our work.

Like her patient, Joan has been hopeless about her own possibilities. She has hesitated to believe she could find and develop her capacity to love. She, too, has nomadically involved herself in relationship after relationship to protect herself from facing her deep sadness and sorrow. Each relationship has been a cynical search and denial of her hopelessness about being able to love. As she tells me about her wanting the patient to return, she cries.

Time and time again, she has been suppressed, beaten down by her family, been given no support, nor has there been any love by her self for her self. She gave up little by little. She settled for relating in a way that sought protection rather than expressed her interest. This does not mean she could not relate with the same person in a different way, but in each relationship she cynically settled for less. She did not see the other possibilities of relating: she could not, because she had to continue her hopelessness, and the relationship veiled the hopelessness of her sorrow. She emphasized that her husband adores her, and she settles for living off what he feels for her. Again this reinforces her hopelessness about ever being able to love. One wonders if deeper still is a feeling that she is unlovable, and his adoration is ill-founded, proving his stupidity and worthlessness.

I wondered more about her hopelessness: she chose jobs that did not call for involvement. They were completely service-oriented, though she "wanted to learn." She did her work without seeing any meaning in the work. Although gifted as a child therapist, she avoided the depth of her patients' love for her and missed sessions when the involvement became deeper. On one occasion when she began to care about the children, she left the hospital.

Hopelessness is functionally important because it keeps the moments of creative rebirth at bay. When she recognized that her discussion of hope for her patient was a beginning hope for herself, she felt a twinge and a tightening in her chest. She cried. I said, "You want her to come back; you want your own struggle for your hidden strengths to come back." I felt we worked together in this moment. It was awesome: the articulation of her hope—a turn to possibility there—we joined in deeply supporting the management of our chaos. We depended on each other to know that hopelessness was a way of obstruction—that there was something beyond what we could know. This is to say, we recognized the presence of a mystery—if she stopped avoiding the struggle, she might be reborn in a new world.

MASOCHISM

She said she felt sleepy. I should say, however, that even as I walked past her in the waiting room, I had caught a glimpse of her that telegraphed an entire ambience, an ambience described only partially by sleepiness. She looked at me coyly, like a little girl who was just coming out of a nap. She said she felt drugged and heavy in feeling and weight. She had been eating a lot. For the first time, however, in one of the eating binges, she could *see* something was happening to her. Usually, she would become angry with herself for the overeating and would go on having to eat. Now she felt somewhat more objective about it and considered it a part of the total dragging process. From all she said and conveyed, it appeared clear to me that she was attentive to the direction of her current biological and psychological movement. Listening to her, though, I felt a certain *drag* in myself, as if she were trying to suck me up. We were both being carried into the primordial soup from which the world emerged. So I was watching with her. I became aware that I had a sexual feeling toward her. In the past, when I had such feeling with her, I felt uncomfortable in accepting such a process. But this time it was different. This time, it was a fact for me. The difference was that I did not simply observe that I had the feeling, but I was aware that *this me* that is now, is in a sexual state. Awareness of the process was me now and substantially an event. I had an existential, hard-core fact represented by a biological process called sexual feeling. To know this was to know there was nothing to be done except to be attentive to the constraints of this feeling. Bubbling into awareness was a memory cassette of how this had happened many times before when I was with a person, male or female, who felt helpless: I would experience a magnetic pull from such a person that seemed to drive me to merge with him or her. I would also feel their need to merge with me. This kind of feeling manifested in the sexual forms and at other times in a need to let go and be taken up by them. I would feel an anxiety about being different that would develop into a helplessness and emptiness. I would seek to dissolve myself so as to relieve this pressure of responsibility for them and me. I think this microprocess is like the primitive orgies in which destruction of the old makes possible a new birth. The first goal in both is an ocean of blurred diffusion with a merger of all distinctions.

I am aware that there was such a process in my past experience with my mother's helplessness: she was not there for me when I was in need; that absence made the experience that I was reminded of (grateful, too, that she reawakens this problem) in this patient's helplessness and my differentiation from her. My rage that there was no one there for me was the context of my early experience. Now, too, I wonder if I can be alone, because alone is felt as similar to helplessness. As a child, I was left in my separateness and I felt pain.

Now?? My movements often obliterate my pain in a search for pleasure through self-obliteration or relief through "sexual action." It was a relief to dedifferentiate, not letting go for rebirth. This *direction* of my system was pulled by the patient who manipulated, wittingly or unwittingly, by her "inability" to take care of herself. Her direction when in tension pretended she could not be in a growing pain of our work. She moved to find her relief. For both of us, uncertainty brought pain so we sought escape to a dynamical disorder.

For several weeks, she talked of her realization that her mother was an evil, sadistic person. The latter had been in a state hospital, diagnosed as a paranoid schizophrenic. Her recent clarity about the cruel coldness of her mother was accompanied by a general lucidity of perception of other realities in her life: she saw that certain colleagues tried to manipulate her and used her to avoid their autonomy; she saw their egocentricity; she saw the lies, insincerities, and hypocrisies of so-called friends; she felt helpless when she began to see so much as she felt more and more alone. She was aware of the responsibility she had in her life. The pain of all this awareness was accentuated on her birthday: she panicked that her brother "would not remember her." She said, "It is very important to be remembered. I do not want to think of myself as so alone, and if he does not call, I feel that I do not matter to anyone."

She recalled a dream from childhood: "I was sleeping in a second floor bedroom and the water of a flood began to creep up to my level. I felt threatened by the waters. I was terrified." She expressed a furious anger at her mother for leaving town two days before her birthday without calling to say goodbye. She asked, "What kind of mother would do that?" The conclusion: a real shit of a person. All this added up to more clarity about the constraint in which we live.

She raged at the malevolence in the world with more and more intensity. As she did, we both discovered that immersion in the chaos meant seeing the evil that her mother represented. This was a confrontation that was not a pleasure. And this moved with my help to the next stage: her perception that the real evil of her mother was how she anxiously did not engage her relationship to the limits of the world.

I stressed that she must confront her own malevolence; that was what really would make it possible for her to see it everywhere else. The way she avoided anxiety corrupted her relationship to all the facts of her life. She was evil when she orgiastically overate because she abused the actuality of her relationship to her body and to time. She filled time with the oblivion she felt as she stuffed herself with ice cream. She was evil when she isolated herself from the moments of anxiety she felt with others. She was evil when she spent her time in front of a television set rather than live with the suffering of her life's discomfort. Each of her actions and movements expressed her direction when she is *alone:* the facts of bounded life, her life, were there to be seen. But she feared that she would see the facts and would be drowned by the implication of their call for action. Then she would be a separate person with the *actuality of time, space, and her own death to engage.* As we looked at all this, I felt we really worked together inside the chaos, slaying the dragon of delusion moment-by-moment.

She had begun the session as a burst of "masochism" in which she moved and escaped from fear rather than live in uncertainty. My sexual process had been remnants of this in me. But more important for our work together, it was my registration and my participation in the *total* process in which *we* moved. The feelings expressed a direction that she *needed help* to oppose. I was able to give her this help by seeing the process in me and *not being taken over by it.* Similarly, our society, with its pleasure orientation in television, advertisements, values, and so forth, corrupts and aids such evil; there are friends who do the same, yet call themselves friends. Our task is to watch for this process constantly in ourselves and in others.

Parenthetically, I also came to my deepest understanding of paranoia. Her mother ran away from the evil ghosts who were chasing her. That woman experienced the anxiety of being in the world in the form of the *rage of "it" at her.* She started out as the world being a tortuous place. To her, her daughter undoubtedly was another source of anxiety, a ghost who created the terror and pain of a possible love and yet another self that she could not engage. My patient represents a transition in history in that she was now facing that anxiety the mother externalized as the malevolence in the world. Ghosts are not ghosts; they are real because she could differentiate the ghosts as *her anxiety* from those people who move in evil ways. She teased out the facts that were there in the world as structured and ordered information: a mother who leaves without saying goodbye. She saw the separateness of the anxiety avoidance. These distinctions were difficult to come by as they catapulted her onto her own feet where she constantly faces uncertainty.

REFERENCES

1. Shainberg D: The Transforming Self: New Dimensions in Psychoanalytic Process. New York, Intercontinental Medical Book Corp., 1973.
2. Shainberg D (ed): Healing in Psychoanalysis. Unnpublished manuscript.
3. Eliade M: Rites and Symbols of Initiation. New York, Harper and Row, 1955.
4. Eliade M: The Sacred and Profane. New York, Harper and Row, 1959.
5. Shainberg D: Consciousness and psychoanalysis. J Am Acad Psychoanal, 3:1975.
6. Shainberg D: Telepathy in psychoanalysis:: An instance. Am J Psychother, in press.
7. Shainberg D: Transforming beyond the self. Unpublished manuscript.
8. Kelman H: Kairos: The auspicious moment. Am J Psychoanal, 29, 1959.
9. Kelman H: Communing and relating. Am J Psychoanal, 18:77–98, 1958; ibid. 18:158–170, 1958; ibid. 19:73–105, 1959; ibid. 19:188–214, 1959.

Paul Olsen, Ph.D.

Recognitions of the Soul

Because I am going to deal with such an ostensibly esoteric and elusive idea as the soul—the recognition of which has had a profound impact on both my life and work—I want to set the experiences and thoughts emerging from that idea within a rough context of how I view my work. I am an analytically oriented psychotherapist who, in a relatively traditional manner, takes detailed histories of my patients' lives; who is highly aware of concepts such as transference, countertransference, resistance, and working-through; who clarifies and interprets; who basically heeds Wilhelm Reich's advice to peel the onion of character armor.[1] Not convinced of the sanctity of these constructs, I nevertheless keep my eye on them.

While I am fond of my patients and feel deeply connected to them, I avoid being "nice" or friendly as substitutes for technical procedures that propel treatment. I try not to fill gaps in my technique with "warmth" or "positive regard," then attempt to call it "humanism."

Yet I am going to define psychotherapy as follows, as I have come to see it: A contact not just between two people engaged in some sort of interpersonal activity on a seesaw of transferential distortions and the "real" relationship, but a communion of two souls—a conception which for me expands therapeutic possibilities and, indeed, enriches relationships in general.

A glance at traditional literature reveals that Jungians are married to a belief in the soul: one needs a calculator to tally references to it in Jung's *Collected Works*. June Singer, an analytical psychologist, titled her by now famous book on treatment *Boundaries of the Soul*.[2] From a different direction comes *The Doctor and the Soul*[3] by the existentialist, Viktor Frankl. But the term is almost impossible to locate in psychoanalytic writing, or for that matter in the mass of literature generated by the newer therapeutic modalities such as Gestalt, bioenergetic analysis, and primal therapy—all of which I am prone to label as mechanistic, or materialistic, or both. The soul seems to have no room in the canons of these disciplines. Or perhaps it is denied, unknown, or even studiously avoided—the latter a strong conclusion after examining *Psychoanalysis and the Occult,*[4] a book that does not contain a single indexed reference to the soul. Yet the soul is the brain and backbone of the every occult philosophy and practice, even black magic.

There have been several more recent references to the soul, but only in the context of "soul murder," a term apparently coined by Schreber[5] and discussed by W. G. Niederland in his modern reassessment of Freud's famous case.[6] Soul murder, as applied to Rudyard Kipling, is the subject of a study of the writer in the 1975 edition of *The Psychoanalytic Study of the Child.*[7] However, it is questionable if "soul murder" has anything at all to do with the soul. It seems, rather, to be a current attempt to infuse drama into the tired vocabulary of theory and psychopathology.

In my discussion of the soul, I want to make very clear that I am partly dealing with a kind of empathy (for lack of a better word) that is refractory to research efforts. Researchers have attacked this empathy as if it were an entity, a thing, a cluster of attitudes or traits, a semantic enigma that the magic of other terminologies may hopefully unlock. We can hardly define it, let alone catalogue or measure it, because the empathic possibilities that emanate from the soul, as with all nonintellectual dimensions of the therapeutic dyad, do not conform to the limited capabilities of our "scientific" instruments of measurement. Probably it is high time that we turn our gaze in a different, nonscientific direction—which may not be too terribly difficult if we allow the fact that any system that recognizes the presence of nonobservable psychodynamics cannot correctly be labeled a science. (I have always found it fascinating that many psychoanalysts who faithfully accept one body of nonobservable data rigidly oppose the "reality" of another body of nonobservable data. Years ago Edward Glover wrote a book called *Freud or Jung?*;[8] why not Freud *and* Jung?)

So there is something unquestionably occult in the therapeutic connection—occult in the true sense of a body of data not easily understood and therefore unknown *for a period of time.* If we are to assess, or even *see,* this connection we must leap to a different dimension, a dimension that encompasses the capacity for the experience of beauty and love, and the use of the experience, once recognized, to understand that all is possible. This is the importance of the soul; it is what it is and thus defines itself, and it represents for me the core of the psychotherapeutic process, that which allows psychotherapy to be a *process* at all.

I am not a religious person in any traditional Western sense, and so in a peculiar way the existence of the soul is perhaps more meaningful for me than for members of organized faiths. What I mean is that I have no investment in regarding the soul as an entity that may be lost or saved. I see it as a collective force that links person to person, people to people, people to nature, to space, to—if you will—all that exists in the universe. It is what connects you, the reader, to me, the writer; neither the words nor even the ideas on this page really connect us. The soul is *why* we are able to communicate, and in truth, no two human beings can ever be out of communication. It can only be a matter of more or less, good or poor, but never *not*.

This is my framework in relating to my patients on the deepest levels: the personality, with its complexity of psychodynamics, is merely a layer beneath the surface of behavior. This layer forms the matrix of individual differences which determines how we do or do not get along with each other in the context of cognitive processes that more or less "communicate" a string of contiguous words that we almost understand. But beneath the personality is the *real* intrapsychic life, the soul—that which underlies all individual differences, binds us all together, and leads us to the potentialities for true communication. It is what makes us a species; it is, as Eastern thinkers have urged for centuries, the essence holding all together. It is *that* important.

The idea of soul as the binding force of all life in nature (not an idea simply that people have a lot in common) has wrenched me emotionally from a position I once called humanism—a position which I now see as an ability to relate to others with good feelings and as a reflexive conviction that all people have a right to life as well as a right to experience it as they see fit. I might add that this position still does not permeate most psychotherapy as practiced. Patients are still too often misperceived as sick, neurotic, psychotic, or whatever; and patients are too often not regarded as people—let alone people with souls—and that is why it is necessary to begin with humanism before approaching a recognition of the soul.

Humanism, and this is crucial, must be *felt:* it must spring from the confines of the intellect into an intensely emotional, automatic response. A therapist needs to experience it deeply, then live it: not in selected situations or specific encounters, not as a matter of choice, but as a way of life as vital and yet as unobtrusive as breathing. In one way, the end of the humanizing process resembles *satori,* which D. T. Suzuki[9] defines in part as an intuitive looking into the nature of things in contradistinction to the analytical or logical understanding of it. . . . Or we may say that with satori our entire surroundings are viewed from quite an unexpected angle of perception.

Intuitive understanding must transcend analysis, or humanism is not really possible, remaining only an intellectual or socially acceptable posture. You cannot unselfishly like or love or form an attachment to what you analyze; you can only try to keep the bits and pieces, the fragments, from running through your fingers. Which is why we therapists are always wondering where the patient is *at:* since we do not see all of ourselves we are not seeing all of the patient and so are always in pursuit of some fragment of personality, some behavioral manifestation, some "line" to deepen, some elusive psychodynamic with which to play hide-and-seek.

By intuitive I mean reflexive, and that means knowing what to do without the obstruction of thinking. Hopefully we have all experienced moments of intense connection with our patients during which everything felt, said, done, is right—absolutely *right,* an almost blissful sense of harmony that cannot be defined in less than spiritual terms. In the psychotherapist who is progressing toward a recognition of the soul, such connections grow more frequent, the moments extend in time, often subtly but sometimes dramatically.

Since we live in a culture of drama, it is usually the *moment* of drama that informs us of the nature of our humanism: whether it is reflexive or not, indeed even if we have any at all. Whatever happens in the drama is either defended against or assimilated. That which is assimilated into consciousness and hence into intuitive understanding is then a part of us and so must change us. I am utterly convinced that if I do not permit my patients to change me, to contribute daily to my emotional and spiritual growth, then I must do something else to earn my living. Because otherwise the practice of psychotherapy becomes, at best, a supreme misunderstanding; at worst, a criminal act.

A moment of drama that provided so much clarity for me happened with a patient to whom I refer as one of my greatest teachers. He had been in treatment with me for more than five years, a large, tough-looking man, but with an air of gentleness that hovered about him like some delicate aura playing along and around jagged plains and edges. He could remember being angry only twice in his life, and twice he carried his anger, and himself into a hospital. He often dreamed of a razor-sharp pendulum that he would grasp with his hands and push away from him into the darkness; for a moment it would be gone, then suddenly, horrifyingly, sweep back at him, swinging closer and closer to his head while he stood paralyzed, terrified, appalled, his mouth agape in a silent scream.

In time he began to feel his anger, even express it, but not often. One day in my office, rage began to fill him: his flesh seemed to swell with it, his face red and quivering; then he sprang to his feet and in the same explosive movement lashed out at his empty chair and knocked it over. He stood there, having swung out his pendulum again, waiting, panicked. I *found* myself standing with my arm around his shoulders; I had no idea I had gotten to him so quickly; no sense or thought or physical movement. I was just there, intuitively, reflexively, profoundly connected. We looked at each other's eyes, then into them, and the room, the air, was suddenly deep and soft, totally free of pain, totally free of differences.

I cannot say *what* happened; I can only describe it. The *Chandogya Upanishad* is right. The person seen in the eyes is the self. The innermost self. Perhaps the soul.

The profundity of the connection I experienced that day—again, there was no thought or planning in any of it, and that is the crucial point— moved me to an understanding that people are spiritual beings. A leap into the knowledge that we are all bound together by something far more powerful than traits or characteristics or language or needs. As a result I seem to hear more in what my patients tell me, including what they occasionally tell me about myself. And I take that very seriously: what they say is far more accurate than "transferential." And I am feeling a great sense of love in sessions, a reverence for the other person; it is just there, in the room, without words. And always that growing sense of infinite possibilities.

What, then, are some of the possibilities in a recognition of the soul?

Returning to my belief that human beings can never be totally out of contact or communication—a belief I consider one of the absolute foundation-stones of successful psychotherapy—leads me to illustrate this idea by citing a kind of paradigm laid down by a seventh-century mystic named Avva Dorotheus. This mystic believed that people (in our context, read this as the two people involved in the therapeutic relationship) who achieve the closest contact are enabled mutually to reach God. The idea is schematized by visualizing a center like the hub of a wheel or a sun from which extend an infinite number of spokes or rays or radii. There is a person on each of two adjacent radii. The closer these people come together, the closer they move toward the center which, although Avva called it God, we may call the soul, a place where individual differences vanish, and unity, oneness, is experienced. This image has really nothing at all to do with the loss of identity through what lately we have come to call pathologically permeable ego boundaries—a theoretical construct whose very mention arouses so much anxiety in one (or two) of the people in the treatment room. Rather, it is akin to the Hindu's eternal and most profound identification of human with human, human with all, the concept of oneness, of *Thou art it.*

> *Ahan-sa* or *'han-sa* (pronounced *hong-sau*) is literally "I am He." These potent Sanskrit syllables possess a vibratory connection with the incoming and the outgoing breath. Thus with his every breath man unconsciously asserts the truth of his being: *I am He!*[10]

Of great importance in this age-old metaphorical wheel is that the soul, one's essence, is revealed, felt, and absorbed *via* an intensely committed relationship with another—which, with accuracy, we might easily call love or, for the most mystically inclined, transcendental love. But certainly not a purely erotic love as we are familiar with the term. Nor is this a regression. It is the discovery of union, of harmony through a kind of happy fusion which reveals the self.

Conversely, the wider the gulf between two people, the farther they move from the center of the wheel toward some distant, blurry circumference; and thus the further they are from a recognition of the soul. Yet even in this distant dimness, there is still contact and the potentiality of a brighter one.

The metaphor of the wheel obviously suggests an interpersonal relationship of great intensity, yet with an important distinction: the two people *go together* into a radiant, revelatory center, *both* glimpsing, finding, experiencing their souls. In the setting of psychotherapy, one does not, by definition, go it alone—unlike the yogi, who achieves the experience of the center (cosmic consciousness), *then* becomes suffused with a transcendental closeness to others. In short, the therapist *must* go with the patient, the patient with the therapist, each in turn leading the other until they are finely attuned, until a greater consciousness is revealed to both.

What we are searching for here is the extension of all human possibilities and, consequently, the extension of awareness or consciousness. That is, the profound and unmistakable identification of the self with its boundless spiritual dimensions; the liberation of human existence from at least a few cells of its mundane, boring, driven, compulsive, materialistic prison. Without this extension, psychotherapy is to me a questionable proposition and the practice of it a questionable endeavor.

If the therapist is able to immerse himself fearlessly in the oceans of his patient's existence, he will understand that the mysterious "something else" always sought after by the patient is the dimension of spirituality within and not merely some grandiose primal fantasy, readily analyzed, amenable to theorizing—but gloriously refractory to dissolution. Hopefully, following this immersion into the vast mythic originality and creativity of the patient begins a journey *through* the complexities of the psychodynamics into a recognition of the unity, even sameness, of human life beneath the mirages of the "unique" personality.

Anything less, and the patient must stop abortively; he cannot move past the limitations of the therapist's vision, the limitations of the therapist's soul. More concretely put, no person in therapy can proceed to point eight if his therapist's scale of possibilities stops at point seven.

Of course, there is little doubt that within the limitations of a seven-point therapeutic setting patients frequently become more "practically" oriented, sexually active, and materialistically inclined. But I believe these goals essentially to be substitutes for the patient's connection with his spiritual qualities: sexual prowess may increase, but he still may not understand and feel the difference between "having sex" and making love. This materialism is too often reinforced by therapists who are mired in the delusion that material achievement is the *sine qua non* of success in psychotherapy as well as in life. In such a setting a deep part of the meaning of human existence has been amputated. Stark blacks and whites have become arranged into highly intricate patterns held together by grays—but they are blacks and whites and grays nevertheless.

Quite obviously, I am not in sympathy with these exclusively materialistic goals and would ask the therapists of such "successful" patients: "How do you know if they couldn't have gone much, much further?" If it really happens that a patient is not ready to go very far, then so be it; but a context of infinite possibilities must still be established in the therapeutic relationship, or else it is *fact,* not conjecture, that the patient will progress only as far as he is allowed.

Actually, that certain people can "only go so far" is highly debatable anyway if therapeutic progress continues to be assessed via our embarrassingly fruitless measures—particularly research, which still seeks some "objective" truth. We may never know how far a person may go if the person, as patient, has not had an opportunity to soar, to touch the heights. I don't think that we may *ever,* except in arrogance and stupidity, state "how far" a patient is capable of growing as long as he is bound into the grave limitations of our accepted therapeutic systems, which are simply societal systems in microcosm.

However, as therapists we must always ask ourselves how far *we* can go. Because this is the debt that we owe to those people who have placed themselves in our hands. If we can admit our limitations, we will at least know that we limit our patients because we see only aspects of their lives and never the whole of them.

I have too often seen a phenomenon in friends, colleagues, and patients who have left past therapists—that is, when they arrived at their therapists' limits, the general concept of *resistance* was introduced powerfully into the treatment. Efforts were made to analyze or, more accurately, to analyze away, get rid of, that which the therapist did not understand, envision, imagine. This was invariably followed by attempts to analyze the *transference resistance* when, in fact, no such thing existed. What was taking place under the rubric of transference resistance was the therapists' intense anxiety; so great were the threats to the therapists' identities and perceptions that they helplessly stood and fought to preserve their systems. The very need to call what was occurring "transference resistance" is an almost poignant clue to the head-to-head nature of the combat.

At that point the intact patient terminates treatment. The less intact patient comes to regard his imaginings, visions, and creative fantasies as sick and, at least for a time, will guiltily recede into some sort of compliant plasticity. And in the latter case the therapist, *with no conscious awareness whatever,* will feel that he has reoriented his patient to treatment and to reality.

A tree grows in the earth, but it is not created by the earth. A seed is neces-sary. This seed may be in the soul, or absent from it. When it is there it can be cultivated or it can be choked; when it is not there it is impossible to replace it with anything else. The soul (if soul it may be called) lacking that seed, i.e., inept to feel and reflect the world of the wondrous, will never put forth the living sprout, but will always reflect the phenomenal world, and that alone.[11]

What I have come to see and to treasure is the truth—and truth it is—that the human being is, in his spirituality, his soulness, capable of incredible, even cosmic feelings, leaps, and fantasies. And too often such people, as patients, are responded to with the therapist's envy—that is, "Who are *you,* the sick one, to experience such things when *I* can't?" At the same time we cannot want for a patient what we cannot locate in ourselves as a want. I would affirm that any assessment we attempt to make of a patient—that is, where the patient *is,* not in a session but in his life—is not a reflection of our science but of ourselves. It cannot be otherwise, particularly in regard to the soul. For I may *have to* believe, by sheer weight of evidence, that my patient has a "good sex life" even though *I* do not; but if I do not believe that I have a soul, then my patient cannot have one either.

I am well aware that I seem to be advocating the proposition that only a very special kind of person can be therapeutic in the sense of recognizing the soul and in working with the implications of that recogni-tion. That is exactly what I am saying: the specialness of such a therapist resides in the recognition itself. No training analysis can provide it, nor can any other kind of analysis unless it encompasses a spiritual dimension that is rooted in feeling and intuition, but not in theory or intellectual abstractions. It must emanate from the therapist, be a seamless part of his existence; the perception of larger dimensions must be as reflexive as his humanism. Which is why, when a young therapist once asked me if the reading of a particular theorist might be helpful in working with patients, I replied that ten works by this author were not as valuable as a single novel by Dostoevsky.

The purpose of the comment was to focus upon a way to gain some degree of access to the soul—through art. As a matter of fact, so much of what I have written here is beautifully illustrated by Peter Shaffer's play *Equus,* not only in the literature of the work itself but also in an aspect of the controversy surrounding its opening. Believing the essence of the play to be concerned with a patient-therapist relationship (rather than the emergence of the doctor's soul through a sudden identification with a young man), many members of the psychiatric community publicly expressed outrage at Shaffer's "distortions" of psychotherapy. It was painful to read the criticisms because they were both incredibly concrete and defensive—and ultimately disheartening. Almost all stated that the stage psychiatrist was "sick." Yet what he experienced was the opening of himself via his patient—apparently a massively threatening idea, that two human beings, in this case a doctor and patient, can walk a path of enlightenment when one of the pair is blatantly "schizophrenic."

Art has always had a habit of bringing such conflicts into sharp relief, because *true* art has no investment in maintaining social roles, and so it has the power to deeply offend while revealing its truth. But, less controversially, it also has the power to stimulate recognitions of the soul. It has for centuries dealt directly with visions of the soul and may well be the most productive way of opening a person to the core within— which is why we identify with the protagonist of a literary work, the subject of a painting, even with the emotion in something as ostensibly contentless as music. What we identify with is the great commonality in these works, the threads of existence inherent in all humanity; we do not identify with the quirks or idiosyncrasies of a hero or antihero but with the larger meanings beneath the relatively superficial personality. And therefore we are catching a glimpse of our own souls, of our beauty and power and immortality.

Because all things are connected, as I finished rereading this paper my eyes drifted to a bookcase and were caught by a dogeared copy of Freud's *Leonardo da Vinci: A Study in Psychosexuality.* Opening it, I stared at the Mona Lisa and was struck by a new recognition. For years I had wondered—as millions of people have wondered—at her enigmatic smile. More than a decade before I had seen her exhibited in the Louvre fronted by an endless queue of people making the same enquiring comments, asking the same questions: Who is she *really?* What does her smile *mean?* The burning necessity to decipher an expression that, to my knowledge, no other work of art has ever stimulated.

Seeing her again, even in a poor black-and-white reproduction, it all seemed clear to me. I had the fleeting thought that, unlike most oil paintings, she might be framed behind glass—the sort of effect sought by the British painter Francis Bacon, an idea of identity achieved by the face of the viewer superimposed on the face of the subject. But then I decided that such a mechanism was much too artificial, a gimmick that simultaneously says something yet nothing and so falls into flatness.

I realized that she is not just the reproduction of some historically unidentifiable woman caught in an inexplicable pose. She is Leonardo himself.

The greatest artist is he who expresses what is felt by everybody. But how does he do it? By being more subjective than others. The more he expresses *himself,* i.e., his innermost being, the nearer he comes to others. . . . The secret of art is that it reveals the supra-individual through individuality, the "not-self" through the "self," the object through the subject. Art in itself is a kind of paradox. . . .[12]

Still another possibility of Avva's wheel: the profound contact with others through a universal subjectivism, the knowledge of the self to perceive the commonality of all. The painting is in no way an objective representation of anything, and therein lies its genius, its incredibly magnificent truth.

Because what we are looking at in the Mona Lisa, what we desperately attempt to understand via our hopelessly limited "objective" cognitive abstractions, is a face redolent of the inner soul—the knowing smile of bliss, the omniscience and omnipresence, the total connection of within and without.

What we have never been able to articulate, yet know so well, what has drawn us so magnetically to the face in that painting, is the vast spiritual potentiality within ourselves. We have been gazing not at a picture but at a mirror of the profoundest kind. We have been gazing awestruck for hundreds of years into the depths of our soul.

And have never been able to put it into words.

REFERENCES

1. Reich W: Character Analysis. New York, Farrar, Strauss & Giroux, 1970.
2. Singer J: Boundaries of the Soul. Garden City, N.Y., Doubleday Anchor Books, 1973.

3. Frankl VE: The Doctor and the Soul. New York, Knopf, 1955.
4. Devereux G (ed): Psychoanalysis and the Occult. New York, International Universities Press, 1953.
5. Schreber DP: Memoirs of My Nervous Illness. London, Wm. Dawson & Sons, 1955.
6. Niederland WG: The Schreber Case: Psychoanalytic Profile of a Paranoid Personality. New York, Quadrangle/The New York Times Book Co., 1974.
7. Shengold L: An attempt at soul murder: Rudyard Kipling's early life and work. *In* Eissler RS, Freud, A, Kris M, Solnit AJ (eds): The Psychoanalytic Study of the Child. New Haven, Yale University Press, 1975, pp. 683–724.
8. Glover E: Freud or Jung? New York, Meridian Books, 1956.
9. Suzuki DT: Essays in Zen Buddhism (First Series). New York, Grove Press (Evergreen), 1961, p. 230.
10. Yogananda P: Autobiography of a Yogi. Los Angeles, Self-Realization Fellowship, 1975, p. 460f.
11. Ouspensky PD: Tertium Organum. New York, Vintage Books, 1970, p. 197.
12. Govinda A: Creative Meditation and Multi-Dimensional Consciousness. Wheaton, Ill., The Theosophical Publishing House, 1976, p. 17.

Sabert Basescu, Ph.D.

Anxieties in the Analyst:
An Autobiographical Account

> *In the family in
> which I live there are
> four people of whom I am
> afraid. Three of these
> four people are afraid of
> me, and each of these three
> is also afraid of the other
> two. Only one member of the
> family is not afraid of any
> of the others, and that one
> is an idiot.*
>
> Something Happened,
> by Joseph Heller

I am used to being told by people I see in psychotherapy that I seem so calm and unruffled. I know I appear that way and it really does reflect an aspect of my being as a therapist. It's not that I make any effort to appear that way. It's just the way I am. But it's not the whole story, not by any means. When I make a point of noting the stream of thoughts and fleeting feelings that flow through me during my work, I am amazed at how many things I am uneasy about and afraid of.

For example, whenever someone I'm seeing (I don't really think of the people I see as patients, or clients, or analysands, and I usually feel a twinge of uneasiness—see what I mean?—when I refer to them that way, so I mostly refer to them as people I see or work with. But that can get to be semantically awkward at times, so I sometimes refer to them as patients and put up with the twinges.) Well, when someone I'm seeing begins to describe himself (there's another one of those problematic designations that gives me a twinge because I can anticipate the reactions of the liberated women in my life to it. I am going to resolve that one in this essay by using "him" when the person I'm thinking of is male, and "her" when she's female.) as despairing or discouraged or hopeless (and in this line of work that is a fairly frequent occurrence), I immediately expect it to be the beginning of a criticism of me. Since I've never become completely calloused to criticism—even criticism I can successfully pass off to myself as transference—I start to feel some sense of unease. The discomfort can disappear pretty quickly (especially if it's clear that I'm not being criticized, or even if I am), but it can also linger on and become more intense.

Criticism of me has taken many forms—that I don't say enough, do enough, explain enough, react enough, care enough, give enough (once even that I don't charge enough). Also, that my clothes are too square or too informal, that my office is too quiet, or too noisy, or too small, or too uncomfortable, or too cozy. That I go too fast or too slow, that I understand too little or too much, that I'm too healthy, too well-adjusted, and too secure (this paper should set that straight!) to empathize with what life is like for somebody with problems. The list goes on. That I don't go deep enough, that I don't sleep enough, that I move around too much in my chair, that there's not enough fresh air, that I'm not a Jungian, that I sound just like a Freudian, and why don't I do hypnosis. It may sound funny, but if you don't believe that a continuous daily barrage like that takes its toll, you ought to see a therapist . . . or be one.

Since very few people are crazy enough to miss the mark completely, most such comments have their kernel of truth. I find myself having two kinds of anxious reactions to these kernels of truth. When they link up with things I've been told by others, especially my family, I worry about what's the matter with me and about the difficulties others have in living or being with me. And I worry about how my work as a therapist would be different, that is, better, if I were different.

Sometimes—not too often—the barrage gets to be too much for me. I've reacted by thinking that the person was about to quit therapy. I was flooded by feelings of failure and worries about lost income. I thought of who it was that referred him to me and who would know about his quitting and what they would think about me—and felt intensely uncomfortable. Just then I felt a wave of relief at the thought of his quitting. I wouldn't have to be exposed to this buffeting about any more. I wouldn't have to struggle against feeling demoralized. And besides, I could really use the free time. I did such a good job on myself that I was almost disappointed when he didn't quit. In fact, quitting wasn't even on his mind.

It is much easier to contend with such worries when I'm feeling generally good than when I feel low or self-doubting. But even feeling good doesn't prevent the worries from registering.

You would think that, given my sensitivity to criticism from the people I work with, I would rejoice in expressions of praise or gratitude from them. No such luck. That's not to say that I don't like the fondness and respect for me that this kind of work often generates, but it brings with it a fair share of anxious concern and uneasiness—some of it even more problematic for me than that caused by criticism. We therapists have all learned that the admiration, attraction, idealization, and so forth coming our way has mostly to do with somebody else, is probably masking some pretty angry feelings, and is elicited by the structure of the therapeutic situation (see, I know the rules). But there are times when I think maybe it really does have to do with me. After all, I'm a pretty good guy in many ways. (My mother thinks I'm great.) Why shouldn't somebody have good feelings about me, especially if I'm tuned in and the work is going well? I can experience that without too many twinges of anxiety as long as it doesn't happen too often. But if I start to feel that I *need* the admiration, the love, the affection, the praise, I get very anxious and guilty. There are so many opportunities and temptations for self-aggrandizement and self-gratification in this kind of work, and since I'm no more calloused to admiration than I am to criticism, it's very easy for me to feel suspicious, and then anxious, and then guilty in the face of praise from my patients. Many times I'm right!

I once had a dream that a woman I was working with was like a rag doll—my rag doll—the floppy kind whose limbs and torso I could put in any positions I wanted—and I did! I put her arms around me and her legs around me, and it was sexy and great. And I woke up with a start! The whole thing suddenly got too obvious. Of course, it made what was going on in the sessions painfully obvious, too. She and I were accomplices in setting me up as the powerful manipulator and her as the obedient puppet. We were both getting our respective neurotic kicks from that combination. I can't say I felt too good about myself with the realization. Then I started to wonder why I had the dream about her that night. I couldn't recall anything striking about that day's session with her, but I did remember a fight I had had with my wife that night, after which I felt self-righteously angry and unappreciated. It seemed pretty clear then; if I couldn't get the treatment I deserved at home, I surely knew where I could get it and apparently had been getting it. The next thing that hit me was the realization of what I was really angry at my wife about. She wasn't willing to be my rag doll. Then I felt terrible all over again (about me, but really good about her). Ah, well. All in a day's work—and a night's dream. That's the trouble with this profession. It keeps you working day and night. The person who told me I didn't sleep enough was right.

Praise is more problematic for me than criticism when the praise makes me feel caught in a cover-up, my cover-up. As I think about it, it's not surprising that the self-doubting feelings I'm willing to acknowledge in the face of criticism must be less of a threat to my self-esteem than those I keep under the wraps of admiration from others. The moral of the story is that it is better to look a gift horse in the mouth—as self-depriving as that feels—than to turn your back and risk getting kicked in the head.

There is another kind of "spoiler" that I feel required to be at times that makes me uneasy—the spoiler of the other person's good feelings. It is not unusual for troubled people to endow the external objects of their environment with the power to make them happy. A new possession, a promotion, a trip, a new relationship, a new twist of any kind may be the occasion for a surge of good feeling and the announcement that "all my problems are solved." When somebody who has been suffering latches on to the illusion of joy, I don't feel especially good about being the one who says, in effect, "You are kidding yourself." This leads to people saying things like, "I felt pretty good when I came in but now I feel lousy again, thanks to you." I don't feel anxiety about this, since I know that the new experience is more likely to be a positive one if it is not expected to provide something it cannot provide. But the immediate experience for me may be of the other person's disappointment and anger, and I don't find that especially pleasant.

Perhaps the most unpleasant experience that I confront in my work as a psychotherapist is the experience of feeling intimidated. By intimidated I mean scared and paralyzed, knowing full well that something is wrong but feeling helpless to do anything about it, although knowing I should be able to do something about it. I'll give you an example of what I mean.

The very first time I ever saw Mary, a bright and energetic five and a half year old who had just been banished forever from kindergarten because of her disruptive behavior, she entered the playroom and began to destroy it. Without even a "Hello," she managed to dump three shelves of toys on to the floor and was stomping on them by the time I overcame my surprise and got out of my chair to stop her. Subsequent sessions continued to be messy (in more ways than one), and I established the procedure of announcing, ten minutes before each session was scheduled to end, "We have to clean up now." "We" turned out to be a euphemism for "I", since Mary didn't see much need for any cleaning up, that is, until one session in which she used, or rather, abused finger paints. She placed a large sheet of paper on the floor and began with the paints innocently enough. Then she discovered the creative possibilities inherent in elbow painting, wrist painting, chin painting, and knee painting. I made my clean-up announcement fifteen minutes before the session's end that day. But Mary was full of surprises. She decided the room needed cleaning, and she was determined to see the job done properly. She ran around the room wiping at spots on the walls, windows, shelves, floor, and furniture. Covered with finger paint as she was, each wipe smeared a rainbow of color on whatever she touched, and she became ever more enthusiastic about "helping" me clean up. And I became ever more tense and helpless to end the session (which was by then overdue) and get her out of there. Some time later, when a colleague asked why I didn't just take her firmly by the shoulders and walk her out of the room, I realized that I was in such an impotent rage that touching her would have been like hitting her, and that was what I was afraid I would do.

I think my fear of being destructive or attacking is always at the root of my feeling of being intimidated by the people I see. I'm really intimidated by the possibilities of my own anger when I can't allow myself to be angry because I feel I shouldn't be. I shouldn't be angry just because someone is self-righteous, or self-justifying, or presumptuous, or overbearing, or skeptical, or rigid. I wouldn't be angry unless I felt that this was going on at my expense, that my needs were being thwarted, especially the need to experience myself as effective. Come to think of it, my feeling intimidated arises only when I feel ineffectual with people I see as effective—when I see myself as a competitive loser. It takes two to make for competition. When I'm one of the two and a patient of mine is the other, I feel guilty about being competitive and angry about being a loser. Until all of that comes to light, I am intimidated and to some extent paralyzed.

A woman telephoned for an appointment. When she arrived, she introduced herself quite pointedly as "Dr. R." She was a forceful, attractive, articulate, impressive-looking career woman about twenty years older than I, on a university faculty, nationally known as a leading authority in her special field, a field somewhat related to my own. She was also referred to me by my psychoanalyst who was a friend of hers. (I assume I don't have to spell out the loaded impact on me of that array of presenting facts.) In our work together, she often said things like, "I've been using

such and such a teaching method with my students and it works marvel-
ously. You really ought to try it." Or she would tell me, in the course
of discussing a problem of hers, what a favorable reaction an audience
had to one of the many speeches she gave. In addition, she was an avid
reader of the literature of the social sciences and always assumed I read
everything she did and more. She would say something like, "I've been
reading Blabberman's books, which I'm sure you're quite familiar
with. . . ." More often than not, I was not only unfamiliar with it but
hadn't even heard of it. I rarely acknowledged that.

The combination of her style, my problems, and the special needs I
had in this situation to prove myself left me feeling increasingly tongue-
tied and impotent. In session after session, I felt like a child disguised
as a psychoanalyst, about to be found out. I was a loser. Finally, out of
desperation, I told her I felt intimidated by her. She bolted upright, thoroughly surprised, and said, "How could you be frightened of me? I'm
so frightened of you." That surprised me as much as what I said surprised
her, and it was the beginning of the end of that anxiety-laden impasse.
In fact, the whole interchange had an unexpected payoff in that she realized
part of her difficulty with her faculty colleagues followed exactly the same
pattern. She was frightened of them without realizing that their behavior
toward her was indicative of their feeling intimidated by her.

Although this very troublesome situation had something of a "happy
ending" attributable (maybe) in part to my saying what I felt, don't think
that I am advocating that therapists should lay out their anxieties for
their patients to react to as a general policy. In view of what I have
already described about my own reactions to people telling me about their
bad feelings, I could hardly think it desirable to dump an added load
onto people who are seeing me because the loads they're carrying are
already too much for them. I felt driven by my feelings rather than in
touch with them, and I was not really clear about what was going on
with me until after the experience passed its peak. I think my anxieties
can be generally useful to me in my work when they are not getting the
better of me. Then they can serve as clues to understanding what is going
on in the relationship. It would be easy to assume that because I felt
intimidated by Dr. R., she was trying to intimidate me, especially since
her colleagues also felt intimidated by her. Some therapists would immediately confront her with trying to intimidate others and in that sense hold
her responsible for their feeling intimidated. I would prefer to examine
her behavior in relation to her feelings rather than mine, namely her need
to bolster her self-esteem by impressing others. My reaction is helpful in
understanding something about the impact of her behavior on others, an
impact that she did not intend and was puzzled by but frequently, although

not always, encountered. Even if, at some less focal level of consciousness, she did intend to frighten others, I think that could be best brought to awareness by first focusing on what she did in relation to what she was aware of feeling.

However, the whole issue of disclosing myself in my work as a therapist is one that is shot through with nagging anxieties for me because I wonder what my real intentions are when I answer personal questions or deliberately describe something about myself—an experience, event or feeling—and I wonder about the kind of impact it has on the other person. I know that the conception of the role of the therapist has evolved from that of the anonymous reflector, through that of the participant observer, to the current standard of the therapist as human being. It is not so easy for me to be a human being. I think it would be easier for me to be a mirror. The rules for being a mirror are more clear-cut than the rules for being human. I think the people who say you should "just let it all hang out" are trying to make being a therapist, which I think is a hard job, into something easy or at least something that sounds easy. (Even "letting it all hang out," which I am trying to do here, is not easy. When I first started to study psychology, my grandfather, who was in the insurance business, would say to me that he was a psychologist, too. He said he had to be in his work. That made me furious.)

A therapy relationship is not a mutual relationship for me, although there are certainly aspects of mutuality in it. It is not a friendship, although there are qualities of friendship about it. It's not love, marriage, or parenthood either, although there are analogies to those relationships. As a therapist, my awareness of purpose is very different for me from other truly interpersonal relationships. That is, the purpose for being there, the purpose for the relationship existing is always an overriding presence which exerts a pressure on me that I am more or less aware of all the time. That awareness does not exist in the same way for me in other kinds of relationships, even those that can be described as purposeful. The combination of my awareness of purpose and the feeling I have that being open and "human" is desirable is, I think, what gives rise to my moments of doubt about what is going on when I talk about myself or expose my feelings (or avoid talking about myself).

Am I looking for attention or creating an impression? Am I playing a role? Am I giving in to pressure? Am I cooperating with avoiding something? Am I serving my needs or the other person's? (I realize, incidentally, that serving my needs has its place and therapeutic value in my work, but that doesn't simplify the problem of my doubts. It complicates it.) Am I conveying understanding by describing a similar experience of my own? Am I being reassuring by saying I have experiences like yours?

Am I just being me as a way of saying, "It's all right for you to just be yourself"?

I saw a young man of twenty, an only child, whose father had been killed a month before he was born and whose mother had committed suicide when he was fourteen. He had spent some time in a reformatory and in a military academy before his mother died. After, he was adopted by a gang of thieves as their mascot, and he lived in a house with them and their "molls." Then he lived alone and was essentially an isolate. The point of these facts is that, in the lexicon of our profession, he had never had an adequate adult male identification model. Nor had he ever had a suit of clothes.

In one of our meetings, he talked about his clothes, or rather the lack of them, and then asked me where I bought my clothes. The context led me to feel the question had to do with both clothes and father figures. I answered that question as well as a few others having to do with the cost of my suits and men's clothing stores in New York City. (He had been in this city only a few months.) Then he asked whether I shaved with a blade or an electric razor. That question puzzled me, and I asked why he wanted to know, since he had been shaving for a number of years. I supposed he could have still been trying to find out what kind of a man or father I was, or what kind of questions I would answer. He said he was just curious, and then he quickly and sarcastically asked me how often I had intercourse with my wife and if I had extramarital affairs. I didn't answer those questions but rather commented on his sarcasm and suggested that something about my answering his earlier questions made him anxious.

I felt clear during the session itself about what I was doing, but I was beset with doubts after it. Should I have answered the first questions in the fatherly way that I did? And if the first, why not the others? Was I made uneasy by the sexual questions, and was he reacting to my uneasiness? Or was he made anxious by the exposure of his own need for a father and the responsiveness it evoked in me? There were other questions then and even more now in retrospect. My point is that as the value of self-disclosure by the therapist has become recognized, it has provided me with, among other things, additional opportunities to worry and wonder. It is much easier to avoid all self-disclosure than to have to decide what is or is not desirable to express. But is it more therapeutic?

Money makes me anxious, too. Getting it or having it doesn't, but dealing with it does. I am referring mainly to the problems created by fees for missed appointments—when to charge for a missed appointment and when not to. I know of procedures that avoid such dilemmas, like charging for all appointments whether kept or not, for whatever reason, or charging a regular monthly fee. These procedures keep the therapist from having a financial stake in any judgments made. They also facilitate a guaranteed annual income. I also know of therapists who do not charge for *any* appointment cancelled in advance (the meaning of "in advance" varies from hours to days), but these therapists tend to have other sources of financial support.

I don't feel comfortable (as yet, although I could imagine it happening) in either always charging or never charging for cancelled appointments. (Of course, I always charge for an appointment missed without any notice given. Or do I? What about the person trapped in a stalled subway train for two hours on the way to the appointment? Arranging a make-up appointment spares me some such dilemmas.) So I end up with a set of rules of thumb that work well (that is, keep me and the people I see agreeable) most of the time but which confront me with disquieting decisions and conflicts some of the time.

In discussing my anxieties as a psychotherapist, I have, up to this point, focused on the interpersonal occasions for my uneasiness. There are other sources of anxiety for me that have to do with theoretical views I have that I experience as differing from traditional or predominant views. My attitude toward personal history is such an issue. I think that what is significant about the past is active in the present in such a way that a full understanding of what is going on now is sufficient without necessitating an understanding of how and why it got to be that way. I realize that, oftentimes a person's history can be helpful to the therapist in clarifying the structure of present behavior, especially if the therapist is interested in how things got to be the way they are. But that just isn't a major interest of mine in psychotherapy and, therefore, not one I frequently resort to in my attempts to understand the nature of the other person's world. I think a knowledge of history is necessary for a theory of development but not for expanding one's awareness. I don't feel uneasy in stating that, but I sometimes do feel anxious in operating on that basis. I believe that I am not as attentive to or familiar with the personal life histories of the people I see as most therapists are. And that can make me anxious. Am I lazy? Am I missing something I shouldn't be? When I read about or hear elaborate case histories tracing the development of pathological patterns from the potty to the present, I think to myself, I can't do that with the people I see. Maybe I should be able to. Everybody else seems able to.

However, I believe there are a number of routes to the same goal— the increased awareness of self and experience. Dreams, fantasies, personal history, current experiences, and the patient-therapist relationship are all relevant areas deserving of attention. Different therapists use them differently because of varying interests, sensitivities, and skills. My own interests are less in the area of personal history than in other areas. Therefore, I don't as often rely on a person's history to shed light on what's going on with that person as other therapists might. That's not to say I never do.

I have a similar ambivalent feeling about the emphasis I place on the related issues of choice and responsibility for oneself. Although I adhere to the concept of unconscious processes and their influence on behavior, I think they are often dealt with in psychoanalytic work in a way that induces passivity, and a discounting of the effectiveness of a person's will. (I think this is what underlies the meaning of the statement that psychoanalysis is the disease for which it purports to be the cure.) Someone I see, a psychologist, said to me, "I haven't done a lot of things I know I ought to do because it would take a conscious decision and a struggle to do them. That seems unnatural. I've been waiting for them to happen spontaneously." On the one hand, it is striking that consciously deciding something and struggling to implement it gets equated with unnaturalness. On the other hand, it is exactly what could be expected from the omission of will.

Most often, unconscious content is seen to be the consequence of childhood repressions. I think it is also the consequence of conscious choices. That is, the ways in which one chooses to structure his or her world influences the nature of one's unconscious experience. What is unconscious is a function of the self and its projects and is determined by them. Unconsciously determined behavior is a result of prior choice and commitment. In that sense, the unconscious influences consciousness and consciousness influences the unconscious. Psychoanalysis has traditionally concerned itself with the former, not the latter. I think I try to emphasize the latter (without neglecting the former), but I do it with recurring twinges of trepidation.

I feel anxious because I experience myself in a minority and that minority does not have a long-standing or extensive theoretical tradition. Volition is a topic that is notably absent in personality theory and psychoanalytic literature. Psychoanalytic work is so filled with intangibles. Consequently, so much depends on personal judgment, and it is easy for me to raise doubts about mine. I wonder if I overemphasize responsibility for one's behavior and oneself. I can substantiate my views theoretically, but I become uneasy when confronted with comments like, "I can't get myself to do it differently," or "I don't know why I do things like that. I certainly don't want to."

There are times when personal concerns, as opposed to professional ones, preoccupy me. Since I find it very difficult to listen to another person when that is the case, I try to lay aside my personal anxieties when I work. I have found the best way for me to do that is to concentrate on what is bothering me and to be as clear about it as I possibly can. I try to set aside some time before my sessions in which to do this. I don't orient myself to trying to resolve my personal anxieties but just to being clear about what bothers me. It is as if I am making a list of things to be attended to at the proper time. Having that list seems to leave me freer to stop worrying about those things than trying to ignore them does.

I have attempted to present a wide-ranging sample of the kinds of experience that make me anxious in my work as a psychotherapist. I have by no means exhausted the list of problematic issues and situations that make this work something other than the idyllic enterprise it is sometimes romantically portrayed to be. It has for me its fair share of rewards, joys, and deep satisfactions, but I think I am more aware of these feelings in between sessions than during the sessions themselves. When I think of the changes in my anxieties as a therapist over the twenty-five years I have been one, the single most important change is that I am continually less anxious about being anxious. I accept it and expect it as part of the work. The more I can do that, the better able I feel I am to use my anxieties as a resource for understanding and clarifying the structure of the interpersonal world in which I find myself.

POST SCRIPT

My work as a therapist is not the only thing about which I sense anxieties. At this point I feel uneasy that I have created an image of myself as so beset with anxiety that my ability to function effectively is highly questionable. I fear that I might have presented myself as anticipating criticism at every turn, as thoroughly intimidated, as continually in need of reassurance, as indecisive, as unaware of the significant events in the lives of the people I work with, and as paying only lip service to my theoretical convictions. Do you think anyone without a great deal of self-assurance could risk all that?

Avrum Ben-Avi, Ph.D.

On Becoming an Analyst

The venture into psychoanalytic training is a dual process. There is the relatively straightforward and demonstrable procedure of fulfilling requirements and the more personal process of "becoming an analyst." The first has to do with satisfying formal requirements, such as completing courses, meeting the specified number of supervisory hours, and even demonstrating one's personal fitness to the faculty and/or to one's colleagues. You put in the time, do the work, think and act within the prescribed code of the group with whom you are training, and in due course you are, at least outwardly, an analyst. Here, I am interested in dealing with the more personal aspect of the experience which is not as readily definable. When is one acceptable to oneself as an analyst?

It might be virtuous and modest to simply state that becoming an analyst is a long process and let it go at that. The truth, of course, is that it is a lifelong process which runs a course that is determined by a variety of circumstances during one's career. It is not merely a matter of getting more knowledge and experience. The inner experience of becoming an analyst is not simply additional, but rather an algebraic sum of positive and negative personal transactions. It is a developmental process of acquiring, modifying, and discarding theoretical and clinical knowledge as one becomes a competent and confident professional. I will describe some of the early concerns, experiences, and attendant anxieties that were a part of my becoming an analyst. As will be noted, these comments will be determined in part from the particular place and time of my training, while some of the account will result from the nature of the profession.

The major emphasis will be on personal experiences and observations.

In what spirit does one undertake to become a psychoanalyst? Some seem, at least outwardly, to proceed with what appears to be considerable confidence and cool to embrace what others approach as an awesome adventure. There is no doubt that I fell into the latter group. Is it possible that what distinguishes one group from the other is represented by the degree to which they show the trepidations they have? Or are there indeed such considerable differences in the ways in which people approach training in this field? The initial decision to venture into analytic training rests with the person himself. In viewing the disparate characters of one's colleagues, it is quite mysterious as to what could be the common factors fostering such a choice among such a wide range of personalities. Indeed one may well ponder the function, or at least the usefulness in earlier days, of the religious having had the experience of "a call" for performing somewhat similar functions before the days of modern psychiatry. In reviewing the literature on primitive cultures, one finds that those functioning as medicine men, shamans, and the like were exposed to certain selective procedures in order to be nominated for these "professions." The qualifications or method of selection varied from culture to culture, but there does appear to have been some *community* function. Whether by physical deformity, heredity, or emotional deviation, some observable quality clearly established them as candidates for the "therapeutic" role. These functions might be filled by those judged the most stable and intelligent, those senile or frankly psychotic, transvestites, those physically deformed or manifesting other variations on the "therapeutic personality." What is apparent is that there was a mark, a distinctive aspect of the individual to which the community looked in its acceptance of the individual in the role of therapist. Currently, psychoanalysts nominate themselves—so they have only themselves to hold responsible for what ensues.

I will describe two very personal incidents. Although they are both rooted in my own character, there is a distinction between the two. In the first, "reaction to mail," I was to a degree influenced by the time and setting in which I was trained. The second, "who me?" will relate a singularly personal response to my viewing myself as a psychoanalyst. Before discussing "reaction to mail," I would like to describe the setting, at least as I experienced it, in which I was trained.

During the past twenty-five years, there has been an increase in the variety of training centers and in the number of analysts. Familiarity with and attitudes toward psychoanalysts have undergone considerable change. Fewer in number, less in evidence either in professional or social life, the psychoanalyst was, during my training, surrounded by an aura of knowledge, wisdom, and powers which today is realistically much less in evidence. However, it may very well be that to a degree he is still a victim of overestimation. The image of the analyst has been affected by the general changes in attitudes toward authority figures, as well as to changes in the attitudes toward professionals as a group. Also the mystique of the psychoanalyst has been altered with the Americanization of the field.

The specific setting in which I was trained was of significance in affecting my personal reactions. My training in psychoanalysis was taken at an institute devoted to the training of psychiatrists. Anyone who was not a physician was in a distinct category in the eyes of a majority of the faculty, graduates, and fellow students. The nonmedical candidates (psychologists) were supposed to represent and prove themselves as a chosen minority supposedly especially talented or gifted. This circumstance was hardly likely to endear one to any of one's fellow students who happened to feel insecure or especially competitive. Particularly threatened were some of the younger medical faculty who had recently graduated and were interested in establishing themselves in the institute hierarchy. Preference for training of nonmedical applicants was given at this time to professors of psychology, which also set them apart and might have contributed to the unease for some of the other members of the community.

This institute was also in its early days of establishing itself in the community of both medicine and psychoanalysis.* There were recurrent crises having to do with charters and joining or being admitted to various professional organizations, either as an institute or as individual members. In almost all these issues, questions about the role that the psychologists played in the outcome of any of these dilemmas was always in the air. Although the candidates sat in the same classes and were expected to participate in identical seminars, the curricula were printed separately in the catalogue. One had simply to read the listing of the courses to see that they were almost identical, but they were listed discretely for heaven knows what reason. To jump ahead for the moment, although I did not know it at the time of my studies, when I did graduate and receive a certificate, it was "in recognition of the satisfactory completion of the prescribed courses offered to clinical psychologists." As I have said, this was in the early days of becoming established. There were also repeated considerations to ask the psychologists to sign statements to the effect that they were primarily being trained to do research or use the training to function better as teachers rather than practice as analysts. To the credit of the faculty, I don't think that they ever actually exercised this

---

* It should be pointed out that this institute, over the years, has become clearly committed to training psychologists. It has recognized their talents and achievements as psychoanalysts. Many of these graduates function on all levels of its teaching and administrative staffs.

hypocrisy as had been practiced for years at another training center in New York. To further describe the setting, at the time I was accepted as a student, there had been graduated, I think, only one psychologist. Actually, I'm not even sure that the one had been graduated. I did know that there were a couple of psychologists who were in advanced standing and also that a few had been dropped in previous years.

So here we have the setting: an institute just getting underway, in the process of being permanently chartered, eager to be accepted by the medical and analytic societies, and dedicated to the training of medical people, which was willing to accept for training a limited number of "specially talented others." Because of the work of other psychologists who happened to be geniuses and especially stimulating teachers and writers, a number of us were to be given training. Lest this seem too one-sided a portrayal, I add that this represents that aspect which fostered the flourishing of my own anxieties and fears. There were in the institute highly placed faculty who openly and clearly supported the training of nonmedical candidates. I don't know if they were a majority, but it was evident that they exerted a significant power and influence in the governance. Undoubtedly, some of my concerns about my fitness for analytic training would have surfaced regardless of how inviting and congenial the milieu might have been. But it was clear that to the younger medical colleagues the presence of the psychologists represented a threat to their being accorded the status in the field that was not an issue with the more established faculty. So while there were rumors and petitions for the exclusion of psychologists from training, the senior members of the institute generally opposed such moves. That might have quieted the concerns of the others, but it rarely stilled my own preoccupations, as will be seen in my relating the following incidents.

One of the experiences that reflects the trepidations with which I approached psychoanalytic training follows. This was the apprehension with which I greeted mail that included a letter from the institute. It occurred to me repeatedly that the letter would be a notification that I had been dropped from the student body. This was not uniformly the case, thank God, since there was a constant flow of letters of various kinds informing us of meetings, class changes, lectures, and the like. However, it was frequent enough for me to remember it very clearly and to recall my attempts to understand it. There was, of course, no reality that I know of to support my fears. It was difficult to judge where one stood in the estimate of teachers in the lecture courses. Attendance was about the main requirement for some of larger ones. In the seminars, by and large, the estimates of the fellow students as well as the instructors were clearly favorable. The best estimate of one's performance at an analytic institute rests on the flow of referrals, especially of one's supervisors. In my case, this had been most reassuring and flattering, although not exclusively so. In the course of my years at the institute, I had six supervisors. Of the six, three indicated by their reactions a high regard for my work. I would estimate that two of the supervisors considered me simply adequate. It seemed to me that they were neither enthusiastic or despairing of my efforts at psychoanalysis. One supervisor would have to be put into the negative side of the balance. She, toward the end of a year's work during a supervisory hour, said something like, "Well, for once you did something right." Although it was a single remark, the message seemed clear as to her estimation of the year's work.

I report my impressions of the supervisors' estimates, because they are generally very important to the candidate and, in my case, gave little evidence that I was considered an inferior candidate. Nevertheless, I was personally uneasy with the role of being one of the supposedly gifted minority who was being given a special chance. There was the feeling at times that we few psychologists were being bussed into the psychiatrists' school. We had to demonstrate our worthiness and gratitude. Perhaps a more apt analogy would be that of a small group of scholarship students in a private boarding school. I felt comfortable as a student in classes with my psychiatric peers, except for the feeling of specialness. Living the role of the worthy, gifted, underprivileged student oppressed me. It bred anger and resentment in me. Being put in this position on an irrational basis, in effect being patronized, fostered discomfort and resentment, both of which I felt loathe to evidence. Both of these attitudes, which I felt I needed to keep secret (suspecting that I alone was afflicted with them), influenced my approach to mail from the institute.

My stay at the institute, if I remember correctly, covered the years 1950 to 1955. During the same period, my other professional activities were also of concern to me. I was in the midst of deciding whether or to what extent I would remain an academic. My turning to psychoanalytic training was partially determined by the feeling that working full time at the university was not fully satisfying. How much of my time and energy I would shift to clinical work was as yet not clear—how much of this the university would tolerate was also not clear. It also occurred to me that there might be conflicts, both personal and administrative, between doing my analytic work and my university appointment. At that time, there were few precedents for psychologists in university positions openly working privately as psychoanalysts. There has been a great shift in the attitude of university administrators in this regard, although envy and hostility of some colleagues still persists. The period under consideration was one in which it was frowned upon, if not clearly forbidden, to be in private work while holding a full-time university position. Since then, it has been recognized that the clinician could not function very well teaching techniques and procedures that he knew only from reading and research. With this, it has been realized that it was important for the teacher of clinical subjects and specifically psychotherapy to have experience actually doing the work.

Another more likely determinant of my "reaction to my mail" was that I did not feel that I was learning enough. I'm not quite sure what "enough" would have been, but there was an abiding feeling that there must be some greater knowledge available, some wisdom that seemed to be reflected in the manner and conduct of the teachers that I had little feeling I was achieving. Now I must have reasoned, if I know that I'm not learning enough, these teachers might also know that I'm not learning much, and out I go. Being at this time an experienced teacher on my own, I was aware of the fact that the dissatisfied student is hardly the teacher's favorite person. In fact, if the teacher is anxious or made more anxious by the student's attitude, the student may very well become the target of retaliation. The teacher may feel that the reason that the student is dissatisfied with what he is learning is perfectly valid in that the teacher does not have enough to offer or cannot present it in such a manner that any self-respecting student should be satisfied. In this case, given the choice between castigating himself for being an inferior teacher or the student for being the inferior one, the student gets the nod. I'm not sure how far I went with this, but I do recall feeling that I was not satisfied with what I was learning, that is, aside from the supervisory experience, and that my teachers might have the same idea.

Over the years, I have been interested in the reactions of students to various aspects of analytic training. There have been a number of detailed studies of this. However, one feature that seems to result from either formal inquiries or casual meetings with students reappears regardless of the institute being studied. In summary, the candidate rates the personal analysis as the most important learning experience and the supervision as generally useful, with variations depending on how well the supervisor-student match fits. There is almost always an overwhelmingly critical review of the class or seminar part of the educational experience. Not only is the criticism likely to be rather severe but also, occasionally, the attacks on the teacher are rather extreme. Certainly there must be some instances in which both the contents of the course and the person of the instructor warrant the most fiendish reports. However, since there is such an over-whelmingly negative appraisal of this aspect of the training, I wonder if what I have referred to above is not operative in many students—namely, that they know that they're not learning what they want or think they should be getting, and so they become anxious about this and then deflect the anxiety from themselves by being inordinately critical. The extent to which the student experiences his own lacks and anxiety or transforms his anxiety into criticism of the teacher will be determined by the character of the student. There may also be diverse reasons for the student's enthusiasm for a specific seminar. Indeed, the seminar may be one in which the student is actually learning material significant for his work. However, in other instances the response may have more to do with a reduction of anxiety than learning. A teacher may project a degree of confidence which to the student means that if he listens he will acquire an antidote to his anxiety and be helped along the road to attaining the teacher's apparent security.

As previously mentioned, the student's evaluations of analytic training attribute considerable value to the supervisory experiences. They report that their work as analysts is strongly influenced by both the person and work style of the supervisor. Although a rather primitive model, the preceptor relationship has been retained as the basic design in analytic training. Why, in spite of all the modifications in technique and theory, does this relationship persist at the core of the training? In my opinion, it prevails because it fulfills the most basic need of the student, the need for reducing anxiety, which is intrinsic to analytic training—an attempt to quell the persistent doubt, "Am I personally suited to function as a psychoanalyst?" One method attempted at reducing anxiety is to find a teacher—one who has apparently "arrived"—and to emulate him, to follow his lead and route to the desired goal. The student's choice of teachers and supervisors is determined more by the hope for reducing anxiety than by the desire to increase one's technical skills. Admittedly, an increment in knowledge and skill may very well be reassuring and help in reduction of anxiety. But the basis for the choice of this particular person was that, hopefully, he could serve as a model and help with anxiety rather than simply transmit a given amount of technical instruction. The student analyst chooses teachers he esteems and whom he feels reflect the personal qualities for doing analytic work. There is a need to hope and expect that there are figures in the world to whom we may look for guidance and leadership, as well as to use as models, especially in anxiety-producing situations. The searching for models, whether teachers or others, need not be a negative experience and may be a part of the experience of any professional training. The ubiquitous yearning for both enduring and transient transferential figures in the course of one's life has been well documented in the analytic literature. We may therefore attribute a portion of the distortion of one's teachers to the need for powerful and admired transferential figures. To the extent that the teacher functions to increase the student's confidence in himself and his choice of profession, there will be a decrease in the stake the student has in his irrational image of the teacher. The irrational transferential aspects of the student's image of the teacher may then very well be dissipated. However, it may become a destructive experience if the teacher's anxiety compounds that of the student's. For example, if the teacher, out of his own anxiety, fosters the overestimation by the student—in other words, increases the student's awe—the student becomes even more discouraged of ever becoming an acceptable member of the analytic community. It is thus truly unfortunate if the teacher is only too willing to foster the transferential images that grow out of the student's anxiety.

The transmission of knowledge is certainly a fundamental function of psychoanalytic education. However, teachers, especially supervisors, should realize that students are more centrally concerned with their personal suitability than their deficiencies in knowledge of theory or technique. It is when the ignorance is felt to be a reflection of personal inadequacy rather than naivete that the student's grave concerns are touched. The supervisor who recognizes this can therefore be extremely useful to the student. If, however, the supervisor is made anxious by the student's admiration and proceeds to try to impress the student even more, he is dooming the student to escalating self-doubts.

My teachers rarely revealed anything about their concerns or difficulties in the analytic work. They were, generally, kind, thoughtful, and certainly useful. However, they offered little to indicate that the anxieties and doubts that assailed me and other students were or had been familiar to them. So sparse were these revealing comments that I recall, with pleasure, even now, the welcome with which I received these rare utterances. One teacher once remarked, in a rather offhand way, "As a young man I was quite neurotic." What a relief it was to hear that. At last, some indication that he, the esteemed and eminent teacher, and I might belong to the same species. It was one of the most telling, useful, and reassuring remarks that I had heard in the many years of training. Another time, in discussing psychoanalytic training with one of the major faculty members at the institute, focusing on the function of supervision, she said, "Well, I think that the main function of the first supervisor is to help the candidate feel as if he belongs in the profession." Wow! What a different emphasis. In most of the contacts with teachers and faculty the emphasis is just the opposite, with the student trying to convince them, in spite of his own fears and doubts, that he belongs in the field. This experienced teacher was acknowledging as a generalization what I had harbored as a deep personal concern, namely, that in spite of being engaged in a training program, with a growing acquisition of knowledge and skills, there was an abiding doubt common among students concerning their personal fitness to function as psychoanalysts. She was letting me know that this was a general problem, one which she recognized existed in students and which she had perhaps experienced herself. I was quite sure that this was really meant as a commentary on the training function of supervision and not merely a personal reassurance. Our discussion was not a part of a supervisory hour but occurred in a social setting when we were discussing and evaluating various aspects and functions of analytic training.

A final incident, the most human and perhaps the most telling, occurred at about the time that I was to graduate from the institute—it might have been after I had graduated, since I continued with certain supervisors for some time after finishing formal training. At this time, an important issue was being considered at the institute which aroused intense feelings and was causing opposing factions to be formed. The aroused passions, fed by strivings for power, prestige, ambitions, and competition, were in danger of actually affecting the useful functions of the institute. During a meeting with one of the founding members, I mentioned my surprise at what I considered the inappropriate behavior of certain faculty members. Her answer was simply to reach for the institute catalogue, turn to the faculty listing, and say, "As an exercise, let's find an analyst for each member of the faculty." We spent an interesting couple of hours working up a list of analysts who might be useful to each and every member of the faculty. This was done in a serious and respectful mode. There was no sense of criticism or negative judgment, merely a forthright recognition that the behavior of these people under certain conditions revealed a need for continued exploration of the self which could use the participation of another. This was indeed a particularly striking quality of this teacher. In addition to her genius as a teacher, theoretician, and clinician, she had that rare gift of approaching everyone with respect. Hearing her speak to someone it was impossible to discern whether she was talking to a friend, a colleague, a patient, or a student. She approached each as a person worthy of her regard and was respectful of their sensibilities.

As we all know from the earliest writings in psychoanalysis, spontaneous utterances can often be the most revealing. It is, I think, suitable that in trying to describe my own reactions to what I view as the considerable but often neglected personal reaction to the demands made on students that one such "slip" be discussed, as it was for me a revealing and distressing incident. In training, there is this paradox: you are supposed to become well adjusted in the course of the training, uncover the amnesias, and confront the conflicts and problems; but in the process of doing all this and contending with these pressures, you must, at the same time, represent yourself as being very much in control. It is quite all right to reveal how crazy you used to be, even indicate the current stresses and strains, but there must always be in the air the very clear understanding that all of this is definitely under control. It is fine to indicate an awareness of a problem as long as it is recognized and being worked on. In many instances, it is even required that you at least identify and name the problem, especially if this is a problem which at the time and with that particular group happens to be a sign of self-awareness or a way station on the road to health. This may vary from simply identifying oneself as obsessional rather than hysteric to being in the process of sublimating or in the midst of a catatonic episode, all very acceptable, even desirable, depending upon the group to whom this revelation is made

My unwitting remark, I am afraid, did not fit into the category that I have just described. In fact, quite the contrary, as you will see, it was a very clear indication of low self-esteem which, in my particular parish, was not admired. This occurred when one of the teachers whom I respected very much, one who had indicated high regard for my analytic work in supervision, told me that she had referred a patient to me. I blurted out, "Oh, he won't want to see me, he knows me." She simply shrugged her shoulders, and we went on with the supervisory session. I should say, *she* went on with it; I was not quite there for the rest of the hour. I alternated between discussing my patient, thinking how to say something to her to recoup, and trying to reassure myself that the remark did not really reflect my dismal evaluation of myself, not only as an analyst but also as a person. After the hour, over a cup of coffee, I tried very hard to soothe myself. What I had meant to say was that since the man she mentioned had been a student of mine, we knew each other and that there would be some embarrassment on his part to be analyzed by me, since we have many friends in common, would meet at various places, and so forth, and that she would understand. As I've said, I tried, but fortunately it didn't work. I had not said that we knew each other—I had said he knows me. The implication was clear—anyone who knew me would not want to be my patient. From this it followed that only people who did not know me would voluntarily be my analysands and then that it was important for my patients not to get to know me—that is, if I was to remain in practice. How was I doing this on a daily basis, and what was I trying to hide? What did this man know about me that would eliminate me as an analyst for him? I tried to think about what our contacts had been and what had passed between us. How had I revealed to this man those qualities which would eliminate me as a potential analyst? Of course, more to the point, how could I reveal to my supervisor my own fearfulness and sense of unworthiness?

I started by considering our relationship—that is, mine and the young colleague. Actually, our contacts had been rather limited to an infrequent lunch at an institution where he was interning and which I visited as a consultant. Among the more personal habits that he might have been privy to was that at lunch I preferred my pastrami lean. He might also have gotten the idea that I was reticent and a bit ill at ease in the hospital situation, since most of the staff had had more clinical experience than I, who, until that time, was more involved in the teaching and training function. My consultant function was not clinical but rather to coordinate the academic and clinical training of the students during the internships. In this regard, he would recall that at the time that he was stuck in designing his doctoral research on a topic he had been interested in for some time, I had helped him develop its final form. Actually, as I reviewed our limited association, what I could recall was definitely positive. In desperation I tried the explanation that, after all, patients and analysts were supposed to have very little or no extra-analytic association which, in this case, was not possible. Perhaps that was what I meant by saying "he knows me." But our institute was not so committed to this edict, which is actually rarely achieved anyway, as evidenced by the incestuous relationships that develop in almost all training institutes. That rationalization just wouldn't work. The problem had to do with why I felt that someone who "knew" me would not choose me as an analyst. Incidentally, this man never did call me, although not for any of the reasons considered here. He was interested in becoming a candidate at the institute after completing his doctorate and was limiting his choice of analyst to those who were training analysts.

The question remained, what did I think I revealed of myself in casual and professional contacts with this man that would disqualify me from consideration as analyst? How was I different with patients? Outside the office, I was freer, less careful, more variable and revealing of my moods and feelings—in other words, I was myself. As analyst, I was patterning myself after the people, real and imagined, with whom I had studied. I was using as a criterion for my behavior the figures whose papers, books, and biographies I had read and about whom brilliant anecdotes were repeated. The role I had assumed as analyst was less revealing and less spontaneous than that as colleague. As analyst, I was trying to be the calm, older, thoughtful sage. How would this fit with his seeing me when I was phobic about fat on pastrami, compulsive about taking coffee breaks, and paranoid about revealing to the staff how little clinical experience I had had. I had accepted the idea that I had to be different, someone special, when I was in the analyst's chair. Partially, I was suffering from the implied and sometimes explicitly stated graduation requirements of analytic institutions. The graduate is an example of what analysis can do. He becomes an object, a result of analytic work, and assumes the burden of being a living demonstration of analysis. It therefore becomes necessary for him to engage in a series of charades; first with his teachers, then with his colleagues and patients. After all, the qualities that are required for graduation will also bring referrals. This is tolerable, if undesirable. The real burden is maintaining this illusion within oneself. What is fostered is a greater concern with how one looks than with who one is. With my slip to this supervisor, I feared I had blown my cover. The proper concern for me in reviewing this slip was: what did I know about me that I felt necessary to keep from view during analytic work? I realized it was not possible, if even desirable, to declare a moratorium on my anxieties, conceits, values, and conflicts as I assumed the analyst's chair. What I perceived as the expectations of others as well as my own aspirations were beyond my grasp. Thus, my inability to satisfy the real or imagined demands of others or indeed my own expectations were fostering the anxieties revealed by the "he knows me," and so forth. My doubts about my professional competence were due not merely to my level of training and experience but rather to my limited ability to deal with my own anxieties and problems in living. I went back into analysis.

It is impossible to work as an analyst with confidence and assurance if one is disappointed in the results of one's personal analysis. We start working as analysts largely on the basis of faith. We have read theory as well as clinical papers. We have heard prominent practitioners lecture and discuss clinical material. It is, however, as a patient that we first experience the workings of psychoanalysis. It is in this setting that the specific workings and efficacy of the method may be experienced. There is the potential hazard that limited benefits from one's own analysis may be considered a limitation of the process. It has been repeatedly remarked that the significance of the training analysis has precisely the function of demonstrating to the student analyst that psychoanalysis works. When there are only partial gains in one's own analysis, one may react by questioning the process, the competence of the training analyst, or oneself as a proper candidate for analysis. It is a happy event when all three—analyst, psychoanalysis, and oneself as patient—get top marks. To which of the three factors the student analyst attributes the limited benefits of his experience will certainly affect his future professional role and functioning. Given that the analysis is generally successful, the student is faced with the situation where the method is deemed adequate, his analyst is competent, and he gets passing grades as a patient. So he knows that his analyst can do the job—but can he?

This is a significant stage in the professional development of the student. Although he has not been the analyst, this is the first time that he has been intimately involved in a successful analysis. Knowing others who have found analysis extremely useful falls far short of this crucial personal event. However, the student analyst must still have serious questions about his own capacity to be a psychoanalyst. It may take years of effort before he can actually experience the results of his own analytic work; that is just the nature of the practice. For years he operates on faith, supported by his own analytic experience, helped by the regard of teachers and peers, but essentially and eventually he has to see what he does with patients. During these years while one is struggling with the work, trying to develop competence and confidence, one is exposed to the work and publication of prominent scholars. One wonders, are they doing the same work, are they assailed by the same doubts, complications, and vagaries that plague me?

It is important to come to realize that what is written usually represents a considerable condensation. These writers do not mean to misrepresent themselves but rather to focus and sharpen the points they wish to make. There is often a decidedly selective communication. What is written is not necessarily characteristic of our work, but the best part of what we know and do. Sometimes the writer may be describing the high points, those moments or episodes in his work where he most nearly achieves that to which he aspires. This is not to diminish what is written or lectured but rather to put it into proper perspective. I think it is very discouraging for a student to read a clear, concise description of the analysis of a patient, presenting the work in definitive steps and stages, when, in actuality, this represents a distillation of years of work. What was a series of ups and downs, gains and dead ends, is then described in retrospect with clarity and precision. Many of these papers continue to appear, and if others respond to them the way I did early in my training, they are less than useful. We all have times of discouragement. The work seems a maze of contradictions and confusions. One can deal with this, as these times are interspersed with others in which the satisfaction of one's efforts and feelings of accomplishment are experienced. However, it is especially difficult to sustain oneself at the beginning if one reads in the literature or listens to experienced colleagues describe with magical accuracy the ways in which they deal or have dealt with patients in their daily practice. None of this seems so terrible to me now. Much of the sting of these memories has been softened by years of what I consider to be productive work.

There is also reassurance to be gained from sharing with colleagues these thoughts and experiences. And, it is gratifying to hear others validate from their history similar and sometimes identical concerns, anxieties, and apprehensions. One wonders about those who do not have such professional and human concerns. But the professional mythology is perpetuated.

As one proceeds with the work, the experiences, and the successes as well as the failures, one feels in a position to challenge some of the myths and traditions of the profession, specifically those not validated by one's own work or that of one's colleagues. There is an even firmer basis for evaluating some of these propositions and that is to test them against the experiences in one's personal life. That remains one of the most revealing and significant sources of data on which to base one's efforts in this field. A teacher of mine once said that she learned her psychiatry by observing her friends and colleagues. Certainly, if one includes oneself as a subject of such observation, one finds the richest source of testing the postulates and principles of psychoanalytic work. Although we develop our understanding of human behavior by study and observation, be it of books, teachers, patients, or ourselves, we inevitably test the hypotheses that we use in our work in the conduct of our own personal lives.

SUMMARY

I have tried to describe some of the personal experiences and observations that have shaped my development as an analyst. The emphasis has been on some of my early experiences, with particular attention to the anxieties and questions which, at that time, were of importance to me. It may be that, to some extent, the field has loosened up considerably, both in terms of what is expected of the candidate and what the candidate expects of himself. There is, however, still a relevance to these factors for the beginning analyst, as I now observe in my role as teacher.

Although it is true that there seems to be less of a need for the current candidates to represent themselves as paragons of adjustment, there are still the hurdles of screening, selection, evaluation, and graduation which tend to threaten the student. Whether the emphasis is on clinical ability, conceptual talents, or emotional stability, there is always in the offing the judgment which, to my mind, leads to the anxiety associated with being on display. Added to this is the pressure for the student to earn a living and therefore to want to impress one's colleagues and teachers with one's skill and ability. This frequently results in a collusion, a group display of confidence and understanding in areas in which our knowledge remains strikingly limited. As long as the more experienced practitioners and teachers continue to distinguish between what they reveal to the students and what their private concerns are in the consulting rooms, there will be a perpetuation of a variety of myths, traditions, and misleading ideas as to the reality of working as an analyst. This, in turn, makes it even more difficult for the younger members of the profession to realize their true talents and competence.

Just as what is written about clinical material is selective and incomplete, so also is what any of us reveals about ourselves to others. However, it is urgent that what the teacher reveals should not be restricted to those qualities that reinforce the fanciful images created by the student out of his security needs. This can only foster in the student the adoption of a chronic professional pose with an invitation to enduring self-deception. As a rebellion against these early restrictions, one may observe in later years a flowering of personal eccentricities and vanities.

Erwin Singer, Ph.D.

The Fiction of Analytic Anonymity

Wer den Dichter will verstehen
Muss in Dichters Lande gehen.
(If thou wouldst know what poets felt,
In poets' lands thou must have dwelt.)

Goethe, 1819*

Some years ago, while discussing Goethe, Santayana,[1] in one of his essays, fully acknowledged Goethe's shortcomings. Such criticism, justified as it was, is a rare literary event. But Santayana also pointedly portrayed Goethe as the "philosophical poet" of inner turbulence and flux and of the insights attending familiarity with internal turmoil. This knowledge led the most prominent of all German writers to a highly moral position, yet a stance singularly devoid of the banalities of moralizing. I have chosen to introduce my essay with his aphorism because it harbors profound implications for the excruciating task of the psychoanalyst, even though it was penned long before formalization of his therapeutic art came into existence. Indeed, only he who risks experiencing the poet's world and in doing so admits familiarity with it can meet the poet fully. But he who chances to expose himself *by* hearing truly his fellow's anguish and ecstasy can hope to be met equally exposed by him. In any genuine meeting, both participants stand equally bared before each other, and the moral fiber of such an authentic encounter precludes the trivia of moralizing.

* Translation mine.

From their very beginnings the psychoanalytic literature and institutes dedicated to the training of psychoanalysts have insisted that a person seeking preparation for the practice of this art must be willing to be a patient himself, must be a person prepared to scrutinize himself in infinite detail. And *willingness* to do so is all one may rightfully expect; we may ask if anyone can claim with honesty that he is really eager to face his own abyss of affect and associated agonies. Originally Freud,[2] and many since him who also deemed it essential that future analysts engage in self-examination before they try to aid others in such efforts, thought of this process as "training analyses," procedures designed to familiarize candidates in firsthand fashion with methods and techniques of the endeavor. Simultaneously, they expected that in the course of a "training analysis" and subsequent periodic reanalyses the analyst would develop so profound a familiarity with his own up-to-then unconscious promptings that it would help him recognize similar unconscious tendencies in his patients. And furthermore, it was hoped that this self-investigation would free him to meet turbulent passions in others, unworried about their potentially touching upon aspects of his own inner flux. After all, it was reasoned, an analyst aware of his inner life is not too much in need of avoiding those affective realities of his patients that parallel his own struggles. Clearly, it was implied, the higher the analyst's level of consciousness, the less he will be tempted to selectively dissociate communications likely to bring to awareness previously unconscious material. There will be less need to avoid the patient in order to avoid himself. When Sullivan[3] exclaimed, "We are all simply more human than otherwise," he restated succinctly both Goethe's insight that only efforts to travel through seemingly unfamiliar lands enables one to meet the poet and Freud's recognition that only self-confrontation may bring in its wake the possibility of courageously encountering other fellow human beings.

All this makes perfectly good sense and has been for years part and parcel of that credo which analysts of all persuasions feel free to support. And yet for some years now the suspicion has grown within me that this deep insight advanced by Goethe and others before him and by Freud and Sullivan and their epigones since contains, paradoxically it may seem, the key to understanding one of the most troublesome stumbling blocks of the psychoanalytic process. In a previous paper,[4] I have suggested that analysts often appear peculiarly reluctant to comment insightfully and incisively on their clients' communications lest their remarks reveal all too well that they have grasped the patient's subtle message. They seem fearful that their insight would make self-evident that the analyst, too, "has been there," at least at some point in his life. Their empathic grasp, they correctly sense, would betray pointedly that the basic precondition for empathic communion is given, that is, personal knowledge of the experience under scrutiny—or as common language has it, "it takes one to know one."

The obvious thought suggests itself that our insights about ourselves resemble the only windows available to us for contemplating and understanding the world outside. Genuine understanding of another person's life becomes inevitably a function of intimate contact with one's own existence, and, I might add parenthetically, these windows of self-recognition represent the only valid escape route from the horrors of loneliness.* It follows that nobody can ever talk about anybody but himself or herself, even though, perhaps especially when, they are engaged in penetrating discussion of others. The process I have had occasion to call "expansive projection,"[5] as juxtaposed to what is usually referred to as "defensive projection," makes itself immediately heard. This process is at one and the same time the foundation, the vehicle, and the expression of all intimate exchange. Therefore, neither I nor anybody else may rightfully say, "You are . . ." or "She is . . ." I may imply only, "In your presence *I* tend to feel . . ." or "When you do what seems to *me* . . . then *I* think. . . ."† Apparently, what analysts so fondly think of as interpretations are neither exclusively nor even primarily comments about their clients' deeper motivations but first and foremost self-revealing remarks.‡ If the analytic process represents a series of situations in which all the patient's acts, be they commissions or omissions, reveal him if we had the courage to grasp the revelations' meaning, then exactly the same must be true about the analyst. The crucial difference between the two rests in what is hopefully the analyst's less defensive posture and his fuller realization that both participants inevitably reveal themselves to each other, were they willing to see and hear what is to be seen and heard.

Of course, I am not talking about the analyst merely sharing with the patient events or facets of his life, although this, too, undoubtedly happens at times, and such sharing may not be as destructive to the process of inquiry as some seem to think. No, I am talking about a much more subtle process in which the patient, in exposing the structure and content of his concerns, simultaneously reveals what Fromm[6] once called the person's private religion or the genuine hierarchy of values by which he lives no matter what fancy pretenses he may cherish or proffer. And similarly,

---

* For a sensitive and provocative discussion of a related issue, see Fromm-Reichmann.[17]

† These thoughts parallel Schimel's.[18]

‡ Other authors have dealt with this and related subjects from varying vantage points. Among them, see Kaiser,[19] Jourard,[20] Searles,[21] Tauber,[22] and Tauber and Green.[23]

the structure, focus, and content of the analyst's response to the patient reveals the analyst's private religion, no matter what his pretenses to himself and others. Let me illustrate with a clinical excerpt.

Quite some time ago, while working with a young woman whose mode of communication was so confusing to me that I could grasp the meaning of her statements only on the rarest of occasions, she related one day in language and organization of material much more comprehensible to me an episode of years gone by. It was an instance in which her father—a man of whom she had always felt ashamed, whom she rejected whenever the opportunity to do so arose, and whom she had denigrated and humiliated mercilessly—had shown her unusual kindness and tenderness. Somewhere in the middle of relating this episode and the devotion clearly reflected in the father's actions, she began to restructure and shade the events so as to belittle his efforts on her behalf. Oh, she allowed, he really had not done all that much for her, and furthermore he had looked and smelled dirty while laboring for her, and besides all this he seemed so clearly outside the much more "refined" rest of her family.

As she spoke, two things happened. She became progressively agitated, rambling, and returned to her usual rather incoherent manner of speech; and I, preoccupied with the image of the touching scene she had described, felt deeply moved by the man's efforts to comfort his daughter. Suddenly I felt forced to comment, "Did you feel so guilty then and even now that you must talk that way?" As if quite startled and struck by surprise, she bolted up in her chair, looked straight at me, and asked in what was for her an unusually serious vein, "How do you know this?" I did not answer but merely returned her gaze. After a while she sat back, nodded her head, and simply added, "I know how you know." I felt exposed—I *was* exposed. Years later, when we terminated our work, she returned to this moment of meeting, musing about how she had experienced, at least temporarily, a sense of liberation brought about by her recognition that I, too, must know the burden of having betrayed and the unbearable length to which one will go to deny guilt associated with betrayal.

I am not insisting on the validity or the appropriate timing of my comment. It would also be easy to imagine that in the course of the episode she had described, the little girl had been sexually aroused, and one might therefore be inclined to focus the inquiry on this potential aspect of the events. Certainly, some of her descriptive terms, her references to her father's looks and to his smell, her increasing anxiety while relating the story, leading once again to disorganized speech lend themselves readily for the development of such inferences. I merely insist that if the analyst's comments are to be relevant rather than "correct" or "deep"—though obviously I maintain that relevance is synonymous with genuine precision and depth—then they must unavoidably touch upon his experiential realm. In their relevance the analyst's comments must willy-nilly expose him to the patient as much as the patient is exposed to him.

Hand in hand with this recognition there has grown over the years another realization within me. I now know that I am in urgent need of sharp self-examination when I catch myself working very hard to be "accepting and understanding" of the patient. I have grown suspicious that my working so hard to help the patient feel accepted reflects my distrust of his willingness to accept *me* and that somehow I have grasped some inclination on his part to be rejecting of *me*. By such a rejection I do not mean his refusal to enter analysis in a formal way with me. Such rejections are easy enough to take and not infrequently denote the person's unconscious sense that our particular interaction may be too burdensome for both of us and therefore not as fruitful as one might hope it to be. No, I mean by rejection here a process potentially much more devastating: the likelihood that the patient may reject me as a human being and that he may, in a critical, controlling, and derisive manner, deny the reality of my experience—that I am of consequence. At such moments, I seem to fear an undermining and rejection of my reality because, contrary to psychoanalytic folklore, patients are not the only ones concerned with acceptability as human beings—analysts are also, or at least this analyst is. Again, let me illustrate with a clinical example.

I was once consulted by a man who, before seeing me, had "interviewed" three other analysts but claimed somewhere in the middle of our meeting that he had decided to work with me. He explained that he wanted to work with a nonmedical person and the other three had been physicians. When I inquired how this entered into his decision, he said something about physicians being too "clinical and cold." This remark did not impress me as valid, particularly since I knew all three quite well as genuinely concerned, empathic, kind, and highly competent analysts. And so I commented along these lines. Well, he said, he had been in analysis before, in another city, with a medical analyst, and he insisted that his experience with this man had been disastrous. There was not enough time left to investigate what he had found so "disastrous," but the thought crossed my mind that even if that were true, it reminded me of a man who, once having had a tough piece of roast beef, had decided to become a vegetarian. Indeed, a strange reason for such a decision. But I did not express this thought, somehow "concerned" that the man was not "prepared" or "ready" for such a comment and that he might feel "put down" or "rejected" by it. I let it go with a skeptical expression on my face, a puzzled shrug of the shoulders, and slightly raised hands suggesting we would have to see what this is all about. I recommended that we meet in a few days again, allowing each of us some time to reflect on our meeting and to exchange on that occasion notes on our thoughts and reactions. To this he readily agreed.

That evening I ruminated about our conversation. In the course of the double session—I usually meet for initial consultations in a double session—he had told me a good deal about his reasons for having sought help earlier and why he was contemplating renewed analytic exploration. Among them, he mentioned some rather superficial suicidal gestures, some verbal expressions of violence toward members of his family, and his wasting his life as a dilettante by dabbling in various artistic pretensions in the hope of impressing most anyone he met. His family's considerable wealth, which he considered his own, allowed him to indulge himself haphazardly in his fancies. But time was passing by. Now, at the end of his thirties, he knew he had contributed nothing. And while he did not put it this way—indeed at one point he resented my use of the term bitterly—he did think of himself as some strange type of lounge lizard.

While reflecting on our meeting, things became clearer. I had felt flattered and thereby controlled, and I had to ask, had this perchance been his intent. Hadn't he tried to control others by feigned violence against them or himself? And clever fellow that I thought he was, wouldn't he prefer working with a psychologist who, he could imagine, would feel professionally more insecure than a psychiatrist—ergo, more capable of being intimidated and controlled than one of his medical confreres?

The picture seemed rather obvious, for clearly there had been enough time to at least start exploring at its edges. Yet I had let it go. Why? No doubt it was unpleasant and disappointing to reencounter childish competitive feelings in myself, tendencies that I liked to think of as long past and buried. But disappointment with oneself is, at least in part, the inevitable lot of the analyst—that much I know and accept—and had I not caught these silly neuroticisms easily enough in the evening, why had I avoided them during the session? Sadly, I had to face the fact that investigations along these lines would have revealed me (and heightened my anxiety quite early in our contact) as one who knew about the desire to control, to manipulate, and to intimidate and about the devious ways such desires can take, including the use of flattery and playing on the insecurities of others. How else would these possibilities come to my mind? Was *I* ready to stand exposed this way; would the patient accept me as one who knew about such devious motives and maneuvers? It had never been a question of his being ready and his need to be accepted. Much more it was a question of my anxieties along these lines.

Once again I feel forced to repeat that our insights about ourselves—perhaps I ought to say more modestly, my insights about myself—represent to me a double-edged sword. They potentiate my insight into the patient, but this insight, in turn, potentiates his deeper knowledge of me. They make me realize that relevant comments about him are inevitably revealing of myself, and therefore my courage to bare myself via pointed reflections and the posing of pertinent questions is constantly tested, for the therapist's question, "Will the patient accept me if he knows me?" always hovers in the background.

This brings me to three related themes central to our therapeutic concerns. I believe that the preceding discussion bears implications for aspects of our theory of psychopathology, for our notions as to what is therapeutic in psychotherapy, and for our theoretical ideas concerning termination of analytic work. Let me take one issue at a time, using as my point of departure a complaint every analyst must have heard all too often. One of the most common laments of patients insists, "I feel so exposed and embarrassed and angry. You know so much about me, and I know nothing about you. It isn't fair."

To the first issue, the question of a theory of psychopathology: It seems to me that a patient's "ignorance" about the analyst, unless it is a conscious ploy, a somewhat psychopathic fake and pretense employed for whatever manipulative reasons, depicts precisely what is wrong with him—indeed, it describes the very nucleus of *all* psychopathology. It reflects that the patient has abandoned a birth right and a fundamentally given human capacity: to hear what can be heard, to see what can be seen, to grasp what can be grasped.* Those among us who maintain a vision in which psychological well-being is defined by the courage to know oneself rather than by adherence to prescribed behavioral norms always understood psychopathology as a form of cowardliness, its particular modes of expression, and their often disastrous consequences. Hopefully, we have stated this understanding without pompously preaching courage when we encounter an example of the universal human propensity to look away when passing the mirror. I think that among those who broadly define themselves as "depth psychologists" there are no crucial differences in their acceptance of this definition. All of them apparently view this all too human avoidance of self-confrontation and self-recognition as the hub of psychopathology, various syndromes simply describing the spectrum of maneuvers and avenues available to all of us in our quest for self-deception. Where psychoanalytic schools of thought, of course, do differ is on the question of precisely what human beings so studiously avoid noticing about themselves and what is responsible for the development of such cowardliness and its specific manifestations. In brief, their arguments are not about the definition of psychopathology but about their respective metapsychologies.†

If it is true that through self-knowledge and self-recognition analysts become capable of grasping the essentials of their patients' lives, and if, conversely, it is also true, as I have argued, that through their newfound

---

* Contrary to popular belief, this also includes the very abandoning and/or crippling of the patient's intellectual acumen, a development convincingly investigated and presented by, among others, Rappaport, Gill, and Schafer.[24]

† While the rigid adherence to metapsychological systems undoubtedly has its deplorable and often overly reductionist consequences, it must also be noted that various metapsychologies simply reflect their proponents' and adherents' visions of man, and therefore they cannot and must not be avoided. Their dangers lie not so much in the propositions they advance but in the unfortunate tendency of their often being employed as closed rather than open systems.

or rediscovered self-knowledge patients grasp the essentials of their analysts, then psychoanalytic success seems to me readily definable. It expresses
itself in the patient's ultimately becoming as conversant with the analyst's
personal visions, his psychological operations, and his hierarchy of values—
including the discrepancies between what he professes and by what he
truly lives—as the analyst, hopefully, has become conversant with these
central aspects of his patients' lives. Therefore, I feel inclined to comment,
when listening to the lament of the patient that he knows nothing about
me, "That's your trouble. You could know as much about me as I know
about you. Yet it seems as if you do not want to know, either about
yourself or about me." Of course patients do not *actually* know details
of their analysts' lives, such details ranging from food preferences through
favorite leisure time activities to idiosyncratic sexual practices. But in
themselves these data are as inconsequential as all data *qua* data happen
to be. They are merely trivial bits of information. For data are of significance only to the extent to which they illuminate broad issues and phenomena. In our discipline, bits of historical, behavioral, and reactive data are
of consequence only if they illuminate and thereby help the participants
grasp by direct experience and/or inference aspects of their own or the
other person's character.* While patients have quantitatively less data to
draw upon, there is a wealth of qualitatively significant and poignant information about their analysts at their disposal—if they were only courageous enough to avail themselves of it. I say "courageous enough" because
I have insisted that to know about the other in depth requires penetrating
confrontation with oneself. And therefore a patient's ability to grasp the
meaning of the analyst's life denotes a rather heroic achievement, a remarkable willingness to know oneself and thereby know the other. Growth to
such a point may well denote that termination is around the corner.

As the title of this paper and the discussion suggest, I am convinced
that the whole notion of analytic anonymity is fictitious. I would be tempted
to call it a myth were it not that this term in the context of our work
has been preempted brilliantly by Szasz.[7] It seems to me that this anonymity
is an artifact carefully maintained by an analytic *folie à deux*. It minimizes
the rawness but also the excitement that a full encounter will bring. Obviously Freud, too, was not overly impressed by the substantiveness or importance of "analytic anonymity"—all protestations to the contrary notwith-

* Food preferences, occupational choices, and often even preferred athletic activities
are clearly such bits of data, analytically irrelevant except insofar as they may illuminate
wider issues in the patient's character style. For instance, I have noted that "a passion for
tennis" may reflect the person's fierce competitive strivings expressed not only in sublimated
fashion but in a truly elegant manner, aggression in spotless and perfect whites, so to speak—
or so it was, at least in a not too distant past.

standing—if we are to lend any credence to the Wolf-Man's[8] account of his work with Freud. Furthermore, even a superficial reading of Freud's description of some of his work[9] makes it quite clear that he was never an "anonymous" analyst. Incisive mind that he was, he must have realized that try as one may, one cannot be anonymous, that one's very effort to be that would in itself be most self-revealing. And, finally, how could he have thought otherwise? Didn't he recommend an evenly hovering attention as the analyst's most productive orientation when in session with his patient so that his own reactions and associations may freely come to the fore, eventually to be communicated to the patient in what he called "interpretations"?[10]

I would like to add a brief postscript to this part of the discussion, even though I have touched upon the issue in an earlier paper.[11] I believe that the warnings offered there bear repeating. Self-evidently, neither the inevitability of the analyst's self-revealing behavior nor the derivative recognition that "analytic anonymity" is a fiction can be construed as license for his engaging in self-important chatter, self-indulgent ruminations, or intrusive diversions, no matter how tempting such digressions may be. I suspect that the temptation for such "time out" is always with us and in it we recognize how difficult our work is and how eagerly we therefore may look for a respite. Disciplined opposition to such temptation and careful examination of its meaning is part and parcel of the daily struggle the analyst must suffer, but in his self-discipline and self-examination, he reveals to the patient that he, too, must struggle, that the struggle against primitive narcissistic indulgences is always with us, and that it can be carried on, at least at times, successfully.

But to return to the mainstream of the discussion, not only do I think that psychopathology equals self-imposed ignorance about oneself and therefore about others, and not only do I believe that the patient's courage to know himself is often strikingly reflected in his courage to know the analyst, but to me of even greater theoretical and practical importance is the recognition that the patient's profound and realistic knowledge of the analyst as a representative of his fellow men—past, present, and future—enables him to live authentically, in mutuality, in solidarity, and in communion. The development of such intimate personal knowledge represents to my mind the true meaning and the glorious promise of the dissolution of the Oedipus complex and of paratactic distortions. This realistic sense and grasp of the other's life line offers us the chance to "forget," not in a repressive sense but in the sense of designating as old business what indeed is past history; only such knowledge enables us to forgive, perchance with sadness—not to maintain grudges in madness—and to resolve—again in sadness rather than in madness—that the suffering we have caused others need not be perpetuated. This willingness to forgive, to put aside, and to resolve demands has as its foundation the recognition that the analyst—as were our elders—is potentially as limited, as pathetic, and as heroic as we are. This recognition then enables us to contemplate in sadness and perhaps with bittersweet humor our shared destiny of folly, shortcomings, and courageous heroism; and it reduces the power of the neurotic banner of self-righteousness.

Obviously, this process does not lead to happiness in the conventional sense of the word but leaves us indeed sadder, perhaps even tormented, and yet I shrink from saying wiser and substitute instead more conscious and alive. This sadness, which seems to me the inevitable outcome of any searching self-investigation and therefore of any successful therapeutic encounter, must not be mistaken for or equated with depression. Unfortunately, this question is all too common in the superficial use of language, observations, and concepts that can be noted all around us. Indeed, I have the firm conviction that sadness and depression are mutually exclusive states. If depression is understood as a sense of total futility engendered by injured narcissism, that is, by injury to a fictitious though highly cherished (because presumably very impressive) self-image, not by injured self-love in Fromm's[12] sense (for how could true self-love ever be injured?), then sadness may be understood as the exact opposite: as a burst of rich and authentic affect, albeit sorrowful in nature, brought about by the realistic though painful recognition that life has been wasted and destroyed.*

I am not in the habit of making promises to people who consult me, even when they pressure me to do so. When such pressure is exerted, I am much more inclined to inquire about their tendencies to test my sincerity. Experience has taught me that the more intense this pressure, the more the patient knows that I have nothing I rightfully may promise other than my efforts and hopefully some skill in conducting a joint inquiry about his life and the premises on which he has built it. Yet I must ask myself, If our efforts were to be fruitful, what may the person facing me expect? And I must reply, Fewer illusions but less depression as I have defined it; also more sadness, yet with it more aliveness and hope; more separation and with it, paradoxically, more intimacy and less loneliness and isolation.

In two beautiful essays, Ehrenberg[13],[14] has discussed what she calls the fine edge of therapeutic intimacy. If the growth of one's capacity to develop intimate knowledge of personal experience and, through it, compa-

---

* The amount of cultural conventions designed to minimize sadness as if it were an affective state to be shunned is amazing. Many seem to prefer anger, depression, and similar feelings to sadness, finding ample cultural support in these efforts. Indeed, these affective states can easily be seen as defenses often avoiding or masking sadness.

rable knowledge of the experience of others, if this growth represents our aim, then the very nature of the analytic exchange must be the starting point for this growth. The nature of such a growth-producing exchange demands first and foremost that the analyst divest himself most strenuously from all exercise of what Laing[15] so pointedly calls "mystification," without engaging in equally debilitating intrusiveness. Not that one can really practice mystification on people unwilling to be treated in this way; as I have said earlier, we are all rather transparent to those who want to see. But to repeat, patients, perhaps all human beings, are not too eager to see. And so I must conclude that the nature of the therapeutic effort in the analytic encounter is the nurturing of therapeutic intimacy furthered by the absence or at least the minimization of efforts in mystification, even when the patient tempts us—indeed, as is so often the case, even when the patient persistently tries to seduce us into being mystifiers, when he tries to "transform" us, as Levenson[16] has it, into what are to him psychologically familiar characters. Implicit in Levenson's presentation is the thought that one need not worry about the development of transference; it is always all too much with us and so is the patient's attempt to force countertransference upon us. The steadfast refusal by the therapist to be transformed in this fashion and his continued authentic self-revelation through the pursuit of his thoughts and reactions as they are triggered by the patient represents to me the therapeutic effort of psychoanalytic work.* This process may, of course, acquaint the analyst with unpleasant truths about himself, and these unpleasant truths will become apparent to his patient, too. This may seem embarrassing to some, but in the genuine spirit of our work, it is exciting and rekindles hope.

I cannot close without inserting a note of caution. Our efforts to avoid mystification, with the attending likelihood of increasing clarity about and awareness of inner and outer reality, may, perhaps inevitably does, lead to some at least temporary sense of unreality and disorientation in the patient.† The unreality of our patients' lives has become all too often their reality. A shift in relatedness to oneself and the outside world as represented by the analyst, if based on authenticity, turns the patient's world upside down, reduces his neurotic hope for certainty, and is therefore invariably anxiety provoking. These are the moments that test the analyst's convictions. They require that he reveal himself even more than he has done up to now by resolutely desisting from offering reassurances and similar operations. In desisting from such reflexive follies and by pursuing the exploration, with its inevitable and mutual denouement, he reveals

---

* Also see Singer,[5] Chapter 10.
† For a detailed and penetrating presentation of this possibility, see Bonime.[25]

that he, too, knows the agony of uncertainty, that he, too, is subject to common sorrows, but that he also deems it possible to go on despite them.

REFERENCES

1. Santayana G: Three Philosophical Poets. Cambridge, Harvard University Press, 1910.
2. Freud S: Analysis terminable and interminable (1937). *In* Freud S: The Standard Edition, vol. 23. London, Hogarth Press, 1953.
3. Sullivan HS: Conceptions of Modern Psychiatry. Washington, The William Alanson White Psychoanalytic Foundation, 1947.
4. Singer, E: The reluctance to interpret. *In* Hammer EF (ed): Use of Interpretation in Treatment. New York, Grune & Stratton, 1968.
5. Singer E: Key Concepts in Psychotherapy. New York, Basic Books, 1970.
6. Fromm E: Psychoanalysis and Religion. New Haven, Yale University Press, 1950.
7. Szasz TS: The myth of mental illness. Am Psychol 15:113–118, 1960.
8. The Wolf-man: The Wolf-man. New York, Basic Books, 1971.
9. Freud S: Fragments of an analysis of a case of hysteria (1905). *In* Freud S: The Standard Edition, vol. 7, London, Hogarth Press, 1953.
10. Freud S: Recommendations to physicians practicing psychoanalysis (1912). *In* Freud S: The Standard Edition, vol. 12. London, Hogarth Press, 1953.
11. Singer E: The patient aids the therapist. *In* Landis B, Tauber ES (eds): In the Name of Life. New York, Holt, Rinehart and Winston, 1971.
12. Fromm E: The Art of Loving. New York, Harper, 1956.
13. Ehrenberg D: The intimate edge in therapeutic relatedness. Contemp Psychoanal 10:423–437, 1974.
14. Ehrenberg D: The quest for intimate relatedness. Contemp Psychoanal 11:320–331, 1975.
15. Laing RD: The Divided Self. London, Tavistock, 1960.
16. Levenson EA: The Fallacy of Understanding. New York, Basic Books, 1972.
17. Fromm-Reichmann F: Loneliness. Psychiatry 22:1–15, 1959.
18. Schimel JL: Tell it like it is. William Alanson White Newsletter, Winter, 1969–1970.
19. Kaiser H: Emergency. Psychiatry 25:97–118, 1962.
20. Jourard SM: The Transparent Self. Princeton, Van Nostrand, 1964.
21. Searles HF: The informational value of the supervisor's emotional experience. Psychiatry 18:135–146, 1955.
22. Tauber ES: Exploring the therapeutic use of countertransference data. Psychiatry, 17:332–336, 1954.
23. Tauber ES, Green MR: Prelogical Experience. New York, Basic Books, 1959.
24. Rapaport D, Gill M, Schafer R: Diagnostic Psychological Testing. Chicago, The Year Book Publishers, 1946.
25. Bonime W: Depersonalization as a manifestation of evolving health. J Am Acad Psychoanal 1:109–123, 1973.

Kenneth A. Frank, Ph.D.

Conclusion: On Being A Psychoanalyst

I set out to compile a volume of papers elucidating aspects of the analyst's subjective and personal involvement in the practice of psychoanalysis. Such a volume, I thought, could serve a valuable instructive purpose by addressing this generally neglected, if not avoided, subject. I believe the volume has realized its goal, both with happy revelations and with more sobering ones, and hope it has shed light on the true foundations of psychotherapy.

Reading the candid disclosures of the contributors, with their various psychoanalytic orientations, it is difficult, and consequently illuminating, to find a common thread which unifies their endeavors into a whole fabric of psychoanalysis.* The volume includes representatives of the Freudian orientation, of the cultural-interpersonal approach, for example, of Horney and Sullivan, of the English school, including the object-relations point of view, and of others more difficult to classify. Clearly, under the rubric of psychoanalysis, we find many divergent theoretical formulations and technical procedures—an observation which, as we shall see, underscores the potency of the human dimension in psychoanalysis.

All the contributors to the volume may be identified as *psychoanalytic* psychotherapists, in that all espouse a theoretical depth psychology and implement, in their own ways, a psychotherapeutic procedure including transference analysis which rests upon the belief that persons grow as the result of deepened self-awareness and insight into unconscious conflicts.

---

* Psychoanalysis and psychoanalytic psychotherapy will be treated interchangeably, as in the Introduction (cf. p. 2).

The particular techniques emphasized in performing the psychotherapeutic task—for example, a focus on the experiencing process, on the caring connection between patient and analyst, on the transferential distortions, or transference neurosis, within the psychotherapeutic relationship—all intimately interrelated, are ultimately a matter of personal conviction. It becomes apparent that the practice of psychoanalysis is on one level an interpretive art, blending technical principles with those of personality theory, and drawing importantly from the unique personality of the therapist. Accordingly, Greenson points out that the psychoanalytic situation is one of the few places where science, art and creativity all come together. On another level, we are reminded of the psychotherapeutic potentiality of the patient-therapist relationship, *per se*. For example, Guntrip emphasizes that the psychoanalytic collaboration, in addition to the transference relationship, includes the "real-life" interaction of two unique persons in all its complex possibilities; if within that collaboration one finds a genuine "good object" in the analyst one will be profoundly strengthened by it. In a related vein, acknowledging the importance of the affectional relationship, Greenson speaks of the analyst as a peculiar and unique combination of researcher and parent, and Kelman stresses the "caretaker" functions of the therapist.

The volume helps to clarify aspects of the complex interrelationship between a practitioner's personality, theory and technique. The contributors seem to rely upon defined personality theories in varying degree. Some appear to adhere rather closely to a particular theory; others seem more relaxed about theory and inclined to follow more directly the data of their therapeutic experience with a patient. We observe that theory and practice enjoy a mutually enriching relationship. As Rosenfeld emphasizes the critical role of a sound grasp of Kleinian theory in improving his work with patients, Guntrip underscores the opposite: that theory must be improved with the insights derived from psychotherapeutic practice. While there is general recognition within the field that one's technique is modified in accordance with one's personality, Bruch goes a step further, suggesting that one's choice of a personality theory is a matter of individual personality and that we select a theory which is personally appealing to us. As for patients, what is suitable to one practitioner is not to another, nor necessarily to that same practitioner at a later time in his career. Guntrip goes further in exploring the relationship between one's personality and theoretical position. He asserts that one's theoretical position must be rooted in one's psychopathology. Accordingly we may understand why it is possible to find "defenders of every variety of faith" in psychoanalysis, and disagreement about such basic psychotherapeutic issues as the role of interpretation: for example, whether interpretation is, in and of itself, mutatively effective, or whether it is effective as an expression of a profoundly understanding, and consequently mutatively effective, personal relationship.

In considering Guntrip's reflections upon his personal psychoanalyses with Fairbairn and Winnicott, it appears that there is no uniform correlation between one's theory and technique; there may be conflict between one's intellectual views and his personality as it effects his capacity to implement those views as a psychotherapist. We see how a traditional theorist, without fully realizing it, may be innovative in practice, and vice versa. Thus we must be critical in evaluating a practitioner's formulations about what he does, or has done, that has been helpful to a patient. Guntrip also asserts that, depending upon the "natural fit" with a patient, the person of the practitioner may ultimately be more important to the patient's change than one's technical approach, including "critical" interpretations a therapist might make.

A sense of the individual personalities of these analysts emerges from their papers. One is challenged to speculate, from the feeling as well as the content of each paper, about the possible experience of being in psychotherapy with these very different human beings. Some seem more patient, nurturing and gentle; while others seem more active, confrontational and forceful. Some appear to be more formal, intellectual and precise; others more casual, intuitive and guided by impression. Some are more questioning, moderate and modest; while others are more extreme, bold and opinionated. Despite these individual differences, all seem deeply interested in and curious about people, respectful, caring and appreciative of them, profoundly dedicated to helping them, and uniformly humble in at least one respect: there is a recognition that the analyst, when effective, can claim only to have helped release the previously inhibited, but nevertheless existent growth capacities of patients; there are no claims of having "cured" or even having changed them. This is well illustrated, for example, by Guntrip's comments on "post-analytic developments."

In reading this material, a recognition develops that each person's psychotherapy is unique, an odyssey of sorts, revealing novel developments as one's life course unfolds with the therapist. A theory of personality, of psychopathology and of technique provides the analyst with technical guidelines and rough expectations, but still a great deal occurs in an individual's psychotherapy that cannot be known beforehand. Despite the procedural routine defining the structure of the psychoanalytic situation, there is relatively little which is precisely predictable about the actual therapeutic experience with patients. The therapist can anticipate developments from his knowledge of theory, prior psychotherapeutic experience, and intuition, but he never knows exactly what lies ahead. This requires a spontaneity that challenges one's ability to meet the unknown constructively. Each patient presents a new world to explore and to attempt to understand. Though there are principles, there are no technical formulas. Guntrip and Khan, for example, stress the need to remain flexible with theory, and to modify the therapy to suit each patient's unique needs. Here the metaphor of a road map occurs to me: it provides a formulation, an estimation, about what to expect and how to proceed; yet the real, uncharted exigencies of life—using our metaphor, traffic conditions, a detour, an accident—all determine the actual experience of the journey which is necessarily uncertain and unpredictable. So with the analyst, it is the unpredictable, unfolding experience with the patient with which he must deal, and not formulations about this experience. Ultimately, as practitioners, we must function as well-honed interpretive artists, relying on intuition, timing, insight and empathy, in determining how to apply the principles provided by our theory. As Guntrip reminds us, theory makes a useful servant but a bad master.

While often arduous, the analyst's work affords unusual intellectual stimulation and opportunities for creativity. In lending one's understanding to a patient's developing self-awareness, the analyst is challenged to tap the totality of his experience and knowledge, from the most mundane to the most exotic. As a mastery of psychoanalytic theory and principles of technique, such as dream interpretation, help one to understand and interpret a patient's communications, so do all other areas of knowledge, as varied as carpentry, fashion, athletics, pure science and the arts, to name a few. All knowledge and experience are helpful to the analyst, for the basic language of psychoanalysis is one of metaphor. As psychoanalytic work challenges our intellect, spirit of adventure and creativity, it also moves us emotionally. Each psychoanalytic journey is filled with emotional ups and downs for both analyst and patient. Shainberg has described what might be termed the "peak experiences" in analytic work, those poignant moments of personal transformation, filled with wonderment, which we share with our patients. On the other hand, analytic work can also arouse strong negative feelings within the analyst. Khan has alluded to the potential frustrations of the work; Searles to its innate deprivational nature and associated feelings of futility; and Greenson to an assurance beforehand of accomplishing personally unsatisfying results.

The life of the analyst, we are reminded repeatedly, is often a stressful one. This point of view, as Basescu humorously points out, is in sharp contrast with our patient's frequent idealizations of our lives. There is a need for constant self-awareness and regulation lest the analyst act in an untherapeutic manner toward the patient out of his own neurotic needs. Searles reminds us of the potential dangers of the analyst's unconscious sadism and hopes to perpetuate the patient's disturbance; Bruch of the analyst's vulnerability to intimidation; and Rosenfeld of the psychotic areas within the analyst that require analysis. The analyst must be able to work constructively with a patient's idealization, dependency, seduction, and assault, even though these may arouse discomfort or even strong anxiety if they touch upon unresolved conflicts within the practitioner himself. Many of the authors discuss feelings of emotional depletion. And Singer reminds us that in analytic work there is no hiding—from oneself or from one's patients.

Analytic work, we also see, is technically complicated and often exceedingly difficult, especially with severely disturbed patients.* There is a need to blend, in optimal amounts, giving and withholding, listening and interpreting, activity and receptivity, spontaneity and technical caution, based upon an accurate appraisal of the patient's psychotherapeutic needs. More subtly, there is the need to distinguish our and the patient's realistic from distorted needs and perceptions, the interactions of which are extremely complicated and potentially confusing. Failure to maintain such distinctions may result in an unproductive collusion, as described by Shainberg, or in the extreme, in disabling "feelings of entanglement," as described by Rosenfeld. As the process of self-discovery is never completed, so the technique of psychoanalysis is never fully learned; analysts learn gradually, often painfully, becoming more comfortable and acquiring greater perceptiveness and subtlety as their capability expands with their growing personal and professional experience. We are told by Ben-Avi that the stresses associated with becoming competent as an analyst begin with one's entrance into the profession and continue through a lifelong term of study.

The psychoanalyst has but one tool with which to perform his complex work—himself.† As Singer points out, unless one knows oneself well, one cannot know others, nor perform the psychoanalytic task effectively. A lack of self-awareness results in distorted perceptions and increases the likelihood of subtle countertherapeutic factors, from within oneself, intruding into one's work. It is pointed out that therapists have their share of emotional problems; indeed, that these problems may play a role in motivating one toward a career in psychoanalysis. Several contributors mention

---

* It is interesting that contributors working mainly with schizophrenic patients, for example, Rosenfeld and Searles, emphasize the technical and emotional difficulties of the work in their papers. Those working with less disturbed patients present a more positive picture of their personal experience.

† See Sharpe[1] for a discussion of this topic. Actually, Sharpe refers, in this context, to one's "mind." I find this term less suitable because of its cognitive-intellectual (vs. experiential-holistic) implications.

their training analyses which, far more than mere "training" experiences, are appreciated on a profoundly personal level. Ideally, the analyst should have faced his own previously unconscious conflicts, through analysis and continuing self-discovery, in order to be able to perform the work of analysis in a manner free from insensitivity and defensiveness. In practice, one must be able to accompany the patient into emotionally-charged areas with relative equanimity, even when the material arouses parallel conflicts within the practitioner himself. It is understood that the analyst will have residual personality problems, for he is human; but in the absence of their resolution, the analyst is expected to maintain an unusually high standard of awareness of such problems and to prevent them from impeding a patient's growth. One should also have developed to a high degree those personal qualities which enable patients to rely upon the analyst *in a real way.*

Undoubtedly, the pleasures of the work far surpass the strains. Shainberg speaks of the powerful and inspirational moments in therapy when a creative growing together of patient and therapist occurs; Olsen describes transcendent implications of the therapeutic relationship. We are reminded of the gratifications of helping others, perhaps most poignantly by Kelman, who suggests that creative analytic work must be conducted in a spirit of playfulness. It can be fun, easy, and enormously rewarding. And the atmosphere in the consultation room, contrary to the stereotype, is often light. A helpful intervention is often a song, a joke, an anecdote, or even a nursery rhyme. When the work is developing well, then one can most readily appreciate the patient's positive experiences, personality, and appealing qualities. Often during these periods the patient may be moving well "on his own," as it were, and "psychotherapeutic intervention" by a zealous therapist may, in fact, be experienced by the patient as an interruption. During these periods when the patient requires "only" a therapeutic presence of us, the work is remarkably simple and flowing. The therapist can take pleasure in the patient's smooth, unimpeded movement through the course of psychotherapeutic growth.

There is also the exciting and challenging psychotherapeutic growth process itself to reward us, with all its intricate subtleties and possibilities. The contributors reveal that patients manifest and experience such growth in many different ways and, I am sure, differently with different therapists. Some learn for the first time that another human being, whom they permit to have great emotional importance to them, truly accepts, appreciates, and cares to understand them. According to Guntrip, the traumatized child in the patient is permitted to emerge within such a relationship in a way that enables one to live more fully with the traumatic legacy of the formative years. Several contributors suggest that this relationship is the foundation of subsequent psychotherapeutic developments. Patients, feeling an atmosphere of safety that is provided by a dependable and understanding companionship through what must necessarily be felt as an uncertain and potentially hazardous journey, are freed to take experiential as well as behavioral "risks of growing," within and outside of the therapeutic relationship. Another avenue of growth, emphasizing interpretation, is outlined by Greenson. Early fantasies, associated with irrational affects and anxiety, are introduced to the analyst through transference, free association and dreams. They are met with equanimity, gradually but consistently understood, and their potency is diminished. As the origins of irrational feelings and defensive reactions are understood, they lose their tyranny and parts of oneself are realized which were previously known only remotely, if at all. As Kelman, in particular, stresses, feelings, generally, are experienced as an essential and enriching part of life, rather than anathema. Life's pleasures and pains can be felt more deeply. Rosenfeld, discussing projective identification, shows how through analysis a greater trust of self may develop, and hence, of the other; and how relationships cannot but benefit as the relationship to the self improves. Shainberg, emphasizing the growth process, reveals how defensive patterns are uncovered and new ways replace them; how, as a person becomes one with oneself, a readjustment of priorities occurs, with attendant modifications in life style; and how greater freedom develops, with constructive energy for activity and change replacing a passive clinging to the costly "safety" of the known and familiar.

Usually, but not always attuned to the patient's psychodynamics as they unfold within the therapeutic relationship, the analyst is usually aware of, and gratified by, the patient's changes and growth within the process, even in the absence of dramatic or concrete change. For example, I recall the excitement I felt with my new patient, Roberta,* who had been feeling depressed and resourceless, having participated for several years in an intensely sadomasochistic relationship with a lover. She had lost her capacity to feel anything other than depression and occasional paralyzing glimpses of rage. After only a few months of therapy, she dreamed, with accompanying feelings of awe, of "new rooms" in her house, of "more property" than she had realized. Roberta was beginning to sense the process of self-expansion and discovery. She was beginning to appreciate that there were aspects within herself, and possibilities in living, previously unexplored by her. After an intensely painful, but relatively brief struggle, she would leave the man to whom she felt bound, and move on to re-create a more positive and meaningful life for herself. The exhilaration

* Case material is disguised.

we shared was "only" over a dream, but one which was born of growing self-discovery and awareness, and which, I knew, forecast Roberta's coming liberation.

Psychotherapy had not progressed so rapidly with Bonnie, a "difficult" patient, the course of whose therapy illustrates, in the extreme, the typically uneven course of psychotherapeutic collaboration. Bonnie was a bright, sensual and attractive woman, but had very poor self esteem and was prone to extreme feelings of alienation, deprivation and resentment which sometimes erupted into temper outbursts. At age thirty-five, after six years of psychoanalytic psychotherapy, with sessions held once a week, her gains had been meager. Though less volatile, she was depressed, bitter and continued to lead an isolated and barren existence, with weekdays consisting of a drab, unsatisfying work routine, and weekends spent with household chores spiced only with rationed television viewing. Occasional social excursions resulted in episodic involvements with men who were able to offer her very little, and which resulted in her resentful submission and/ or defiance of them—the former felt to be the only condition of her acceptability, the latter, her rebellion against this ugly self-deception.

Bonnie had begun working with me early in my professional career, and although I had had my fair share of therapeutic disappointments, overall, I had grown to feel satisfied with my efficacy. I assume this was due, in no small part, to the fact that most of the patients who had been referred to me were not severely disturbed and had good prognoses. However, after those years of effort with Bonnie, it was still difficult to detect meaningful progress. I sensed not a glimmer of the growth to come from which to draw hope, and experienced deep frustration in response to her inertia. I frequently reviewed, and considered alternatives to my psychodynamic formulation about her, seeking to correct possible technical error. I sought consultation and considered using techniques which were beyond the parameters within which I ordinarily worked. Among them were a more consistently confrontational analytic approach and assertiveness training.

Just as Bonnie was despairing of ever changing, and as my optimism, too, was failing—a countertransferential cue to the subsequent interpretive focus—we reached a turning point. Very briefly, and condensing the convergence of many factors leading to this positive phase, we uncovered her resentment of my "richer" life. With this, we unearthed her determination to deny me further "enrichment," rooted in past parental sadomasochistic attachments, and manifested by her stubborn refusal to grow. Her apparent cry of despair was, we saw, a perverse cry of triumph. Her former inertia had been a covert maneuver to defeat me; my extreme feelings of frustration, unusual for me, were "appropriate" to her stimulus.

After considerable work in this area, Bonnie was helped to move out of her transferential struggle to deny me the gift of her growth, and to defeat me—us—at the therapeutic task. Afterward she took the process of her self-realization forward, making relatively rapid and substantial gains.

The turning point was marked, in her behavior outside of sessions, by her decision to purchase a bicycle. This event, trivial in the lives of most, but so significant in hers, signalled a readiness to "exercise" herself more actively, positively, and to be more generous to and with herself. From an isolate she became a friend and lover, increasingly on her own more positive terms. She selected people who were able to give, and from whom she could receive more than in the past. At work, concomitant interpersonal gains resulted in greater job satisfaction. She completed the necessary academic credentials to permit her to take the next step in her career, which would bring even greater fulfillment. Bonnie is now, in a sense, "a different person," living an affirmative life which she once dared not imagine possible, but which she buried instead beneath higher priorities of sadomasochistic connection and conquest.

Ironically, Bonnie, whose cynical, mutually destructive fantasy I had nearly accepted, and who had caused me deep frustration and self-doubt during a long psychotherapeutic "drought," eventually enabled me to participate in one of the most thoroughgoing psychotherapeutic growth processes I had ever experienced. The stubbornness of her initial sadomasochistic defenses, and the long wait for her substantial changes actually increased the eventual satisfaction I felt with her growth. Bonnie, whose apparent inertia stimulated strong frustration within me at first aroused a sense of wonder and delight later as I saw her move dramatically to realize her potential. The sketch of Bonnie's therapy clearly shows the need to examine and understand our inner experience, as well as the need for unusual patience and persistence as we conduct the work. The ups and downs which are characteristic of the patient's and therapist's mutual experience are evident, reminding one of Greenson's comments about the "extraordinary difficulties" of a profession which is "terribly rewarding."

I regret that the late Ella Freeman Sharpe could not have contributed a paper to this volume, for she wrote with remarkable sensitivity and appreciation of the analyst's work:

> . . . I personally find the enrichment of my ego through the experiences of other people not the least of satisfactions. From the limited confines of an individual life, limited in time and space and environment, I experience a rich variety of living through my work. I contact all sorts and kinds of living, all imaginable circumstances, human tragedy and human comedy, humour and dourness, the pathos of the defeated, and the incredible endurances and victories that some souls achieve over human fate. Perhaps what makes me most glad that I chose

to be a psycho-analyst, is the rich variety of every type of human experience that has become part of me, which never would have been mine either to experience or to understand in a single mortal life, but for my work.[2]

I resonate with this statement. I regard it as a privilege to play an integral role in the lives and psychotherapeutic growth of my patients. And they have played a very significant role in my growth as a person. In addition to the practice of psychoanalysis, I have varied my professional activities to include research, teaching and writing—all of which are less emotionally demanding of me than intensive psychotherapeutic practice. I welcome an August vacation, and intersperse two more weeks of needed vacation during each year. But I always welcome, too, the reunion with my patients and the resumption of our work together. For me, a patient's growth through our collaboration in psychotherapy is among life's most rewarding and beautiful experiences. I cannot imagine another profession which could offer me such satisfaction.

REFERENCES

1. Sharpe EF: Collected Papers on Psycho-Analysis. London, The Hogarth Press, 1950.
2. Sharpe EF: The psycho-analyst. Int J Psychoanal Vol. xxviii, 1947.